W9-AVM-221

THE SENSUAL GOD

THE SENSUAL GOD

HOW THE SENSES MAKE
THE ALMIGHTY SENSELESS

Aviad Kleinberg

COLUMBIA UNIVERSITY PRESS   NEW YORK

COLUMBIA UNIVERSITY PRESS

Publishers Since 1893

NEW YORK   CHICHESTER, WEST SUSSEX

Copyright © 2015 Columbia University Press
All rights reserved

Library of Congress Cataloging-in-Publication Data
Kleinberg, Aviad M.
The sensual God : how the senses make the almighty senseless / Aviad Kleinberg.
pages   cm.
Includes bibliographical references and index.
ISBN 978-0-231-17470-1 (cloth : alk. paper) — ISBN 978-0-231-54024-7 (ebook)
1. God I. Title.

BL473.K54 2015

211—dc23
2015002483

Columbia University Press books are printed on permanent and durable acid-free paper.
This book is printed on paper with recycled content.

Printed in the United States of America

c 10 9 8 7 6 5 4 3 2 1

COVER DESIGN: Mary Ann Smith

References to Internet Web sites (URLs) were accurate at the time of writing.
Neither the author nor Columbia University Press is responsible for URLs that may have
expired or changed since the manuscript was prepared.

CONTENTS

ACKNOWLEDGMENTS

Work on this book began at the library of the Pontifical Institute of Mediaeval Studies in Toronto, where I enjoyed the hospitality of my dear friends Maruja and Hal Jackman. It continued in Paris at the library of the Institut d'Études Augustiniennes, and the Bibliothèque nationale de France, in Oxford at the Bodleian Library and in my hometown, Tel Aviv. Friends and colleagues read the manuscript or parts of it. Karma Ben Johanan, Brian Stock, Joe Goering, Isahai Rosen Zvi, Tamar Herzig, Maruja Jackman and Francoise Meltzer offered comments, corrections and encouragement. I am deeply grateful to them all.

INTRODUCTION

When I tell people about this book, they often want to know whether I believe in God. I say I don't. Why then, they wonder, do I dedicate so much time and effort to issues that few nonbelievers today find relevant? In fact, they say, it is far from certain that even believers find theology all that relevant. One can be a perfectly good Christian, or Jew, or Muslim, with very little theological knowledge, and one can know a lot of theology and have very little faith.

I must add furthermore that there was nothing "natural" about my choice of subject. I am the son of Holocaust survivors for whom disbelief in a God of justice is a moral duty. I grew up in a secular home and in a secular state. Interest in Christianity was frowned upon. In the Israel in which I grew up, showing sympathy for Christian ideas smacked of unfaithfulness, not to the God of our fathers, but to a ghostly throng of slain and persecuted ancestors. And yet I was, and still am, strongly attracted to these texts, to their concerns and ideals, to their endless dialogue with a being in whom I do not believe.

Why? Probably because of the questions. Religions ask "big questions." Why are we here? What is the meaning of our existence? Why do humans suffer? Why are humans worthy, or unworthy, of salvation? Who is responsible for the way things are? Religious texts are unabashedly engrossed in the sublime. In my fashion so am I. Religious thinkers take existence seriously, treat it as a matter of life and death, invest great talent and great passion in it. I find such concerns and such emotional attitudes strongly appealing, philosophically, morally, and even aesthetically.

But while I am impressed by the questions, I am less impressed by the answers. Perhaps I am too Cartesian, as the French would say, too linear in my thinking. I see loopholes, fallacies, logical shortcuts, and *petitiones principii* where straight logical lines should have been drawn between premise and conclusion. But as long as I'm allowed to get off before the final conclusions are reached, I enjoy the ride. Perhaps "enjoy" does not fully capture it; I'm often entranced by the process. I use the term advisedly. My deepest spiritual experiences have occurred while reading (and sometimes thinking about) religious matters. Unfettered by the unkind rules of strict logic, the religious ride through the big questions is wilder, bolder, more imaginative than any philosophical investigation of the same issues. Like all "straight" thinkers, I am taken by the boldness and beauty of the crooked line.

But is this a fair depiction of religious thought? What is so "crooked" about the thinking of great minds like Augustine and Thomas Aquinas, Maimonides and Nicholas of Cusa? In its own terms, nothing of course. These are not only great thinkers but first-rate logicians capable of detecting a logical fallacy no less than any nonreligious thinker. The problem, naturally, is the hand that these great minds were dealt: it included many a wild card—mythology; dogmata born of historical political compromises, phrased by unskilled theologians; and powerful believers too attached to their weird beliefs. That with these materials the Catholic Church (who started with the worst philosophical hand) has succeeded in forming such an impressive edifice is no less than miraculous. Alas, impressive as it is, it does not hold water—at least not the unholy water that rationalists are willing to drink.

But then my interest in religion is not merely a predilection for crooked lines, combined with an intellectual commitment to straight ones. It is not (just) about me. Because religious thinking is "amphibian" (at least in the West, it is truly committed to both rational and irrational premises), it allows us a glimpse at the moment of passing from one logical sphere to another. And it is an exceptionally interesting moment. It would have been much simpler to hold on to one set of logical rules: either remove everything irrational as all "scientific" postreligious thinkers do, or cling to religious articles of faith *quia absurdum*. Religious rationalists have chosen to live with irreconcilables. The idea that these irreconcilables should be reconciled was formulated quite early in the Catholic Church: "faith seeking understanding," as St. Anselm put it (though the idea is much older, of course). But what I find particularly interesting are not the many moments when the reconciliation was successful, but the moments when it was not, the moments when contradictions could not be reconciled and yet were impossible to abandon, when great ingenuity was required to keep the volatile mixture of religious and philosophical ideas from exploding. Such breaking points, points that stretch to the limit the conceptual muscles of religious thinkers, tell us something important not only about the religious mind, but about the human mind in general. They teach us about the complexity, the ingenuity, and at times the self-inflicted blindness of human thought. These are the moments that this book explores.

One could find them in all areas of religious discourse. In this book, I have chosen to focus on one of the hardest-to-solve dilemmas of "faith in search of understanding"—the sensuality of God. How can the ineffable God, the Being so totally different from anything we can think or imagine be described by Sacred Scriptures in such sensual terms? I have chosen moments when the temptation to be either aquatic or terrestrial was greatest.

My examples come from both Christian and Jewish traditions (using sources from within the historical time frame I feel more or less comfortable with, from late antiquity to the eve of the Protestant Reformation). One should remember that there is no symmetry between the two traditions. While philosophy influenced some Jewish thinkers (most notably Maimonides and his followers), it was, and is, marginal in Judaism. Judaism during the last two millennia has been led by jurists, experts in halacha, who sometimes engaged in mysticism (typically unsystematic). They either ignored many of the most acute theological problems that beset the minds of Christians, or offered them solutions that no systematic theologian would find satisfactory. As a cultural phenomenon, the moments of hermeneutical crisis that this book explores are more typical of Christianity than of Judaism. It is not that one cannot find equivalents to most of the issues in both religious cultures. But such "equivalentism" would give Jewish philosophers a much greater weight than they have ever possessed in their own tradition. The book, then, is "unbalanced." More space is dedicated to Christian thinkers for whom philosophical problems are more troubling than for their Jewish counterparts. But Jewish thinkers were not immune to theological anxieties, and when they arise in their midst, their solutions could be quite different from Christian ones.

Finally, I did not try to trace the full spectrum of attitudes toward the various ways in which one can talk about God in sensual terms. Emptying the sea with a spoon, as the little boy from the famous legend of St. Augustine was trying to do, would require more time and more faith than I have.

THE SENSUAL GOD

CHAPTER ONE

Instability and Its Discontents

Everything moves. I'm not sure when I first realized this. It probably happened when I was eight and got my first wristwatch, or at least that is how I remember it. My parents took me on a trip to Switzerland. When we stopped in Lucerne, they decided that I was responsible enough to get my own timepiece. Watches were fairly expensive at the time. Most of my buddies did not own one. I was rather pleased with it. It was an elegant little thing. I was even more pleased with myself. I had every intention of showing off my new prize when we returned home. But then it happened. As I was proudly gazing at my watch, it suddenly dawned on me: things move. As the second hand was making its rounds, time was passing. The circular movement of the thin strip of metal in my shiny new toy was part of a momentous linear movement that I was somehow part of. We were all part of it—my sister, my parents, the people in the bus, the whole town with its streets, with its parks and trees and monuments. Lake Lucerne was part of it too, as were Switzerland and Israel. All the things that looked stable and immobile to me a minute before were part of a huge movement. All things that moved in their own direction were at the same time being herded by some invisible hand along a single path, the path that my watch measured in seconds, minutes, and hours. It was a continuous, inescapable motion that I suddenly became aware of.

In book 11 (chapter 17) of his *Confessions*, Augustine claims that time is self-evident until we try to give it a formal definition. It is only when we start questioning the self-evident, that our naïve confidence is shattered. In my watch-less state, time did not bother me at all. It had a semantic existence that barley scratched the surface of my mind. Even when I became aware of the existence of time, I was not really concerned with definitions. The only thing that bothered me was the *implications* of time on me, on us. What, in other words, did it mean to live in a world governed by time? I assumed without question the objectivity, the ontological reality, of mechanical time. Not for a moment did I ask myself what exactly it was that clocks were measuring, nor did I pay much attention to the possibility that mechanical time was artificial (in contrast with the "natural" time of the movement of the earth and the planets). I took it for granted that time existed and that clocks were simply keeping record of it, just as cameras were recording things as they "truly" were. What I found absolutely devastating was the fact (I assumed it *was* a fact) that time moves in one direction only. And since we are all somehow implicated in its movement, each passing second signifies not just an external event, but also an intimate personal occurrence. These were *my* seconds, minutes, and hours that were passing as I was ogling my watch. Time was robbing me of my precious hours. At the age of eight, I was obviously not thinking about death or old age. It was simply the knowledge that whatever it was that I was doing (or not doing) was, from the moment the clock marked it, a fait accompli. What's done is done. Too late now to do otherwise. The moment of open possibilities has passed. And even though I had no idea at the time who Auden was ("But all the clocks in the city / Began to whirr and chime: 'O let not Time deceive you, / You cannot conquer Time.'"), I realized that the clocks were tolling all the time; they were tolling for me. Ah yes, I also had no idea who Donne was.

We are carved, thin layer after thin layer, by the butcher's knife of time. In the end, we are gone and the carver alone is left, ever ready to perform his gruesome work on those next in line. The clock is a futile attempt to warn us—futile because nothing can be done but mourn, not the passing of time, but the passing of us.

But is the movement imposed on us from without? Is it time that assaults us with its carving knife, or are the clocks merely our metronomes, ticking the tempo of the inner motions of our self-destruction? We are constantly moving from within, I came to realize. It was not just the blood rushing through our veins, the complex chemical reactions in our digestive system, the storm of electric activity in our brains, and the pumping of air in and out of our lungs. In school, they showed us how under the microscope our bodies teem with life (bacteria, fungi, viruses), and that the food we eat and the water we drink are alive.

We are *changing* all the time. Our bodies are not the solid blocks of matter that I imagined them to be. And the movements within us, I realized, were not regular and circular, but erratic and linear. Time was not the perpetrator, but an innocent observer. Heraclitus was wrong. The river of time is constant and regular. Every second is exactly the same as every other second. The reason we cannot step into the same river twice is that *we* are never the same. With time, I became a follower of Parmenides without realizing it. The child never dies, just as the old man is never born. At any moment, we are exactly one moment old. We grow old by creating ourselves in our own image and likeness.

But the image and likeness of what exactly? As we move blindly toward the future, our past is constantly growing. In retrospect, we might detect patterns: we seem to do certain things in certain ways. But who exactly are "we"? Where is the point of reference, the Archimedean lever with which to move our world? We need to stand still for a moment, but we can't. Only the present really exists, argues the Bishop of Hippo: the past is no longer, the future not yet. But the present is fiendishly slippery. Blink your eyes and it's gone. We simply have not got a foothold on which to be "we."

All the hours of night and day add up to twenty-four. The first of them has the others in the future, the last has them in the past. Any hour between these has past hours before it, future hours after it. One hour is itself constituted of fugitive moments. Whatever part of it has flown away is past. What remains of it is future. That flicker of time which cannot be divided into shorter moments, that alone is what we can call "present." And this time becomes past so quickly that it has no duration.[1]

In the geometry of the soul, like in Euclidean plane geometry, the basic point of reference occupies no space. "We" jump from one point that has no extension whatsoever to the next, similarly lacking extension. "We" try to draw unbroken lines out of these spaceless fragments. Like the humans cut in two by Zeus in Aristophanes's myth in the *Symposium*, the split "I's" crave to be whole, thirst for continuity, want psychological extension. These, argues Augustine, are achieved by turning our fragmented consciousness into a reflective "self." We somehow manage to squeeze into our rapidly vanishing self-consciousness of the present (*contuitus*) the memory of things past (*memoria*) and an expectation of the future (*expectatio*). Memory (as a possibly imaginary record of "our" physical and mental reality) is in Augustine's view what shapes our identity, an identity that is historical and accumulative. The entire project of the *Confessions* is based on the assumption that we are who we remember we are. The answer to the sphinx's question—who are you? Augustine would say—is not a definition ("Man"), but a story ("I"). We are the result of specific historical processes that have made us radically different from others, while sharing the same abstract (and to a large extent useless) common definition. Instead of writing an essay on human nature, Augustine tells in the *Confessions* his own story. Now that story—the events, feelings, and thoughts that have shaped him—depends on *memoria*. In book 10 of the *Confessions*, Augustine offers a lengthy discussion of memory as the storehouse of the soul:

> Memory's huge cavern, with its mysterious, secret, and indescribable nooks and crannies, receives all these perceptions, to be recalled when needed and reconsidered. Every one of them enters into memory, each by its own gate, and is put on deposit there....
>
> These actions are inward, in the vast hall of my memory. There sky, land and sea are available to me together with all the sensations I have been able to experience in them, except for those which I have forgotten. There also I meet myself and recall what I am, what I have done, and when and where and how I was affected when I did it. There is everything that I remember, whether I experienced it directly or believed the word of others. Out of the same abundance in store, I combine with past events images of various things, whether experienced directly or believed on the basis of what I have experienced; and on this basis I reason about future actions and events, and hopes, and again think of all these things in the present. "I shall do this and that,"

I say to myself within that vast recess of my mind, which is full of many rich images, and this act or that follows. "O that this or that were so" "May God avert this or that." I say these words to myself, and, as I speak, there are present images of everything I am speaking of, drawn out of the same treasure-house of memory; I would never say anything like that if these images were not present.[2]

But then who is this expecting and remembering self? The remembering and expecting self starts anew with every reemergence of the elusive, spaceless "present." What gives it the right to claim continuity, to seize the moment, to master the past and the future? Augustine, like Descartes more than a millennium later, conjures up God to be the Archimedean lever. However variable and incomprehensible the world may be, however rootless and senseless the conscious self (the Cartesian thinker), there is always God, the solid rock upon which all the rest can rest. We shall return to this presently, but before we do, we might look at a bolder answer to the problem of the self's instability. It is "hidden" in Plato's *Symposium*, in a discussion of the nature of love. Love, it turns out, has important psychological side effects.

The participants in the *Symposium* present a variety of opinions concerning the nature of Eros. As he usually does, Socrates offers a position that contradicts the views of the other speakers. For Socrates, Eros is not the object of desire but the force that can catapult us from the concrete and material to the abstract and spiritual. Socrates's position is presented from the mouth of the wise woman Diotima. Diotima argues that Eros is not a static "thing" but a process, the inclination to generate and beget "in beauty," because to the mortal creature, generation is a sort of eternity and immortality. It is within this context that Diotima speaks about the problem of the fragmented self:

Even while each living thing is said to be alive and to be the same—as a person is said to be the same from childhood till he turns to be an old man—even then he never consists of the same things, though he is called the same, but he is always being renewed and in other respects passing away, in his hair and flesh and bones and blood and his entire body. And it's not just in his body, but in his soul too, for none of his manners, customs, opinions, desires, pains or fears ever remains the same, but some are coming to be in him while others are passing away. And what is still far stranger than that is that not only does one branch of knowledge come to be in us while another passes away and that we are never the same even in respect of our knowledge, but that each single piece of knowledge has the same fate. For what we call *studying* exists because knowledge is leaving us, because forgetting is the departure of knowledge, while studying puts back fresh memory in place of what went away, thereby preserving a piece of knowledge, so that it seems to be the same. And in that way everything mortal is preserved, not like the divine, by always being the same in every way, but because what is departing and aging leaves behind something new, something such as it has been. By this device, Socrates, she said, what is mortal shares in immortality, whether it is a body or anything else, while the immortal has another way. So don't be surprised if everything naturally values its own offspring, because it is for the sake of immortality that everything shows this zeal, which is love.[3]

Like Augustine, Diotima argues that it is memory that holds the ever-shifting self together. Yet Diotima describes a more complex, more dynamic process. Recollection, for her, is not a simple storage of sense and psychological data, but a re-creation. Knowledge, she says, "is leaving us, because forgetting is the departure of knowledge, while studying puts back fresh memory in place of what went away, thereby preserving a piece of knowledge, so that it *seems* to be the same." Recollection is not a simple backup, knowledge recorded on a surface more durable than the mind, but the destruction of data and its replacement by new data produced by a mechanism that is not described. The new data only "[seem] to be the same." In fact, it is clearly *not* the same, but a variation, just as our offspring are us only in the sense of being produced by us and from us, and not in the sense of being our faithful copies. What we call memory is thus a doppelganger, a distorted version of ourselves. Since we constantly forget the "real" sequence of external and internal events, the sequence that in theory (and only in theory) constitutes our true self, the only thing that allows us to think of ourselves as selves, as a continuum, is the mechanism that we call "memory." But this mechanism is producing ersatz reality. All memory is by definition false.

In Christopher Nolan's film *Memento*, the protagonist, played by Guy Pearce, suffers from short-term memory loss. He uses notes and tattoos to remind him who he is and who the man he is hunting is. Like Diotima's man, the protagonist of *Memento* forgets every morning what he has learned the day before, and needs to reconstruct it so that it "appears to be the same." The problem is that these aide memoirs are open to manipulation. Others can plant misleading information in the forgetful hero's recollection. In the end, the hero (that is, one of the heroes bearing the same name, but an ever-changing identity) does this to himself (if it is really *him*self). He deliberately tattoos misleading information on his skin, information that he knows his avatars will misinterpret. The avatar for whom the new memory is not an external appendage, but part of his inner person—indeed, it *is* his inner person (for we are what we remember, and the reader of the messages has now acquired a radically different memory from the writer of them) will act in ways that are psychologically impossible for the producer of the new memory.

If we seek ontological certainty, then there is little comfort in memory. Augustine thinks that we can remember false things, but cannot remember falsely. Plato (at least in my reading) suggests that this might not be as simple as that. Contemporary studies of false memory agree—we can sense a powerful, Cartesian certainty that is flatly contradicted by recorded data and by others' testimonies. I may be certain of my *contuitus*, my *cogito*, but all I can really say, as numerous critics of Descartes have insisted, is that *a thought* exists. We are not sure there is a thinker, for to give this term meaning, we need a whole array of assumptions that are in the end simply intuitive. Who is the first person speaking? Back to square one—the ever-changing unreliable Self that I have discovered as a child, when I got my first watch.

There is a response to this question that is even bolder than Plato's. It is offered by the great ninth-century Indian philosopher Shankara:

> It is a matter not requiring any proof that the object and the subject whose respective spheres are the notion of the non-ego and the ego, and which are opposed to each other as much as darkness and light, cannot be identified. All the less can their respective attributes be identified. Hence it follows that it is wrong to superimpose upon the

subject—whose self is intelligence, and which has for its sphere the notion of the ego—the object whose sphere is the notion of the non-ego and the attributes of the object and vice versa—to superimpose the subject and the attributes of the subject on the object. In spite of this, it is a natural procedure—which has its cause in wrong knowledge—for men not to distinguish between the two (subject and object) and their respective attributes, although they are absolutely distinct, but to superimpose upon each the characteristic nature and the attributes of the other, and thus mixing the real with the unreal to make use of expressions such as: "That am I" or "That is mine."

. . . This superimposition learned men consider nescience (or non-knowledge), whereas the ascertainment of the true nature of that which is by distinguishing it from that which is superimposed upon it they call knowledge.

The mutual superimposition of the self and the non-self which is termed nescience is the foundation underlying all practical distinctions—those made in ordinary life as well as those laid down by the Veda: between means of knowledge, objects of knowledge and knowing persons, and all scriptural texts, whether they are concerned with injunctions and prohibitions (of meritorious and non meritorious actions), or with final release—moksha. But how can the means of right knowledge, such as perception, inference, and scriptural texts have for their object that which is dependent of nescience? Because, we reply, the means of right knowledge cannot operate unless there is a knowing personality and because the existence of the latter depends on the erroneous notion that the body, the senses and so on are identical with or belong to the self of the knowing person. For without the employment of the senses, perception and the other means of true knowledge cannot operate. And without a foundation the senses cannot act. Nor does anybody act by means of a body on which the nature of the self *is not* superimposed. Nor, in the absence of all that, can the self which in its own nature is free from all contact become a knowing agent. And if there is no knowing agent, the means of true knowledge cannot operate. Hence perception and the other means of true knowledge and the Vedic text have as their object that which is dependent on nescience.[4]

Shankara argues that something true (true knowledge) is based on an error (nescience). Worse, this error—the illusion of a mind-body union—is the a priori epistemological condition for all "true" knowledge. Without nescience no real knowledge is possible. Only by starting from false presuppositions (of being both object and subject, of having a body) and by relying on misleading data (of the senses) can we reach any sort of meaningful knowledge.

We are accustomed to thinking of true knowledge as a slow buildup of tiny, pure fragments of truth that stand in stark contradiction to the vast background of error. Upon error, we are inclined to think, only greater error can be built. But for Shankara, the thinking subject (in contrast with pure thought lacking self-consciousness) cannot develop consciousness without a superimposition, the myth of continuity—continuity between the sphere of the ego and the sphere of the nonego. This brings us back to Plato's *Symposium*: The "I" is an imaginary construct held together by memory. But how can memory be the carrier of continuity without a stable I? Whose memory is it anyway? And if it is no longer the assurance of continuity, how do we know that it reflects anything but the delusions of the particular I that we happen to be at a given moment?

Easterners may be willing to live with a strong tension between falsehood and truth, reality and nonreality, knowledge and nescience. We, in the West, need something stable in the moving, ever-shifting mess that we are. If we are committed to commonsense like Dr. Johnson, we may feel an urge to kick stones. If we have more spiritual commitments, we may call upon God.

CHAPTER TWO

Loving God Like a Cow

"Some people," says Meister Eckhart in one of his German sermons, "want to see God with their own eyes, just as they see a cow; and they want to love God just as they love a cow. You love a cow for the milk and the cheese and because of your advantage. This is how those people act who love God because of external riches or because of internal consolation."[1]

Eckhart despises people who love God for *their* sake. He wants them to love Him for *His* sake. Very well. But who is He? Theologians offer definitions, but they rarely agree. More important, their definitions are hard to understand and even harder to "love." That in itself is not necessarily a problem. Most people do not start from first principles nor do their emotions obey the laws of logic. We can fall in love with a person or a thing simply by coming into contact with the object of our love. We see, hear, touch, smell, or taste something, and behold, we're in love. Explanations come later. That does not mean that sensory data are all there is to it. When we think of it, we tend to assume that beyond sensory data, there is some kind of "true" essence. The senses capture only glimpses, reflections of it. It is that essence that we love. We can, after all, "love" an idea.

But God is not easy to love even as an idea. True, we know things about God's actions. He has created the world, for example, or sacrificed His only begotten son for us, or given us His Torah. But the passage from such knowledge (based, inescapably, on hearsay and sensory data) to the true essence of God is obstructed by the theological idea of the utter otherness of God. The god of the monotheists is the ultimate Other—that which is unlike anything we have ever experienced, sensually or intellectually. Those who claim to have experienced Him in some way usually claim (or the experts make the claim for them) that they have been in contact with a certain approximation of Him (a certain aspect of His power, or some lesser form of being suffused with the divine presence). In fact, the Lord Himself says that direct contact with His essence ("his face") is impossible (or at least lethal) for humans:

> And [Moses] said, "Please, show me your glory." Then He said, "I will make all my goodness pass before you, and I will proclaim the name of Jehovah before you. I will be merciful to whom I will be merciful, and I will have compassion on whom I will have compassion." And He said, "You cannot see my face; for no man shall see me, and live. (Ex 33:18–22)

Even contact with divine approximations, however, is extremely rare. Jews and Christians believe that God revealed Himself (that is, certain aspects of His self) to the entire Hebrew nation on Mount Sinai, but that type of collective revelation had not happened before or since, nor is it quite clear what was in fact revealed, besides the Ten Commandments. If God were to be loved only by those who claim some form of contact with Him, His love would have been a very marginal phenomenon indeed. Yet God is not marginal. For billions upon billions of people throughout history, God has been a central element of their existence. Nor is the love of God performed solely by "highly trained professionals." On the contrary, throngs of people lacking "professional training" say they love God enough to die for Him (and quite as often to kill for Him). They dedicate their lives to and love something of which most of them have only secondhand experience (or more accurately they have secondhand experience of his approximations). They may think they love an idea, but in most cases it is not the professional idea of God that they love. If we asked theologians, they would say that the untrained understand God in a very partial and often incorrect fashion. What they love is never "really" God. They love cows. Or calves.

What do the untrained believe in? Most would acknowledge the concept of an ineffable god, but apart from this acknowledgment (the reasons of which we shall discuss), the theologians' God plays a rather minor part in their religious lives. Humans do not love God for *His* sake. This has nothing to do with either greed or egotism, as Eckhart suggests. It has more to do with the kinds of stories that people are told about God. Since most humans have never had any direct experience with God, they rely on secondhand evidence. Are they allowed to "have faith" in firsthand information? Not without theological interpretation. Theologians (highly trained professionals) are willing to tell others what to make of the God of revelation. The problem is, however, that their descriptions of God are often meaningless for any but other theologians. The main source of information that most people rely on is stories, not definitions. Revelation tells us a little about who God is and a lot about what He did and does. In the overwhelming majority of these stories, the message, either explicit or implicit, is that there are great advantages to loving God, to fearing Him, and above all to believing in Him: "For thus says the Lord to the house of Israel: 'Seek me and live'" (Am 5:4). And while belief is crucial, philosophical insight is not; while belief is for everyone, understanding is for the very few.

But it is not only the poor in spirit who love God for the sake of the kingdom of heaven or for His blessings on earth. The rich in spirit also love Him as we love a cow. The few may seek different advantages, but like the many they ask in the hope of receiving. A mind beset by doubt can be as hard to bear as an empty stomach. If nothing else, believing in God is better than admitting that the world is meaningless. When all else fails, there is always God. Who created heaven and earth? God did. Who made the rough rude sea? God. Who changes the seasons and imposes order on the ominous chaos out there? God does. Who is our insurance policy against epistemological and existential angst? God is. Whether horrible or wonderful, merciful or cruel, He substitutes question marks with exclamation points, fragmentation with continuity. In the chaotic big picture that we face, He brightens up the dark spots, fills the places that we cannot otherwise explain. He is the light that chases out darkness, not by means of human arguments and syllogisms, but by the very mention of His name. We may not really understand the answer, but if we have faith, we shall no longer be troubled by the questions. He was there at the beginning and He will be there at the end. He is alpha and omega. "God" names the unnameable. He is the ultimate guarantee that our existence is not a sequence of passing moments of fleeting awareness without extension. That has nothing to do with "popular" religion. The elite is as troubled by the chaotic nature of human experience as the people, indeed more so. The territory the philosophically inclined find troubling is much broader than what their down-to-earth brethren are upset by. Craving intellectual peace of mind is in no way less result-oriented than the pursuit of earthly happiness. From the outsider's point of view, the intellectuals' obsession with abstractions often requires greater philosophical sacrifices than the "simple folks'" alleged materialism. Of course, there are many other things God can do besides serving as the *ultima ratio philosophorum*.[2] He offers hope to the hopeless, consolation to the downtrodden, justice to the weak, security to the uncertain. He is said to do many amazing things. We love Him *for* them.

But the real issue, as I said in the beginning, is not the lovers—whatever their motives—but the unusual object of their love. Psychologically speaking, there was nothing wrong with the old gods. They provided excellent answers to the hardest existential questions. They ruled the universe and meddled in human affairs. Everything could be explained with their help. In some cultures it still is. Making God a philosophical construct that satisfies one particular set of intellectual obsessions (the tendency of equating matter with existential inferiority) comes with a huge price tag in terms of human emotional needs. Not willing to give up either intellectual or emotional benefits, the monotheists created a hybrid. God may indeed be the rock upon which churches and epistemological towers of Babel are built, but that should not mislead us. God is just as fragmented and incoherent as His creatures/creators. Since He is the answer to radically different questions, He is of necessity full of impossible contradictions. He is distant and close, immanent and transcendent, just and merciful, visible and invisible, and so on.

Theologians do not like contradictions. They are trained to weed out the very logical fallacies that life is made of. God suffers particularly from the theologians' lust for consistency. Revelation does not make life easy for seekers of conceptual consistency. The Sacred Scriptures of the Abrahamic religions were not written by professional theologians and are therefore full of very problematic, at times embarrassing material. Theologians try to save God from the many inaccuracies that people use in talking about Him. The result is a God that doesn't quite fit—you simply cannot squeeze all His attributes, stories, traditions into one working system. And so, like Ptolemy's universe, God has given birth, sprouted cycles and epicycles, retrograde movements and temporary anomalies.

Perhaps instead of saving God for the theologians, we need to save Him *from* the theologians. We need to start with the assumption that God is not one thing, but rather a certain category of explanation, that He is not subject to any logical or metaphysical commitment, and that His contradictions are part of His advantage as a universal key to problems ranging from providing luck to bounty hunters and mates for lonely men and women to providing metaphysical certainty for intellectuals. In other words, the theological God is just one avatar (and not a very popular one) among many. Sometimes the avatars interact with each other, in strong or weak ways (the incarnation may explain God's lapses into materiality), but sometimes they do not. They exist side by side, like precedents in common law. Each is there to solve a particular problem, and they can live happily together, as long as we do not try too hard to make them abide by one set of logical rules.

Intellectuals seek to harmonize discordant voices. Legal systems, they believe, should be consistent, human beings should be consistent, and surely God should at least try to make sense—one sense, that is. Like continuity, consistency, making one sense, is all but self-evident. Groups and even whole cultures can get along quite well without it. In the twelfth century, Pierre Abelard tried to prove to his contemporaries that their faith is full of inconsistencies. In his revolutionary book *Sic et non* (Yes and No), he proved that the holy fathers of the Church were in disagreement—at least prima facie—about very significant theological and philosophical questions. This could not go on, he argued. Abelard offered to rectify this unfortunate state of affairs, and while his particular synthesis was not accepted, his project has become the dominant project of Western culture to this very day. The so-called scholastic revolution made the creation of syntheses its central objective. Gratian's textbook of canon law, published a few years after *Sic et non*, was called *Concordia discordantium canonum* (the Concord of Discordant Canons). Soon a general persecution of discordant canons began, followed by a persecution of discordant human beings.

It is hard for us to imagine the ability to live with inner contradictions as anything but a symptom of personal or cultural dysfunction. We offer *Concordiae* as an act of cultural charity. But such charitable activity can sometimes prove too costly. It creates a dangerous hermeneutical myopia, a tendency not to see what does not fit. We become so dedicated to our synthetic creations that we forget that cultural reality is only possible by taking huge liberties with the rules of logical consistency. By this, I mean not simply that no society can live up to its conceptual ideals, but that it is those very flaws that make it possible. Sociocultural entities are never smooth. They are wrinkled and messy. Instead of starting with a seamless definition of God from which all else must follow, we should start from an impartial look at God's actions and more specifically at the seams that keep the idea of "God" loosely hanging together.

Historians have an inborn predilection for the "actual"—not what *should* have happened but what actually happened. They were reproached by Aristotle for being less philosophical than even poets. All historians care about, he scoffed, is what Alcibiades did and what others did to him. Perhaps that is not all historians care about, but they are indeed convinced that what Alcibiades did and what others did to him is not merely a specific case in some grand point but the unfolding of mental as well as practical possibilities. For humans again and again prove that there are things that should not work in theory that work perfectly well in practice. Indeed, the only way they *could* work is by being "unphilosophical."

If we wish to understand the idea of God in practice, as we think of Alcibiades, it might be useful to stop thinking of Him as a single person or idea (this approach wipes out both history and sociology for the sake of philosophy and sees Him instead as a *group* of persons, persons that unlike the three persons of the Trinity do not converge into a common substance, each perfectly suitable for specific tasks and useful for answering a particular set of questions). It is as if the old gods were grouped together under a single name, without thereby losing their conflicting and contradictory attributes. This does not mean that the One God is a camouflaged pagan god. He is not. The grouping together of needs and obsessions has created tensions that were lacking in the old system and answers that were not available in it. The fact that theologians (rather than mythmakers, storytellers, or lawyers) were made the bouncers in the religious club had a huge impact on the nature of concepts allowed to enter "orthodoxy." But we must not forget that the selection process was, and is, distorted because of the heterogeneous nature of the selection principles, and by the fact not only that the selectors were a heterogeneous group, as Abelard pointed out, but also that they were not operating in a pure environment. They were not playing solely with ideas, but with human needs—social, cultural, and political needs. Once they were allowed into "orthodoxy," ideas about God had to obey the dress code and assume the suitable garb. But the gowns provided by reinterpreters never quite fit. You may declare that the cabbalistic idea of the Sephirot does not contradict the idea of God's oneness, but when one has a closer look at the sephirotic god, one can, and should, have doubts. Certainly, His modus operandi has changed radically. What Alcibiades does and what others do to him is not without interest.

If we want to understand how God "works," we need to watch Him in action, not in the classroom, but in specific situations where people report His presence. But where should we look for Him? He is, after all, everywhere. "There is no place free of Him," as the Zohar declares.3 But if we want to catch Him in the process of transforming Himself from one set of preoccupations to another, in the process of avatar-incarnation, then certain places are better than others as observation points. Cultural phantoms reveal themselves at crossroads, where spheres meet, where complicated and poorly understood abstract principles of high theology meet half-pronounced concrete needs. We can get glimpses of Him in the moments when theoretical premises run into difficulties. We might want to look at the relationship of the theologians' God to the senses—those dangerous "windows" that convey into the unsullied soul the false information of the material world. God, as we know, should be above sensory data. But of course He isn't. He is visible and audible. He has taste, touch, and smell. How is this possible? Surely God has a lot of explaining to do.

And so do we.

CHAPTER THREE

Endless

In one of his sermons, John Chrysostom describes the chasm that separates God from His human worshipers: "Let us call upon him, then, as the ineffable God who is beyond our intelligence, invisible, incomprehensible, who transcends the power of mortal words. Let us call on him as the God who is inscrutable to the angels, unseen by the Seraphim, inconceivable to the Cherubim, invisible to the principalities, to the powers, and to the virtues, in fact, to all creatures without qualification, because he is known only by the Son and the Spirit."[1]

Before we turn to the many avatars of the One God and to their distinctive characteristics, we must have a quick look at the source—the unsullied essence of the One God in its immaculate state, before inaccurate words, dangerous metaphors, and His inexplicable love for His creatures made Him flesh. The God of monotheists is omnipotent. That is His most important attribute. As such, He is *absolutus*—free from all restraint. God's immateriality and His ineffability are aspects of His omnipotence. He cannot be matter, for matter is the passive element of being that form, the active element of being, shapes. In God there is nothing that is not pure action, pure force. He cannot be *fully* grasped, for if the limited human mind could understand Him in his entirety, it would mean that He is not unlimited.

In the Zohar, the great masterpiece of medieval Jewish mysticism, he is aptly called Ein Sof, "the one that has no end," "the indeterminate one." Anything that might suggest that He is, that He *can* be, limited by anything external to Him is by definition false and an insult to God. When God commits blatant crimes against this article of faith, as He does, most scandalously, in the Incarnation, for example, that breach of theological contract must be explained away. Appearances to the contrary notwithstanding, God's absolute power must be "saved." This demands of theologians spectacular feats of metaphysical acrobatics, feats that they perform with amazing skill.

It is all the fault of Greek philosophers. Jews did not concern themselves with such elusive terms as "perfection" and "ineffability." Hebrew is notoriously poor in philosophical terms. Essence? Substance? Metaphysics? The rabbis were not quite sure what they meant. Nor does it matter. The real question is what He, whichever way we define Him, expects His subjects to do. God is the Ruler of the Universe. What exactly does this mean? It means that you don't want to mess with Him. For His own inscrutable reasons, He has commanded us to do things and we try to comply. One is reminded of a famous story about the Buddha:

> Malunkyaputta was meditating thus: "Those views are not explained, set aside and ignored by the lord (Buddha): The world is eternal, the world is not eternal, the world is an ending thing, the world is not an ending thing; the life-principle is the body, the life-principle is one thing, the body another; the Tathagata exists after dying, the Tathagata does not exist after dying, the Tathagata both is and is not after dying, the Tathagata neither is nor is not after dying. . . . I, having approached the Lord, will question him on the matter."
>
> When the sage approaches the Buddha with these questions, the Buddha responds by stating that he has never promised to answer questions such as these. A man who refuses to be enlightened before he finds answers to such questions is like a person wounded by a poisoned arrow who refuses to be healed before he is told exactly what type of arrow it was and given a full profile of the man who had shot him.[2]

"Monks," [says the Buddha elsewhere], "reason not ill unprofitable things such as: Eternal is the world; finite is the world, infinite is the world etc." . . . Such reasoning does not lead to Nirvana. When they reason, monks reason thus: This is suffering (*dukkha*); that leads to the ceasing of suffering."[3]

Jews managed perfectly well without very clear definitions of the Tathagata or systematic theology. Greeks did not. Greeks like definitions and abhor logical contradictions. The history of the three monotheist religions is the history of an impossible encounter between Jewish law, history, and myth and Greek philosophy.

The most significant philosophical school—from the Christian point of view, a point of view that had a deep influence on the two other monotheistic religions—was Platonism. Platonism disdains the material. The platonic soul must not only aspire to a higher, spiritual sphere of existence, but must view materiality as a spiritual infection. While Jews agreed that the spirit is nobler than matter, and that matter, if allowed to become dominant, can hinder man from reaching salvation, they did not see it as something to be rid of. In its proper place, matter is not simply a temporary vehicle of the soul, but a necessary—essential—part of being.

This was not how Plotinus, the great third-century interpreter of Plato, saw it. Plotinus saw matter as metaphysical evil, inescapable for humans, but harmful nonetheless. Plotinus believed in a Supreme Being, the "One." He also had his own version of the Trinity—the One, The Intellect (or mind), and the Soul. This made him very appealing for Christians.

Neoplatonism had a huge influence on Christian thinking. It turned Jehovah, with His likes and dislikes, with His jealousy and wrath, with His favorites and enemies, with His imperfections and impatience, into the ineffable One. The One is not the Lord of History. He is a philosopher's Supreme Being: self-sufficient, untouched by anything, totally transcendent, containing no division, multiplicity, or distinction. The One has no will, for he wants nothing. The one does not think, for thinking implies a distinction between thinker and thought. The One does not love, for that would mean needing something other than himself. The One is pure power. Nothing exists that is not dependent on him, but the One is totally independent. Human knowledge is utterly incapable of grasping him in his true, absolute essence. He is unlike anything we know. Words necessarily fail to describe him. The only way that we may do some justice to him is by "apophasis"—"unsaying." All positive statements about him must be immediately contradicted by opposite statements, thus preventing the mind from the illusion of true denotation. From our limited point of view, the One is Not.[4]

In the late fifth or early sixth century, a theologian assuming the identity of Dionysius the Areopagite, converted to Christianity by Paul's preaching (Acts 17:34), wrote a series of influential works that help translate Jehovah into the Neoplatonic One. Dionysus speaks of the ultimate goal of our journey toward God in terms of a gradual emptying of the soul of incorrect ideas about God, until it is left with total unknowing. This is the closest we can get to God. We begin the journey by praising God, attributing to Him every positive attribute, like wisdom and unity and power. These attributes are not descriptions, but expressions of reverence. Soon, however, we run out of words, since no matter how many adulatory adjectives we use, we remain incapable of "covering" His infinite vastness. Instead of trying such an impossibility, Dionysius argues, we should seek, on the contrary, to negate wrong ways of addressing Him:

> The Cause of all is above all, and is not inexistent, speechless, mindless. It is not a material body, and hence has neither shape nor form, quality, quantity, or weight. . . . It suffers neither disorder nor disturbance and is overwhelmed by no earthly passion. It is not powerless and subject to the disturbances caused by sense perception. It endures no deprivation of light. It passes through no change, decay, division, loss, no ebb and flow, nothing of which the senses may be aware. None of all this can either be identified with it or attributed to it.[5]

God is perfect. He therefore "passes through no change, decay, division, loss, no ebb and flow." But, not satisfied with negating imperfection and materiality in God, Dionysius proceeds to negate the most sacred divine names and theological articles of faith: "As we climb higher, we say this: It is not soul or mind, nor does it possess imagination, conviction, speech or understanding." This is stunning enough, but Dionysius does not stop here:

It cannot be spoken of and it cannot be grasped by understanding. It is not number or order, greatness or smallness, equality or inequality, similarity or dissimilarity. It is not immovable, moving, or at rest. It has no power, it is not power, nor is it light. It does not live nor is it life. It is not a substance, nor is it eternity or time. It cannot be grasped by understanding, since it is neither knowledge nor truth. It is not kingship. It is not wisdom. It is neither one nor oneness, divinity nor goodness. Nor is it spirit, *in the sense in which we understand the term*. It is not sonship or fatherhood and it is nothing known to us or to any other being. It falls neither within the predicate of nonbeing nor of being. Existing things do not know it *as it actually is* and it does not know them *as they are*. . . . It is beyond assertion and denial. We make assertions and denials of what is next to it, but never of it, for it is both beyond every assertion, *being the perfect and unique cause of all things*, and by virtue of its *preeminently simple and absolute nature*, free of every limitation, beyond every limitation; it is also beyond every denial.[6]

Earlier, Dionysius compared negative theology to a sculptor creating a statue. He removes unnecessary material, until he is left with his image. But, of course, Dionysius does not want us to worship an image, an idol. He uses his hammer and chisel to remove *all* content from our discourse about God. His last act is to get rid of the tools. God "is also beyond every negation."

Dionysius wishes to convey a sense of the total otherness of God, of His absolute unknowability. He uses apophatic paradox (neither being nor nonbeing, not immovable, moving, or at rest) and deliberately shocking negations (neither one nor oneness, neither divinity nor goodness). As the absolute Other, God is simply beyond words. "Good" is as false as "bad" in relation to Him. And yet, Dionysius is not totally consistent in his negative praise for the otherness of God. You will note that I have emphasized a number of phrases in the text. It seems that the author implies that God *can* be known and know, though not as He actually is or as creatures are. He also seems reluctant to negate the statement that God is "the perfect and unique cause of all things, and that he is simple and absolute." Obviously, these are important qualities. One could even suggest that it is those qualities that justify the entire exercise. And yet, Dionysius's hesitation to take his negative theology to the limit is telling.

A quick look at Ein Sof might suggest an explanation. Ein Sof is the *Deus absconditus* (the hidden God) of the Zohar. He (it?) is the divine essence, the cause of causes. Like Plotinus's One, Ein Sof, who defies all definition (as his name suggests), causes the creative process to begin without "doing" or "willing" anything. The ontological explosion that is the beginning of the non-God is the "mystical" outcome of his very "being" (if "being" is the right term to describe him/it). The ten Sephirot—the Jewish version (vehemently denied) of the divine persons of Christianity—come into being by a process of emanation. The Sephirot are sometimes referred to as the lights (*Orot* in Hebrew) of Ein Sof. They are aspects of the divinity that are present and active in the world (in different degrees), whereas Ein Sof remains totally detached not only from the created world, but also from his own emanations. In fact, it is not quite clear that the term "emanation" conveys properly the aloofness of Ein Sof. The Sephirot emanated from the first real "being"—the Sephira of Keter (crown). How exactly Keter came into being is not clear. Keter itself can be grasped only to a very limited extent (it is often referred to as *Ayin*, "nothing" or "nonbeing"). The first truly knowable Sephira, Hokhma (wisdom), is called Yesh (being) and it emanated: "yesh me-ayin," being out of nothing (creation ex nihilo thus takes a very peculiar meaning):

> Ein Sof cannot be known and does not have beginning and end . . .
> in Ein Sof there are no wills and no lights and no luminaries [that
> is, the Sephirot are not contained in it though it is their source].
> All those lights and luminaries [the Sephirot] depend on him, but
> have no power to comprehend him. The only one who knows-and-
> does-not-know is the supreme will, the most hidden of the hidden,
> Ayin [Keter]. When [the two next Sephirot whose appellations are]
> "Supreme Point" [Hokhma] and "The World to Come" [Binah] lift
> themselves up toward him, they only sense his "smell," like someone
> who senses the smell of a person's perfume.[7]

Ein Sof is unknown, unknowable, beyond words, like Plotinus's One, like Dionysius's God. Even the divine emanations grasp only faint traces of him. He is therefore practically ignored in the Zohar. Certainly, he pales in comparison with the wild, ruthlessly creative speculations and fervent devotions dedicated to the Sephirot. What is the point in repeatedly saying that God is beyond human words? Wouldn't it be simpler to declare once and for all that God is unknowable and then simply forget about him? "Whereof one cannot speak, thereof one must be *silent*," as Ludwig Wittgenstein famously advises in his *Tractatus*.

There may be two important reasons for speaking about the unspeakable. The first is that the purpose of such speech is not to describe God at all, but to subvert "normal" modes of speech and, more importantly, "normal" modes of thought. It is not unlike the techniques used by Zen masters to shake their disciples out of their conventional thinking patterns.[8] The mystic strives to shake himself out of conventional thought patterns, by meditating on the unknowable God in unconventional ways. Our "normal" ways of thought, as Shankara observed, are hopelessly trapped within the duality of subject and object. We divide and distinguish instinctively. For us, things are either-or. God, unfettered by human logic, is also free of the law of contradiction. He is all things and nothing. We can have metaideas of him (that he is not subject to the law of contradiction, for example), but no concrete knowledge, since all positive statements must be immediately negated to retain the total otherness of God.

So we have the *mode d'emploi* of God, but no description of him as object. As we saw, even Keter, the being closest to Ein Sof, has only an uncertain grasp of him (Keter "knows and does not know" at the same time), but the other Sephirot sense him as a "faint smell"—a fleeting, hard-to-describe sense of presence. This is not knowledge, for Ein Sof is out of reach even for himself (as we said, the term "knowledge" implies duality), but something closer to the unknowledge that Shankara describes as superimposed on the object in order to make knowledge possible.

And yet, when it comes to the ultimate Otherness that we call God, such unknowledge cannot lead to knowledge, but is necessarily a dead end, a dark cul de sac where the mind, suddenly aware of it inadequacy, senses, for a fleeting moment, the possibility of some other "thing," something indescribable, *unheimlich*, something utterly different without being the opposite pole in a duality. Plotinus describes the soul's feeling, as it approaches the One, as a sudden sensation of dread:

The soul or mind reaching towards the formless finds itself incompetent to grasp where nothing bounds it or to take impression where the impinging reality is diffuse; in sheer dread of holding to nothingness, it slips away. The state is painful; often it seeks relief by retreating from all this vagueness to the region of sense, there to rest as on solid ground, just as the sight distressed by the small rests with pleasure on the big.[9]

If apophasis is successful, its endless string of paradoxes, of contradictions in terms, destabilizes the mind. Instead of slipping, as it normally does, from one pole of the discursive duality to the other, it is suspended momentarily in the middle. Dionysius describes it thus: "Renouncing all that the mind may conceive, wrapped entirely in the intangible and the invisible, he [Moses] belongs completely to him who is beyond everything. Here, being neither oneself nor someone else, one is supremely united by a completely unknowing inactivity of all knowledge, and knows beyond the mind by knowing nothing."[10] The Dionysian apophasis, then, could be interpreted as a mental game, a manipulation of the mind, aimed at bringing it as close as possible to a temporary (and in this life it can only be temporary) sensation of otherness: "Soul must see in its own way; this is by coalescence, unification; but in seeking thus to know the unity it is prevented by that very unification from recognizing what it has found; it cannot distinguish itself from the object of this intuition."[11] Those brief moments are followed by a return to our normal dualities. The experience can be acknowledged but not described. It has no content. We can, at best, report the faint traces (the perfume) that it has left in our mind.

But there could be another reason for speaking about the unspeakable. Thinkers like Meister Eckhart were not interested in creating temporary short-circuits in the minds of their listeners or readers. What they wanted to create by their notion of the unspeakable God was a symbolic center of gravity that is totally untouched by the failures of human understanding. To some extent, this was suggested by Paul in 1 Corinthians 18–25:

> For the message of the cross is foolishness to those who are perishing, but to us who are being saved it is the power of God. For it is written: "I will destroy the wisdom of the wise, and bring to nothing the understanding of the prudent." Where is the wise? Where is the

scribe? Where is the disputer of this age? Has not God made foolish the wisdom of this world? For since, in the wisdom of God, the world through wisdom did not know God, it pleased God through the foolishness of the message preached to save those who believe. For Jews request a sign, and Greeks seek after wisdom; but we preach Christ crucified, to the Jews a stumbling block and to the Greeks foolishness, but to those who are called, both Jews and Greeks, Christ the power of God and the wisdom of God. Because the foolishness of God is wiser than men, and the weakness of God is stronger than men.

Paul boldly admits the "foolishness" of the Christian message. The foolishness of God ignores the rules of human wisdom, because God's posited omnipotence implies authority to break all human rules—including the rules of human reason. This is the foundation of Christian mysteries—an authorized defiance of human conventions. The *mysterium absolutum* of the Trinity, for example ($3 = 1$), is not an "organic" consequence of primary assumptions as Aristotelian syllogisms are, but a breach. It is a non sequitur, accepted through "faith" in obedience to God's "will" (or, more accurately, to his particular type of being) as it manifested itself in revelation or in the sacred tradition of the Church.

This submission to God's ontological freedom is not easy to digest. Theologians are constantly trying to limit its irrational aspects. Philosophers and mystics using negative theology apply a whole array of logical-noise-reduction mechanisms that form part of different theological positions. But there is something they all have in common: appearances notwithstanding, in His "true" essence, God is not a coexistence of contradictions, but beyond contradiction. He is beyond reason and not against reason. Particular saving mechanisms may rise and fall, but these fluctuations do not affect the object of speculation. Secure behind His impenetrable walls, God is the Gordian knot that no argument can untangle or cut.

The metaphysical untouchability of the Almighty—His being "beyond" all understanding—is not just a source of aesthetic and psychological consolations. It has other, more practical aspects as well. For God was obviously not content to remain an ontological statement. At some point, somehow, He broke through His magic circle into the world as we know it and materialized in the most amazing ways. The Plotinian One has miraculously "overflowed" in a series of emanations. Ein Sof has amazingly brought Keter (the first Other) into being. The Hidden God of Dionysius has mysteriously become the Holy Trinity that has created the world in which the Second Person has become flesh.

There is great vagueness about how the passage from total transcendence to immanence actually occurs. Plotinus's metaphor of overflowing is remarkably unsuitable for describing a being with no limitation, let alone rims. Other metaphors (love exploding, thought materializing, will taking shape) are as problematic. As a last resort, Plotinus could be interpreted as describing a system that has no ontological commitment a system in which the shifts between the One and the many are but "states of mind" or different modes of thinking about the One. But this would not work for monotheists. Believers in the God of Revelation tend to see the world in which that revelation took place as ontologically "real." The "beyondness" of God in his prelogical state simply releases us from providing explanations for the transition phase. At most, we are to be satisfied with poetic metaphors. How can God suffer the existence of non-God without compromising his oneness? Because nothing is impossible for the Cause of all causes. It is simply beyond *our* comprehension.

Relying on the principle of the perfect answer-that-cannot-be-explained is not just a logical game. God's revealed history and His revealed will arouse numerous logical and ethical problems. Why does God behave in this particular way (destroy his creation in a deluge, for example, and then regret it)? Why does He forbid certain morally neutral things (like eating pork and mixing wool and linen) and allow others that are seemingly reprehensible (like sacrificing a goat to Azazel)? Not just because He can (the pre-philosophical Jewish answer), but because He has reasons. What reasons? His ways are mysterious and His wishes incomprehensible. We may find some explanations in the postlogical state, but the prelogical state remains our psychological insurance policy. It is a case of *petitio principii* (begging the question) in its purest form. Literally, the Latin term means seeking the principle or the first premise. The inexplicable God, who is by definition immune to logical attack, is the rock upon which every church is built. He is there not simply as an insurance policy against effective debunkers, but as the eye of the storm: we may not understand how the divine logic works, but it works and is a logic.

Two brief illustrations might be useful. The first is from twentieth-century Israel, the second from sixteenth-century Germany. Yesha'ayahu Leibowitz (1903–1994) was a Latvian-born Israeli scientist and philosopher. Leibowitz did not have much patience for the poetic expressions of God's ineffability. Since God is unknowable, there is no point wasting words describing his indescribability. But God has revealed Himself (for reasons that are beyond our comprehension) and has given us a long list of demands (*mitzvoth*, the commandments). It is our duty to obey these demands without trying to understand them. Indeed, for Leibowitz the highest form of religious devotion is performing the *mitzvoth* not for any gain or advantage (Leibowitz, like Eckhart, despised cow lovers), but for their own sake (*lishman*). For Leibowitz, proving God's existence was futile and trying to understand Him by human reason sacrilegious. God's authority rested entirely on his inscrutability. With one bold move, numerous difficulties and improbabilities were rendered null and void. The alogical nature of God requires an act of faith. Reason is incapable of comprehending it. But once we have performed this leap (by "deciding" to believe), the rest falls nicely into place and can be handled by means of the system's inner logic.

Martin Luther (1483–1536) also believed in a *Deus Absconditus* and he too thought that this ineffable God had the right to command without giving explanations. In *The Bondage of the Will*, written in response to Erasmus's treatise on the freedom of the will, Luther writes:

> They demand that God should act according to man's idea of right, and do what seems proper to themselves—or else that He should cease to be God! . . . Flesh does not deign to give God glory to the extent of believing him to be just and good when He speaks and acts above and beyond the definitions of Justinian's Code, or the fifth book of Aristotle's Ethics! No, let the Majesty that created all things give way before a worthless fragment of His own creation! Let the boot be on the other foot, and the Corycian cavern fear those that look into it! So it is "absurd" to condemn one who cannot avoid deserving damnation. And because of this "absurdity" it must be false

that God has mercy on whom He will have mercy, and hardens whom He will. He must be brought to order! Rules must be laid down for Him, and He is not to damn any but those who have deserved it by *our* reckoning![12]

God does not demand illogic as a way of approaching existence. Once you accept the basic premise of His perfection *per definitionem*, all else follows—logically. You may be a social and religious critic (as both Leibowitz and Luther were), but at the core of your religious conviction there remains a call for illogic justified by a hidden logic and an unquestioning obedience.

The hidden has rendered us a great service by being the absolutely pure, perfect source of imperfections and infections. It is to infections and imperfections that we must now turn.

CHAPTER FOUR

Credo

Faith does not always require leaps. At times, God is willing to offer empirical proof that will convince even doubters. Here is one scriptural example:

> Then Elijah said to them, "I am the only one of Jehovah's prophets left, but Baal has four hundred and fifty prophets. Get two bulls for us. Let them choose one for themselves, and let them cut it into pieces and put it on the wood, but not set fire to it. I will prepare the other bull, and put it on the wood, but not set fire to it. Then you call on the name of your god, and I will call on the name of Jehovah. The god who answers by fire—he is God." Then all the people said, "What you say is good."
>
> Elijah said to the prophets of Baal: "Choose one of the bulls and prepare it first, since there are so many of you. Call on the name of your god, but do not light the fire." So they took the bull given them and prepared it. Then they called on the name of Baal from morning till noon. "Baal, answer us!" they shouted. But not a sound was heard; no one answered. And they danced around the altar they had made.

At noon Elijah began to taunt them: "Shout louder!" he said. "Surely he is a god! Perhaps he is deep in thought, or busy, or traveling. Maybe he is sleeping and must be awakened." So they shouted louder and slashed themselves with swords and spears, as was their custom, until their blood flowed. Midday passed, and they continued their frantic prophesying until the time for the evening sacrifice. But not a sound was heard, no one answered; no one was listening. Then Elijah said to all the people, "Come to me." They came to him, and he repaired the altar of Jehovah, which was in ruins. And Elijah took twelve stones, one for each of the tribes of the sons of Jacob, to whom the word of Jehovah had come, saying, "Your name shall be Israel." With the stones he built an altar in the name of Jehovah, and he dug a trench around it, large enough to hold two measures of seed. He arranged the wood, cut the bull into pieces, and laid it on the wood. Then he said to them, "Fill four large jars with water and pour it on the offering and on the wood." "Do it again," he said, and they did it again. "Do it a third time," he ordered, and they did it the third time. The water ran down around the altar and even filled the trench. At the time of sacrifice, the prophet Elijah stepped forward and prayed: "Jehovah, God of Abraham, Isaac and Israel, let it be known today that you are God in Israel and that I am your slave and have done all these things at your command. Answer me, Jehovah, answer me, so these people will know that you, Jehovah, are God, and that you are turning their hearts back again." Then the fire of Jehovah fell and burned up the sacrifice, the wood, the stones, and the soil, and also licked up the water in the trench. When all the people saw this, they fell prostrate and cried, "Jehovah is God! Jehovah is God!" (1 Kgs 18:22–30)

The Israelites saw fire coming down from heaven in response to Elijah's prayer, consuming flesh, wood, stone, soil, and even water. But what is the logical value of these "proofs"? If it were a question of who could conjure up a greater supernatural force, Elijah or the prophets of Baal, then the events on Mount Carmel would constitute a decisive answer. But do they prove that Jehovah is the only God? Do they prove that He is the creator of heaven and earth, all-powerful, all-knowing, and benevolent? Fire from heaven is fire from heaven, not proof of the existence of an omnipotent, omniscient, and benevolent God. The resurrection that put an end to Thomas's doubts does not prove divinity or we would have had more gods than there were in the pagan pantheon.

What constitutes decisive proof in religion would hardly ever convince a logician. Religions present as proof evidence that has such strong psychological force that believers disregard *what* is being proven. Miracles prove something, but not necessarily the thing that needs proving. This, however, is not a logical conjuring trick. What miracles provide is what really matters—not a set of building blocks for constructing the hidden God, but psychological assurance. The people who saw fire coming down from heaven at the request of Elijah or those who saw saints perform impressive miracles were not interested in the canons of proof that would be of great importance for a scientist. What they received was proof of being in the presence of a great power. What this power is exactly matters mostly to intellectuals and it is to them that the throngs of overwhelmed spectators leave the task of giving names and exact descriptions.

The dictionary definition of "to believe" is "to accept as true, as real." That sounds simple enough when we play simple true-false games:

"This is a horse—true or false?"

"I can't see it."

"I'm telling you that it is a horse."

"I believe you."

We both know what we are talking about (this is a horse; this is not a horse, but a cow). When I say I believe you, I express my confidence in you. My belief in you leads me to believe in what you say though you provide no evidence.

But what does it mean to believe in God, or more specifically "in one God, the Father Almighty, maker of heaven and earth and of all things visible and invisible; and in one Lord Jesus Christ, the only begotten Son of God, begotten of His Father before all ages, God of God, Light of Light, very God of very God, begotten, not made, of one substance with the Father; by whom all things were made"?

What does "I believe in one God" mean? Let us assume that "I" have a fuzzy instinctive understanding of what "one God" is. But what does "begotten of his Father before all worlds" mean? Do we know what *very God* means? And "Light of Light"? Is it a metaphor? And "begotten, not made"? Are we sure we know the difference? In short, do we need to know *what* we believe in?

If the answer is "no" (I do not know *what* I believe in), the term "believe" becomes just an indicator of a specific state of mind. The believer is in a state of unconditional acceptance in relation to a particular sequence of sounds that might or might not mean something individually, but that may not make sense as a sequence. Do we believe that brrrdfffs are of one substance with grrrdffffs? Unless you tell us what brrrdffffs are, it would be difficult for me to provide a meaningful answer. In *On the Trinity*, Augustine seems to suggest at first that faith makes it possible for the believer to love *without* knowing:

> Who loves what he does not know? For it is possible to know something and not love it, but can one, I ask, love what is not known? If one cannot, then no one loves God before he knows Him. . . . For where are those three [the three cardinal virtues that prepare the soul to perceive God] . . . except in a mind believing what it does not yet see, and hoping and loving what it believes? Even he therefore who is not known, but is believed, can be loved.

But the Bishop of Hippo immediately adds a warning: "But one must be very careful lest the mind, believing that which it does not see, feign to itself something which is not, and hope for and love that which is false (*fingat sibi aliquid quod non est et speret diligatque quod falsum est*)."[1] Faith is not the miracle cure for epistemological uncertainties. Without having at least some idea of that which we believe in, it may lead not to salvation, but to idolatry.

In his typically less charitable way, Peter Abelard describes such faith not as the unpleasant result of good intentions, but as utter folly:

> I . . . composed for my students a theological tractate *On the Unity and Trinity of God*. They had kept asking of me rational and philosophical expositions, and insisting on what could be understood and not mere declarations, saying that a flow of words is useless if reason does not follow them, that nothing is believed unless it first be understood, and that it is ridiculous for a man to proclaim to others what neither he nor his pupils can grasp by their intelligence. Such a man, they said, was branded by the Lord as a blind leader of the blind.[2]

To be meaningful, faith needs understanding. Just how *much* understanding do we need to make our faith meaningful? It seems quite clear that we are not supposed to have a *perfect* understanding of what we believe in. I am not sure I can provide a very accurate zoological definition of "horse," for example, and even if I could, this would only be a partial definition. Knowing "fully" what a horse is requires knowledge of subatomic particles, of mammal evolution, of language and signification. In other words, as Leibniz argued, to know *a* thing "perfectly," one would need to know everything. Only an all-knowing being knows perfectly.

So, while we need to have at least *some* valid knowledge of the things we believe in, we do not need to have a full knowledge of them. How much knowledge is enough? Is it enough to understand the lexical meaning of the words? "Begotten," for example, means "generated by procreation." So if we believe that the Son was "generated by procreation," do we believe what the Church believes? Apparently, not quite. "Begotten," it turns out, could mean very different things.

But am I not attacking a straw man? The Church's declarations of faith do not exist in outer space, after all. The Church has established a fairly elaborate mechanism of catechetical instruction to explain just what is meant by such phrases. "Begotten," when it refers to the Second Person in the Trinity, does *not* mean generated by procreation. Everybody knows that.

Maybe. But things are more complicated than that. It is one thing to say that we "know" what a horse is. We know enough about horses to point our finger at one. More important, this is common knowledge. Most people, when asked, would be pointing their fingers at the same object. "Knowing" what *God* is, however, is obviously much more complicated. Not only is it not a material object, it is, as theologians have conceived it, a particularly intricate and hard-to-grasp notion. It often takes an expert to do God the minimal justice required to distinguish Him from brrrdfffs and grrrdfffs.

In the thirteenth-century, Pope Innocent IV suggested that within the Church knowledge possessed by the few who know a lot can make sense of the faith of those who know very little. Even though most of the faithful cannot tell God from a brrrdfff, it is enough that some people can to make everybody's faith meaningful:

There is a certain measure of faith to which all are obliged, and which is sufficient for the simple (*simplicibus*) and perhaps for all laymen—that is, every adult must believe that God exists and that He rewards all good people. He must also believe in the other articles of the Creed implicitly (*implicite*), that is, he must believe that whatever the Catholic Church believes is true.... [Bishops should be familiar with and capable of explaining—with the help of experts—all the articles of the Creed.] As for the lower clergy, it seems clear that if they are poor and cannot attend school . . . it is enough that they know as simple laymen, and a little bit more (*aliquantulum plus*)—about the Eucharist. For they must know that in the Eucharist the true body of Christ is being produced....

Such is the power of implicit faith that there are those who say that if someone has it—that is, he believes in everything the Church believes—but his natural reason (*ratione naturali*) makes him hold the erroneous opinion that the Father is greater than the Son or precedes Him in time, or that the three persons are separate beings, he is neither a heretic nor a sinner, so long as he does not defend his error and so long as he believes that this is the faith of the Church. In that case, the faith of the Church replaces his opinion, since, though his opinion is false, it is not his faith, rather his faith is the faith of the Church.[3]

Innocent's solution is based on the idea of a division of labor in matters pertaining to salvation. Just as people can benefit from the virtues of others (most notably Christ, but also the saints), so should they be able to benefit from the knowledge of others. Faith, then, is a communal activity. The number of saints—those endowed with heroic virtue—is much smaller than the number of those actually saved (in part, at least, through sharing in the saints' merits). Likewise, the number of people who believe explicitly—that is, who know enough to explain what they believe in—is considerably smaller than the number of those who believe implicitly (that is, who can simply repeat the sacred formulae, confident that others *know* what those formulae mean).

The problem is that quite often even the experts offer a fairly shaky explicit foundation for the common faith. Take, for example, the question of divine impassibility, debated between St. Cyril of Alexandria (376–444) and his heretical critic Nestorius (c. 385–440). It is nicely summed up by Paul Gavrilyuk in his book *The Suffering of the Impassible God*:

> Nestorius claimed that Cyril's formula, the Word "suffered impassibly" [*apathos epathen*] or "the impassible suffered," was a blatant contradiction at best and theological double talk at worst. "The same," Nestorius was quick to point out, "could not be by nature impassible and passible." Cyril should quit speaking in riddles, saying one thing and implying another. If Mary did not give birth to God the Word before all ages, why call her Theotokos? If divine nature did not suffer, why make God the subject of the suffering flesh? If God is immortal, why speak of him as dying in his mortal body? If the claim that God was born of a woman, suffered and died has no literal force, why continue to use such provocative expressions?[4]

Good questions. But then Nestorius was a heresiarch. His insistence on applying ordinary logic to God is dangerous and counterproductive. The God of revelation (unlike the Hidden God) is susceptible to human reason, as long as our reason is willing to accept the data of revelation and of authorized inspiration (in the form of ecumenical councils, for example) as the starting point—a set of alternative axioms from which one can proceed in search of understanding. Thus, the Blessed Virgin Mary is the Mother of *God* and not just the mother of Jesus. We are not allowed to question this, only to try to find the best formulation for describing it. What the correct religious axioms are is not always clear at the outset, but it becomes gradually clearer what the best consensual formulations are (though not always what they mean exactly). There is no point in trying to apply the rules of extrarevelatory logic to the God of revelation. This is beautifully argued by Maimonides (d. 1204), an extreme rationalist stuck with a not-so-rational tradition. Aristotle argues, very convincingly for Maimonides, that something cannot come out of nothing. Jewish tradition on the other hand holds that the world was created ex nihilo. Ideally, one could bring logical arguments to refute the Philosopher. Unfortunately, Maimonides does not find any. In truly Aristotelian fashion, Maimonides sets out to "save the phenomena," which for him include both the world as we can understand it through the use of logic (Aristotelian logic—for Maimonides Aristotle was the wisest among those who relied solely on natural reason) and revelation as preserved in Jewish tradition. To the best of his ability, he is trying to eat his cake and have it:

Assume . . . [that a child] of a most perfect natural disposition was born and that his mother died after she had suckled him for several months. And the man [the father] alone, in an isolated island, took upon himself the entire upbringing of him who was born, until he grew up, became intelligent and acquired knowledge. Now this child had never seen a woman or a female of one of the species of the other animals. Accordingly he puts a question, saying to a man who was with him: How did we come to exist, and in what way were we generated. Thereupon the man to whom the question was put replied: "Every individual among us was generated in the belly of an individual belonging like us to our species, an individual who is female and has such and such a form. Every individual among us was—being small in body—within the belly, was moved and fed there, and grew up little by little—being alive—until it reached such and such limit in size. Thereupon an opening was opened up for him in the lower part of the body, from which he issued and came forth. Thereupon he does not cease growing until he becomes such as you see that we are." Now the orphaned child must of necessity put the question: "Did every individual among us—when he was little, contained within a belly, but alive and moving and growing—did he eat, drink, breathe through the mouth and nose, produce excrement?" He is answered: "No." Thereupon he indubitably will hasten to set this down as a lie and will produce a demonstration that all these true statements are impossible, drawing inferences from perfect [or fully grown] beings that have achieved stability. He will say: "If any individual among us were deprived of breath for the fraction of an hour, he would die and his movements would cease. How then can we conceive that an individual among us could be for months within a thick vessel surrounding him, which is within a body, and yet be alive and in motion? If one of us were to swallow a sparrow, that sparrow would die immediately upon entering the stomach, and all the more the underbelly. Every individual among us would undoubtedly perish within a few days if he did not eat food with his mouth and drink water; how then can an individual remain alive for months without eating and drinking? Every individual among us, if he had taken food and had not given off excrements, would die in very great pain within a few days; how then could the individual in question remain for months without giving off excrements? If the belly of one of us were perforated, he would die after some days; how then can it be supposed that the navel of the fetus in question was open? How is it that he does not open his eyes, put out his palms, stretch his feet, while all the parts of his body are whole and have no defect as you thought?" Similarly all the analogies will be carried on in order to show that it is in no respect possible that man should be generated in that matter.

Consider this example and reflect upon it, you who are engaged in speculation [about the manner in which the world came to be], and you shall find that this is exactly our position with regard to Aristotle. For we, the community of the followers of *Moses our Master and Abraham our Father*, may peace be on them, believe that the world was generated in such and such manner and came to be in a certain state from another state and was created in a certain state, which came after another state. Aristotle, on the other hand, begins to contradict us and to bring forward against us proofs based on the nature of what exists, a nature that has attained stability, is perfect, and has achieved actuality. As for us, we declare against him that this nature, after it has achieved stability and perfection, does not resemble in anything the state it was in while in the state of being generated, and that it was brought into existence from absolute nonexistence.5

Maimonides could have claimed that God simply does whatever He pleases, but he does not. He is trying to save as much of Aristotelian physics as he can. Things, he claims, behave very differently in their initial state and in their mature state (an embryo can live in fluid; a grown man can't). There is nothing miraculous or illogical about it per se. Before the cosmos reached maturity (at which point it began to behave according to the rules discovered by the Philosopher), it obeyed rules that would seem to us as impossible as pregnancy and birth to a person who has never seen either. We are lucky that God divulged the knowledge of this prehistoric state to reliable witnesses—Moses and Abraham. *We* know what Aristotle (the smart kid in a desert island) could not have known. Had we not known better, we too would consider it improbable.

But this is not as simple as Maimonides presents it. Aristotle's argument against creation ex nihilo is not a piece of empirical information he happened to miss or get wrong, like the number of legs flies have (six, not four as Aristotle thought). It is one of the foundations of Aristotelian thought. We cannot add creation ex nihilo as a preamble to Aristotelian physics, as Maimonides would have us do. If our inquisitive child were less interested in the origin of things (and given that there are no females in the island, just as there are no new beginnings in the cosmos, this is a purely "academic" question), he could have lived happily, possessing a perfectly correct understanding of the rules that govern "the world once it has been established and reached perfection." But Maimonides can't. There are too many occasions where Jewish revelation defies Aristotelian logic. When he cannot "save" them, Maimonides tries to isolate them as much as possible, so he does not have to choose. If he must live with contradictions, he prefers to have as few as possible.

Maimonides and other believing rationalists have a problem: they are very strongly committed to their conflicting convictions and are too conscious of them. Most of us find it quite natural to believe "half-heartedly," just as we are capable of making significant decisions based on what a philosopher would consider insufficient data and fuzzy logic. Indeed, one could argue that we make *most* of our everyday decisions that way. Faith requires a particularly fuzzy logic. Nonprofessionals tend to see themselves as living in two distinct and separate reasoning systems. Passage from "earthly" logic to "heavenly" logic is marked by the indicator "this is a question of faith." Each of the systems obeys its own distinct rules (this is a simplified version of the Latin Averroists' theory of "double truth"). Professional theologians acknowledge this duality—at certain points, their reasoning relies on authority, not on syllogism or on observation—but they seek to reduce it as much as possible.

This is partly due to the psychological commitment of philosophically trained religious experts to philosophical articles of faith—a commitment that has become the social norm of the group—at least in the West. It is partly a control mechanism aimed at keeping the flock dependent on pastors, since without it, the advantage of the experts is drastically reduced. The literati do not deny the existence of the two spheres, but offer an elaborate formula for drawing the lines between the areas where the two spheres converge and those where they must remain separate. More important, these rules only apply to them. Others, as we saw, can legitimately live in two separate spheres—"reason driven" and "faith driven"—as long as they are willing to admit that their ideas are inaccurate and tentative. When they encounter an authorized expert, their ideas must give way to his, for no matter how strongly held, they were temporary notions. Those who refuse to give way to the authorized expert are heretics.

But most people never meet an expert, let alone engage him in theological debate. The result is that the object of "simple's" faith is amorphous and unruly. This has the great advantage of allowing "the simple" to hold contradictory convictions, without feeling the intellectual and psychological angst that besets the experts, nor do they need to invest, like their more learned brethren, enormous energies in cognitive dissonance reduction. What St. Cyril spends tomes explaining and what Nestorius nevertheless finds impossible to accept—that the beloved Virgin Mary is both fully human and at the same time Mother of God—the faithful find totally unproblematic. Moreover, the elaborate explanations devised by the experts are completely lost on them. At most, they encounter them as verbal sequences that they accept at face value. For theologians like Bernard of Clairvaux (1090–1153) and Thomas Aquinas (1225–1274), the "Immaculate Conception" of the Blessed Virgin Mary causes insurmountable logical problems (Why stop with Mary's mother Ann? Aren't we getting caught in infinite regression?). But for the faithful at Lourdes, it was enough that the Virgin appearing to St. Bernadette identified herself as the Immaculate Conception. The only "proof" they need is that miracles are daily performed at the site.

But one must not yield to the temptation of making too sharp of distinctions between experts and nonexperts. The difference is in degree, not in kind. Like nonexperts, professional theologians alternate between formal and fuzzy logic and between different levels of commitment to the objects of faith, from explicit to implicit faith. As long as you professed your overall commitment to the accepted norm, you had considerable room for maneuver. Faith is not the declaration of implicit adherence to the norm. It is the thousand liberties taking place behind it. It is, in other words, not philosophical, but historical: it is not what people ought to do, but what they actually do. As we shall soon see, what they do in practice is often as surprising as human procreation was for Maimonides's child.

CHAPTER FIVE

Unimaginable

A Short Digression

Imagine a young boy who is eleven—no, six. He is, according to canon law, *non capax doli*, incapable of sinning. Of course, he can do bad things and entertain evil thoughts, but his mind is not mature enough to process his thoughts, and since sin requires a minimum of discretion, a voluntary acceptance of evil, he cannot sin. Like the rest of humanity, he is born with Original Sin, but at this point—at least from a human perspective—he is innocent *per definitionem*. So far, so good. Ah yes, he's an Amalekite. He walks along the river with his dog Bobo. He hums Amalekite nursery rhymes and eats some Amalekite delicacy prepared by his mother. We have no idea how this particular branch of the Amalekite people has survived. We thought they were all gone, ages ago, but the fact is that Amalekites have survived. Studies conducted by a team of renowned biologists proved it beyond reasonable doubt. These are definitely Amalekites. He is one of them.

Now let us assume that you are an observant, very devout Jew. You did not intend to go to this village; you got lost exploring the river and suddenly realized that you're there. This boy is one of the Amalekites the press has been talking about for weeks. Now here is the dilemma: Jehovah orders quite explicitly to "blot out" the memory of Amalek:

Remember what the Amalekites did to you along the way when you came out of Egypt. When you were weary and worn out, they met you on your journey and cut off all who were lagging behind; they had no fear of God. When Jehovah your God gives you rest from all the enemies around you in the land he is giving you to possess as an inheritance, you shall blot out the memory of Amalek from under heaven. Do not forget! (Deut 25:17–19).

You wonder what it means to "blot out the memory of Amalek"? Well, it so happens that the Bible provides an answer, a story of how the commandment should be acted out:

And Samuel said to Saul, "I am the one Jehovah sent to anoint you king over His people Israel; so listen now to the message from Jehovah. This is what Jehovah Sabbaoth says: 'I will punish the Amalekites for what they did to Israel when they waylaid them as they came up from Egypt. Now go, vanquish the Amalekites and devote to God everything that belongs to them. Do not have pity on them; put to death men and women, children and infants, cattle and sheep, camels and donkeys.'" (1 Sam 15:1–3).

Saul does as he is told—or at least *he* thinks so:

When Samuel reached him, Saul said, "Jehovah bless you! I have carried out Jehovah's instructions." But Samuel said, "What then is this bleating of sheep in my ears? What is this lowing of cattle that I hear?" Saul answered, "The men brought them from the Amalekites; they spared the best of the sheep and cattle to sacrifice to Jehovah your God, but we totally destroyed the rest." And Samuel said to Saul: "Stop and I will tell you what Jehovah said to me last night." And he said to him, "Speak." And Samuel said: ". . . Jehovah had anointed you king over Israel. And he sent you on a mission, saying, 'Go and completely destroy those wicked people, the Amalekites; make war on them until you have wiped them out.' Why did you not obey Jehovah? Why did you pounce on the plunder and do evil in the eyes of Jehovah?" Saul said: "But I did obey Jehovah. I went on the mission Jehovah assigned me. I completely destroyed the Amalekites and brought back Agag their king. The men took sheep and cattle from the plunder, the best of what was devoted to God, in order to sacrifice them to Jehovah your God at Gilgal." But Samuel replied: "Does Jehovah delight in burnt offerings and sacrifices as much as in obeying the voice of Jehovah? . . . Because you have rejected the word of Jehovah, he has rejected you as king." (1 Sm 15:13–23)

So now what? If our explorer wants to obey God, he is supposed to kill a six-year-old boy (and his pet dog Bobo). Of course, he does not want to kill the boy, for his moral instincts (or rather his upbringing) make it very hard for him to spill innocent blood. The Talmud is not unaware of this difficulty:

> When God said to Saul, go vanquish the Amalekites, he said, "if the Torah ordered us to behead a heifer in reparation for the soul of one [slain man found in the field, whose killer is unknown (see Deut 21: 1–9)], how much more [should we be careful] with [the killing] of all those souls [of the Amalekites]. For if humans sinned, what is the animals' fault? If adults sinned, what are the sins of children?" Then a voice came from heaven and said to him: "Do not be overly righteous, nor overly clever." (Eccl 7:16)[1]

Not to be overly righteous and overly clever is all very fine in theory. But in practice, our unhappy explorer should draw his commando knife and slaughter the boy humming Amalekite tunes and his dog. Even for those who are very observant, this is an unpleasant undertaking. He tries to find a way out, obviously. The rabbis sometimes tried to get out of such unpleasantness by creating technical impediments to unwanted commandments. Thus, for example, the law that ordered the stoning of an undisciplined son was surrounded by so many preconditions that it became practically impossible to implement. The law that ordered a redistribution of all land in Israel every fifty years was deactivated in the same way (it is valid only when most of the people of Israel are living in the Land of Israel). There was an attempt to solve the Amalekite problem in the same fashion. The Assyrians, said the rabbis, with their policy of moving borders and populations, made it practically impossible to know who is an Amalekite and who is not. If we found an Amalekite, we'd have to kill him. Sadly (or gladly, if you prefer), we're never going to find one. This particular commandment is going to remain null and void.

But technical solutions are not foolproof. In the Diaspora, nobody really thought that the entire Jewish people would reestablish itself in the Holy Land, the precondition for the reactivation of the agrarian reform of the Jubilee year. At least nobody expected it to occur before the Messianic Age (at which point we will not have to worry about logistics). But circumstances have changed. While the coming of the messiah seems as far as ever, the possibility that most of the Jewish people would live in the Land of Israel no longer seems far-fetched. That is why I started with the assumption that the identification is certain. The rabbis were empirically wrong, then. This is not unthinkable. Except in religious matters, the rabbis did not consider themselves infallible. They were wrong about the way the cosmos works (like everybody else at the time, they believed in a geocentric universe). They were wrong about medicine (no Jew would suggest adhering to Talmudic medicine). It is quite conceivable that Amalekites exist. And if we find them, we are ordered to kill them—no question about it. This is not easy.

But who says religion is easy? Didn't God order Abraham to sacrifice Isaac, the beloved son born to him in old age? We have all read Kierkegaard's *Fear and Trembling*: a real believer, a "knight of faith" sometimes needs to act against his instincts, against his common sense, against his morality. Abraham was willing to sacrifice his own son. Surely, he could be willing to sacrifice the sons of others.

Maybe he could. But could we? More important, would we? Sadly, many of us could and would, but many could not and would not. It is one thing to admire Kierkegaard's knight in the book, but if we met him in real life (our twenty-first-century real life, that is), we would probably think him a monster, or insane, or both. The reason is not that we, unlike our ancestors, lack faith. It is that we no longer believe in the same way. Abraham (or whoever invented him) may have lived in a world where heavenly voices were commonplace and were considered a possibly trustworthy source of information and moral guidance. We don't. Immanuel Kant summarizes it nicely in his *Conflict of the Faculties*:

> For if God should really speak to man, man could still never *know* that it was God speaking. It is quite impossible for man to apprehend

the infinite by the senses, distinguish it from sensible beings, and *recognize* it as such. But in some cases man can be sure that the voice he hears is *not* God's; for if the voice commands him to do something contrary to the moral law, then no matter how majestic the apparition may be, and no matter how it may seem to surpass the whole of nature, he must consider it an illusion. We can use, as an example, the myth of the sacrifice that Abraham was going to make by butchering and burning his only son at God's command (the poor child, without knowing it, even brought the wood for the fire). Abraham should have replied to this supposedly divine voice; "That I ought not to kill my good son is quite certain. But that you, this apparition, are God— of that I am not certain, and never can be, not even if this voice rings down to me from (visible) heaven.[2]

Written in 1798, it is still the essence of our modern attitude. Kant's argument was repeated almost verbatim in Jean Paul Sartre's famous lecture "Existentialism Is a Humanism." Nowadays God is allowed to tell us only what we find morally acceptable. Even if we are willing to accept a "cruel theology" in the afterworld (everlasting damnation)—and many are not—we are definitely not willing to accept it in this world. But in fact, this is not a modern phenomenon (though its "categorical" expression by Kant is new). In all generations, the meaning of the absolute truth of revelation is relativized in order to save it from becoming morally reprehensible (in the eyes of ever-changing human cultures). The rabbis' attempt to heap conditions, glosses, and caveats on some of God's clear and explicit commandments and their attempt to make the Amalekites disappear are signs of our implicit faith in the primacy of human justice. In practical terms, it means that the literal meaning of the text of revelation, while formally maintained, must always give way to the reading that makes it "palatable," for the letter kills but the spirit gives life. Oddly, the rehistoricization of Christian Revelation (nowadays especially, but not only, the rejudaization of Jesus of Nazareth) is meant to achieve the same effect—it removes layers of theology that have become an embarrassment. It allows a culture that no longer believes in its own theology, in the theological Jesus, to reattach itself to the miracle-working Galilean rabbi. Seeing Jesus and Paul in context (the opposite of what almost two millennia of interpreters did) makes it possible for twenty-first-century believers to digest those elements in their religious tradition that they find hard to swallow. It is highly likely that the "historical" Jesus is not the last Word.

And what about our Amalekite boy and his ridiculously named dog? I think he has a good chance of survival. A contemporary Jew, even a very devout one, is probably going to find an excuse to shirk this particular commandment. He might suddenly feel very sick and go see a doctor (saving your own life is more important than killing Amalekites); he might convince himself that the gentile scientists who identified the Amalekites were wrong (or if they were Jews, they were not observant, or if observant, they were not from his particular group); he might suddenly find himself agreeing with the exegesis that allegorizes both the Amalekites and their slaughter.

Unfortunately, moral sensibilities cannot always be relied on. Christianity started as a religion whose founder was opposed to violence of any sort, a man who denied his followers the right of self-defense and ordered them to love their persecutors. It took time, but they learned to reinterpret his words. It turned out that not only self-defense but the mass slaughter of persecutors and would-be persecutors were quite pleasing in his eyes. If it happened to the followers of the Lamb of God, it could happen to anyone.

If I were an Amalekite, I would be very worried.

CHAPTER SIX

Impossible

In the introduction to his commentary on the Mishna, Maimonides lists the Thirteen Foundations of Judaism. Here is foundation number 3, "The denial of physicality in God":

> This means to believe that the One is neither a body nor a force within a body, and is not susceptible to the changing states of bodies like motion and rest, neither in essence nor in accidents. . . . And the prophet [Isaiah] says: "To whom then will you liken me, and to whom shall I be equal, says the Holy One" [40:25]. If he were a body, he would be like other bodies. And everything that appears in Sacred Scriptures that describes him in bodily terms, like walking, standing, sitting, speaking, and so forth, is metaphorical, for as our Rabbis of blessed memory said, "the Torah speaks in the language of men." . . . This third foundation is attested to by the verse, "For you saw no image" [Deut 4:15] meaning that you did not see an image or any form [when you stood at Mount Sinai], because as we have said, He has neither a body, nor is he a force within a body."[1]

For Maimonides, God's incorporeality is attested first and foremost by His being without visible form and image. God may be described in bodily terms, but these descriptions are mere metaphors, imprecise language that complies with the imprecise rules of human communication. Upon careful examination, these imprecisions can be detected and "neutralized."

But Maimonides's "Aristotelized" God was an exception. Most rabbis thought that the "Great Eagle," as Maimonides was known among his admirers, had gone too far in dematerializing God. The sages were much less troubled than he was by Greek metaphysical angst. Consider the following description from the Babylonian Talmud:

> Rabbi Abahu said: "Were it not written [in the Bible], it would be impossible to utter. For it is written [Is 7:20]: 'In that day, the Lord will shave with the razor hired from the other side of the river, the king of Assyria—the head and the hair of the feet, and also the beard shall be entirely removed.' The Lord came to Sanherib, appearing to him like an old man. And he said to Sanherib: 'When you came to the kings of the East and the West, whose sons you took with you and killed, what did you say to them?' And [Sanherib] answered: 'I myself am trembling about this. Can you advise me what to do?' [The Lord] said to him: 'Go and change your appearance.' [He said:] 'How shall I change it?' [The Lord] said to him: 'Go bring me scissors and I will cut your hair off.' [Sanherib said:] 'Where shall I find them?' [The Lord said to him:] 'Go to this house [over there] and bring them.' He went there, and found the house. [And he saw there] ministering angels who had appeared to him as men grinding the kernels of dates. He said to them: 'Give me scissors.' And they answered, 'Grind one measure of kernels' and gave him the scissors. When he returned [to the other side of the river] it grew dark. [The Lord] said to him: 'Go bring light.' So he went and brought light. And while he was carrying the light, he blew on it and the fire caught onto his beard. And [the Lord] shaved his hair and his beard, as it is written, 'And also the beard shall be entirely removed.' . . . Sanherib went away and found a plank of Noah's ark. And he said: 'This is the great God, who saved Noah from the flood.' And he said: 'If I go and succeed, I will sacrifice my two sons to him.' When his sons heard this, and they killed

him, as it is written, 'Now it came to pass, as he was worshiping in the temple of Nisroch his god, that his sons Adrammelech and Sharezer struck him down with the sword; and they escaped into the land of Ararat' (2 Kgs 19:37)."[2]

Strange. So strange that in the English translation of the Babylonian Talmud published by Michael Rodkinson in 1918 the text reads: "The Lord *sent an angel*, who appeared before Sanherib as an old man."[3] It is not just that the supposedly Ineffable God of the Jews took human form, but that He did so for reasons that seem trivial and even ridiculous to us. This Incarnation of the Almighty is not aimed at bringing deep divine messages to humanity, nor does God perform an act that is of great significance. He could have judged the king of Assyria, for example, or smote him down in his righteous anger, but He didn't. Instead, He shaves him (hair, beard, and legs). The just punishment of this great enemy of the Chosen People is brought about by natural means quite unrelated to the episode just cited. The king worships a plank from Noah's ark (probably mentioned here because his sons and would-be assassins flee into the land of Ararat, where the ark landed after the flood). He promises this ludicrous idol that he shall sacrifice his sons to it and finds himself the victim of a preventive strike. We may assume he died with impeccably shaven legs, but we cannot be sure.

It must have been obvious to Rabbi Abahu, as well as to his interlocutors, that Isaiah did *not* mean that God would shave the king of Assyria *literally*, but this, apparently, did not matter. What is particularly striking is the realistic plot worked out by the rabbi. God does not simply emerge from His heaven and shave Sanherib. He disguises Himself as an old man and sends his ministering angels to work in a date-kernel mill across the river. He convinces the king to cross the river in search of scissors. He makes sure that the angels humiliate the king by asking him to grind some kernels (a nice extra not mentioned in the prophecy). He plans the whole thing so that Sanherib, who returns to the "barber" after dark, is sent to bring light and then singes his own beard blowing on it. The only detail left uncovered is, sadly, the shaving of the legs. It may have been skipped for technical reasons (it is not easy to shave legs with scissors), or perhaps it did happen and the rabbi forgot to mention it. Whatever the case,

R. Abahu seems to have considered the prophecy fulfilled ("[the Lord] shaved his hair and his beard, as it is written"). We're not told why it was so important for God to shave the king of Assyria in person. But then his judgments are unsearchable and his ways untraceable.

More striking than the strange tale itself is the statement with which it is opened: "Were it not written [in the Bible], it would be impossible to utter." This formula usually appears in the rabbinic literature before statements that challenge the accepted, "normative" perception of God.[4] R. Abahu, in other words, is fully aware of the problematic, indeed scandalous, nature of his Midrash. An equally shocking Midrash appears in *Lamentations Rabbah*, one of the earliest collections of Midrashim. It deals with the destruction of the Temple. The text describes God's reaction to the destruction of his house:

> At that hour the Holy Lord was crying and saying, "Woe to me, what have I done? I brought my presence [*shekinathi*] down to earth for [the people of] Israel and since they have sinned, I have returned to my previous dwelling, becoming, heaven forbid, a mockery in the eyes of people." At that hour Metatron [the angel serving as God's vicar] came and fell prostrate before Him and said: "Master of the universe; I will cry and you will not cry." [The Lord] said to him: "If you would not let me cry now, I will enter a place that you are not allowed to enter and cry," as it is said, "But if you will not hear it, my soul shall weep in secret places for your pride" [Jer 13:17]. . . . And when the Lord saw them [the patriarchs coming to Him upon learning about the destruction], He wore sackcloth and pulled out His hair, and were it not written it would have been impossible to utter. This is why it is said, "[And in that day the Lord God of hosts called for weeping and for mourning], for baldness and for girding with sackcloth" [Is 22:12]. And they were crying and walking from gate to gate [of the Temple] like a man whose dead lies before him. And the Lord was mourning and saying: "Woe to a king who succeeded in his youth and failed in his old age!"[5]

God clearly has a body upon which he can wear sackcloth and hair that He can pull out. In another occurrence of the formula, it precedes God's declaration that since the destruction of His earthly abode, He has been sitting outdoors and not in the shelter of His heavenly home. As proof, He invites His sons to feel the wetness of His hair "for my head is covered with dew, my locks with the drops of the night" (Sg 5:2).[6] More than the anthropomorphism, it is the overfamiliar attitude toward God that makes us uncomfortable. The God of R. Abahu is willing to compromise His incorporeality for a practical joke, and the God of *Lamentations Rabba* is much too human. He regrets His own decisions. He cries, instead of simply reversing them—He is, after all, almighty. He has to hide from His servants who seem more concerned about His dignity than Him. And He openly declares that He, the eternal and ageless one, has lost His powers in old age. The highly problematic nature of these descriptions did not elude their originators: "Were it not written, it would have been impossible to utter."

But *is* it written? The fact of the matter is that it is quite clearly *not* written. As Maimonides would no doubt have argued, there is absolutely no reason to concoct this epilatory tale on the basis of Isaiah 7:20. Isaiah's text is, as anybody can see, a metaphor. God will crush the king of Assyria, not remove his facial hair with scissors from across the river. Similarly, the call for "weeping and mourning, for baldness and for girding with sackcloth," is a warning for human sinners to repent, not an autobiographical statement of God.

These are not even particularly hard-to-understand verses. One could think of other verses that could more aptly qualify for the formula "were it not written, it would have been impossible to utter." I am thinking of the reference in Genesis 6 to the sons of God lusting after the beautiful daughters of men, or the story of Moses seeing God's back in the cleft of the rock (Ex 33:19–23).[7] One could think, for example, of the strange episode where Jehovah suddenly threatens to kill Moses in the desert:

> And it came to pass on the way, at the encampment, that Jehovah met him and sought to kill him. Then Zipporah took a sharp stone and cut off the foreskin of her son and cast it at his feet, and said, "For you are a husband of blood to me!" So He let him go. Then she said, "You are a husband of blood, because of the circumcision." (Ex 4:24–26)

Or better still,

And he arose that night and took his two wives, his two female servants, and his eleven sons, and crossed over the ford of Jabbok. . . . Then Jacob was left alone; and a man wrestled with him until the breaking of day. Now when he saw that he did not prevail against him, he touched the socket of his hip; and the socket of Jacob's hip was out of joint as he wrestled with him. And he said, "Let me go, for the day breaks." But he said, "I will not let you go unless you bless me!" So he said to him, "What is your name?" He said, "Jacob." And he said, "Your name shall no longer be called Jacob, but Israel [one who struggles with God],[8] for you have struggled with God and with men, and have prevailed." Then Jacob asked, saying, "Tell me your name, I pray." And he said, "Why do you ask about my name?" And he blessed him there. So Jacob called the name of the place Peniel [the face of God].[9] "For I have seen God face to face and my life is preserved." (Gen 32:22–31)

Generations of exegetes have done their very best to explain these episodes in which God appears as a being inexplicably hostile to humans. Why does Jehovah seek to kill Moses, who has been obediently doing His will just a couple of verses earlier? Why does the circumcision of Moses's son by Zipporah appease Jehovah? Exegetes were willing to offer anything but the sort of literal explanation offered by Rabbi Abahu and by *Lamentations Rabba*. Although the "man" who wrestled with Jacob all night reveals himself as God at dawn, the God of Israel to be precise, numerous artists have followed the "canonical" exegesis and depicted the mysterious aggressor as an angel. But Jacob is quite clear that this was neither an angel nor a man. He has, he declares, "seen God face to face." "You cannot see my face," God warns Moses in Exodus, "for no man shall see me, and live." Yet Jacob survived. In fact, he did not simply live to tell the tale. He struggled with God and with men and prevailed. Why did God attack Jacob in the form of a man? How is it possible that the nation's sacred name was given at the end of a struggle in which the Almighty was vanquished by a human and *forced* into blessing him? Surely, "were it not written, it would have been impossible to utter."[10]

One would expect the rabbis to be involved in a process of defusing theological bombs in Sacred Scriptures. Instead, our Midrashim detonate unproblematic statements. It seems that while the rabbis do at times deliteralize certain passages in the Torah, at other times (and we have just seen a few examples) they are quite willing to go in the other direction and reliteralize what are quite clearly metaphorical statements.

The rabbis of the Talmud, and many of their successors, are quite unshocked by the idea that God has a body. "The question," writes Alon Goshen Gottstein, "of whether the rabbis believed in a God who has form is one that needs little discussion and therefore is of lesser interest. . . . Instead of asking, does God have a body? We should inquire, what kind of body does God have." [11] The Bible describes bodily aspects of God quite often, not only in what we now think are the earlier layers of the text, but also in later strata, most notably in the epiphanies described by Isaiah (chapter 6) and Ezekiel (chapter 1). In fact, while our implicit assumption is that the "natural" course of theological development is from material to spiritual and from the concrete to the abstract, the rabbis' God is in general *less* abstract than at least the prophetic God. The rabbis of the Talmud do not simply disregard the Greek obsession with incorporeality. They are quite uncommitted to the idea of divine infallibility and omnipotence. While God is indeed Master of the Universe, He is far from perfection. As in the Bible, He is given to mood swings and to often-inexplicable likes and dislikes. But the rabbis' God is not simply a powerful and capricious ruler who can be prevented from using His power in harmful ways by favorites who know His soft spots. The rabbis of the Talmud add psychological depth and self-awareness to their God. [12] He does not just change His decisions, but also regrets His *mistakes*. They depict Him as willing to acknowledge weakness and at times moral and intellectual inferiority. We saw this in *Lamentations Rabba*, but it is given a particularly bold expression in the famous story of the dispute between R. Eliezer son of Hyrkanos and R. Yehoshua, where the former represents the minority opinion and the latter the majority one. The dispute concerns the halachic status of a specific type of oven. The issue itself is of no consequence. What matters is the way the dispute unfolded:

> On that day Rabbi Eliezer brought forward every argument in the world, but they did not accept them from him. He said to them: "If the *halacha* agrees with me, this carob-tree will prove it!" Thereupon

the carob tree was torn a hundred cubits out of its place (others claim that it was four hundred cubits). They said to him: "No proof can be brought from a carob-tree." Again he said to them: "If the *hala-cha* agrees with me, the stream of water will prove it!" whereupon the stream of water flowed backward. They said to him: "No proof can be brought from a stream of water." Again he said to them: "If the *hala-cha* agrees with me, the walls of the schoolhouse will prove it!" where-upon the walls inclined to fall. But R. Yehoshua rebuked them, saying: "When scholars are engaged in a *halachic* dispute, what authority do you have?" So they did not fall, in awe of Rabbi Yehoshua, nor did they resume the upright position, in awe of Rabbi Eliezer; and they were standing thus inclined. Again he said to them: "If the *halacha* agrees with me, let it be proved from Heaven!" Whereupon a Heav-enly Voice was heard saying: "why do you dispute with Rabbi Eliezer, seeing that in all matters the *halacha* agrees with him?!" But Rabbi Yehoshua stood up and said: "It is not in heaven" (Deut 30:12). Rabbi Yirmiah explained: Since the Torah had already been given at Mount Sinai we pay no attention to a Heavenly Voice, because you have writ-ten in the Torah at Mount Sinai, "Turn aside after many" (Ex 23:2).

Rabbi Nathan met [the prophet] Elijah and asked him: What did the Holy One Blessed be He do in that hour? He answered him: he smiled and said: "My sons have defeated Me, My sons have defeated Me."[13]

"My sons have defeated me." Twice. He is not even outraged. He smiles![14] And the divine defeat does not end with God's readiness to toler-ate Rabbi Yehoshua's talking back, throwing at God his own words. The final irony is in Rabbi Yirmiah's proof text. The verse the rabbi is using is in itself an example of the rabbis' exegetical omnipotence. The original wording—upon which the rabbis established the idea that at any moment the law is not a reflection of the absolute truth of divine utterance (the opinion of Rabbi Eliezer, for example) but the *consensus sapientium*—is as follows: "You shall *not* follow a crowd to do evil; nor shall you testify in a dispute so as to turn aside after many to pervert justice." God, in other words, says the opposite of what His sages claim He is saying. When they wish to make sure that their mastery of the text is absolute, the rabbis use another verse, this time from Psalms (119:126): "It is time for Jehovah to act; they have broken thy law." In their reading it means, "It is time to break the law for Jehovah."[15] It is humans who decide *when* the time is.

The rabbis refuse to see God as omnipotent, omniscient, or infallible. They are quite prepared to argue with Him, knowing that they can defeat Him, just like Jacob-Israel in the crossing of Jabbok. They do not hesitate to portray Him in all kinds of ways: as a great king and as Judge of the World, but also as a half-naked old mourner, as a barber, as a man sitting outdoors, getting wet from the rain and dew, and as a heavenly observer graciously losing an argument. All those images (and many others, as we shall see) are not just metaphors for God, they are God's avatars. Beyond those avatars, there lies the ineffable source—God as an incomprehensible ontological force. The ontological source is there to save appearances, but appearances themselves—and those include all God's concrete manifestations—behave according to the rules of human knowledge and need. That means that while the Hidden Lord's commandments—eternal and unchanging, but also meaningless—are absolute, the allocation of meaning through interpretation is a human affair: "it is not in heaven."

In a more discrete fashion, St. Augustine would concur. The real prophet, he notes, is not the person transmitting the message, but the person revealing its hidden meaning. It is Joseph, not Pharaoh, Daniel, not Belshazzar.[16] Without the authority of the Holy Church (the one authorized—human—interpreter of revelation), says Augustine, he would not believe Sacred Scriptures.[17]

TRULY DIVINE AND TRULY HUMAN

Judaism remains to this day a religion with weak philosophical sensibilities. It could be argued that Maimonides is the only major halachic authority until the modern era with a strong commitment to systematic philosophy. For the rabbis of the Talmud and many of their descendants, the contradiction between the Hidden Lord and the God of revelation is better left unexplained. It works in ways that defy ordinary logic and is of little consequence in the everyday life of religious experts dedicated mostly to action (what a Jew must do) rather than abstract ideas (what a Jew must believe). One can be a great rabbi without a systematic theology.

Christianity is different. As the importance of Jewish converts to Christianity shrank, the importance of gentiles, deeply influenced by Hellenistic modes of thinking, grew. The decision to accept the Jewish Scriptures "as is" meant that Christian thinkers, accustomed to the modes of thought of the philosophical schools of their time (mostly Platonism, but also Stoicism and Aristotelianism), had a momentous task of reinterpretation before them. The now-obsolete commandments, strange myths, all-too-human histories, wisdom literature, and prophecies had to become "relevant" *malgré eux*.

Making systematic sense out of problematic texts was a challenge, but Hellenistic culture had a long tradition of doing just that. What are the writings of Plotinus if not a radical rereading of Plato? Turning the commandments of Leviticus into allegories and the histories into elaborate prefigurations was relatively easy. More challenging was the task of turning the Galilean rabbi, Jesus, into the Son of God. First, there were all those Jewish titles that he came with: What is the meaning of "messiah"? What exactly is the "Son of Man?" What is the Son of God? The Jewish idea of sonship (a "son of God" is someone who enjoys divine favor, like the king of Israel and the entire people of Israel) was soon replaced by the idea that since a son is like his father, the Son of God must somehow be like God. Now, unless there are to be two Gods, the Father and the Son (and then, in a weaker sense, the Holy Spirit), the Son must be one and the same God. The greatest problem, from a philosophical and a psychological point of view, was not the fact that there was more than one God, but the Incarnation. One could argue that the divine persons were different manifestations of the one godhead. But why would the eternal logos, God, the divine Son, choose to soil Himself with human flesh? Wasn't it the aspiration of every rational being to rid itself of matter? And how could the divine ever fuse with something as base as flesh?

In his work on the Incarnation (*De carne Christi*, On the Flesh of Christ), written against the second-century heresiarch Marcion, Tertullian gives voice to the horror a well-educated Roman gentleman felt toward the idea of God choosing to be conceived and born as man:

> So if your repudiation of embodiment (*corporationem*) is due neither to the supposition that God would find it impossible, nor to the

fear that it would bring him to peril, it remains for you to reject it and arraign it as undignified. Beginning then with that nativity you so strongly object to, orate, attack now, the nastiness of genital elements in the womb, the filthy curdling of moisture and blood and of the flesh, for nine months to be nourished on that same mire. Draw a picture of the womb swelling up daily, heavy, uneasy, unsafe even in sleep, uncertain in the whims of dislikes and appetites. Inveigh against the shamefacedness of the travailing woman, which ought to be respected at least because of the peril involved or because of its sacred nature. You shudder, of course, at the child passed out along with his afterbirth, and of course bedaubed with it. You think it shameful that he is straightened out with bandages, that he is licked into shape with applications of oil, that he is beguiled by coddling. This natural object of reverence you despise, Marcion. . . . But there is no doubt that *Christ* loved that man who was curdled in uncleanliness in the womb, who was brought through organs immodest, who took nourishment through organs of ridicule. For his sake he came down, for his sake he cast himself down in all humility even unto death, yea, the death of the cross. . . . If these are the constituents of man whom God has redeemed, who are you to make them the cause of shame to him who redeemed them, or to make them beneath his dignity, when he would not have redeemed them unless he had loved them?[18]

As always, Tertullian's rhetoric is very effective. His deliberate dwelling on what for men of his time were the most unpleasant aspects of human birth to prove God's love of man (and Marcion's hatred) is no less than brilliant. But the rhetoric should not conceal the fact that it wasn't really propriety that was troubling the philosophically minded. It was the Christian insistence on mixing unmixables—divine and human, atemporal and temporal, necessary and contingent, unchanging and changing. Tertullian has no patience for such philosophical qualms. To God, nothing is impossible except what is against His will:

You say, "the reason why I deny that God was really and truly changed into man, in the sense of being both born and corporated in flesh, is that he who is without end must of necessity also be unchangeable: for to be changed into something else is an ending of what originally was: therefore change is inapplicable to one to whom ending is inapplicable." I admit that the nature of things changeable is bound by that law which precludes them from abiding in that which in them suffers change—the law which causes them to be destroyed by not abiding, seeing that by process of change they destroy that which they once were. But nothing is on equal terms with God: his nature is far removed from the circumstances of all things whatsoever. If then things far removed from God, things from which God is far removed, do in the process of being changed lose that which they once were, where will be the difference between divinity and the rest of things except that the contrary obtains, namely that God can be changed into anything whatsoever, and yet continue such as he is? Otherwise he will be on equal terms with the things which, when changed, lose that which they once were—things with which he is not on equal terms, as in all respects so also in the outcome of change.[19]

Neither Marcion nor Tertullian deals with the full range of metaphysical problems raised by the Incarnation (neither was a very systematic thinker). Insisting, as Christian orthodoxy does, on the *real*—not simply perceived—presence of God in the world, on His involvement in history as object and not just as subject, creates an impossible quandary for a systematic thinker. But Tertullian is not deterred by what is impossible for humans. To God, nothing is impossible except what is against His will: "Nothing is on equal terms with God: his nature is far removed from the circumstances of all things whatsoever." The contradiction between the Hidden God and the God of revelation is acknowledged and then dismissed. It is in *De Carne Christi* that Tertullian makes some of his most famous claims on the necessity of believing that for God nothing—no matter how absurd in human terms—is impossible:

> I am saved if I am not ashamed of my Lord. *Whosoever is ashamed of me*, he says, *of him will I also be ashamed.* I find no other grounds for shame, such as may prove that in contempt of shame I am splendidly shameless and felicitously foolish. The Son of God was crucified: I am not ashamed—because it is shameful. The Son of God died: it is immediately credible, because it is absurd (*credibile est quia ineptum est*).

He was buried, and rose again: it is certain, because it is impossible (*certum est quia impossibile*).[20]

On a certain level, believing that everything is possible for God is simply claiming that dogma takes precedence over reason. Some of the things that we believe make no sense—were they not written (or rather accepted by sacred Christian tradition), they would be impossible to utter (or, more accurately, impossible to understand). This means that reason is switched off at certain critical points in the theological system and continues to operate (and even dominate) at all others. "Simple" believers may not be bothered by this, but the intellectual must be able to switch, heroically, from one mode of thinking to the other. The exact locations where these switches occur are not always obvious, as the theological consensus on which Tertullian-style faith is founded is constantly shifting, but this must not result in historically induced relativism. At any given moment, the inspired consensus of the Church is absolute and infallible. The split personality that this system requires must be as fiercely denied as the heretics' assertion that God cannot be "truly" one and "truly" three. He—for whom nothing is impossible—can.

Marcion was one of the few thinkers who sought to rid Christianity of its split personality. He thought that the Old and the New Testaments were incompatible. He thought that the Lord of the Old Testament was too carnal, too interested in blood sacrifices, and too quick to punish and kill in the name of justice to be identical with the loving and forgiving God of the Gospels. The emotionally unstable and vindictive God of the Jews, argued Marcion, was a lesser divinity, a demiurge who created the material world. As anyone who has eyes can see, he did not create it well. The Jewish religion was nothing but false hopes and empty rituals. Jewish prophets were expecting a royal messiah who would win wars for them. Christ has nothing to do with all this. He is not the continuation or fulfillment of the Old Testament, but its radical upturning. The spiritual God, a God of love, did not become flesh. He made himself visible as a fully grown man. The earthly Christ was a phantasm, since bodies are neither worthy nor capable of salvation. Christ preached a radical new message, reversing the moral values of the Creator and His representatives. The devotees of the Creator refused to listen and were damned. Sinners, who had nothing to lose, were saved. The enemies of the new message arrested, tormented, and crucified a mere phantasm. The passion and crucifixion were not "real" in the carnal sense. They were a symbolic rejection of the values of power and vengeance. They released mankind from the clutches of Jehovah.

After Christ's "death" and "resurrection," His gospel was falsified by people who either failed to understand it or were doing the work of the Creator. Marcion believed that the true salvific message of the spiritual God could be found in ten of St. Paul's epistles (Marcion excluded 1 and 2 Timothy, Titus, and Hebrews) and in a revised version of the Gospel of Luke from which all references to the Old Testament as a source of true doctrine and all "carnal" references to Christ had been removed.[21]

At first glance, Marcion's theory of the demiurge and his denial of the corporeality of Christ would make him a Gnostic, but this would be wrong. Marcion does not advocate a secret knowledge (*gnosis*), directed only to the initiate. The redemptive message of Christ is addressed to all. The demiurge plays no important role in his economy of salvation. He is not the metaphysical evil force of the dualists who seeks to harm for harm's sake. Many of the Creator's actions are the result of a misguided sense of justice. Marcion used methods resembling those used many years later by Quellenforschung—he tried to make sense of the sacred texts by assigning them to different authors and by "identifying" interpolations based on his preconceived ideas of coherence. If it is to achieve coherence, argued Marcion, the new religion should abandon its Jewish baggage. The Old Testament simply doesn't fit the message of the New. In the name of coherence Marcion discarded the Incarnation, not because the corporeal Christ is unseemly, but because he cannot be incorporated into a systematic monotheistic worldview without constantly having recourse to Tertullian-style strategies of making sense out of nonsense.

The Church, as we know, refused to forgo either its old Jewish baggage or its new Greek cargo. Least of all was it ready to give up its most important mystery. Like Judaism, it chose incoherence. Unlike Judaism, it felt deeply uncomfortable with it. This was a fatefully fruitful choice.

CHAPTER SEVEN

A Short Discourse on the Spiritual Senses

In one of his sermons on the Song of Songs, St. Bernard of Clairvaux speaks of the immateriality of God: "Surely He did not enter through the eyes, because He is not colored; nor [did He come] through the ears, since He does not make a sound. Nor [did He come] through the nostrils, since He does not mix with the air but with the mind; nor does He mix with the air who has made it (*nec infecit aerem sed fecit*). Nor does He enter through the throat (*per fauces*), since He is neither eaten nor drunk; nor by touch, since He is not palpable."[1]

St. Bernard is quite certain that it is not through our senses that God enters the human soul. In the next chapters, we shall see that sometimes that is exactly what He does. But first something needs to be said about a particular manner of sensing—sensing spiritually.

We all know what the senses are. In the West we count five—sight, hearing, touch, smell, and taste. Before we become the thinking machines that we are so proud of ourselves being, we are sensing machines. We experience the world through our senses. We see it and hear it and touch it and taste it and smell it. When we start reflecting on the meaning of all this, "all this" very often means the endless sense data that our retinas and eardrums, our skin, our tongues, and our noses transmit to our brains. How much of it is reliable? How do we know that the messages transmitted are not inadvertently, or deliberately, distorted, or even totally fabricated? After all, I—the thinking man in the Cartesian attic, who is blind, deaf, anosmic, suffering from acute peripheral neuropathy and ageusia—only know what the senses tell me. We know that the sense organs of other creatures convey a radically different world picture. Dogs can hear sounds that we cannot hear and smell odors that do not reach us; eagles and bees see details we cannot discern. If we had the senses of other animals, wouldn't our mental world be very different? And how do we know that what we see is what we get? A bee not only sees things we cannot see, but sees in a radically different way. Numerous generations of epistemologists and (fewer generations of) brain researchers have been struggling with these very questions: Do we "really" know what we know? What if our sense organs, on which our rational ruminations are based, distort the data of the "real world"? Many have given up on the "real" world altogether. Trapped in our minds, notes Kant, the only "reality" that matters for us is mental reality. As for what "really" happens "out there"—only God knows.

How God knows is a categorically different question. God's way of knowing is hard to imagine, let alone understand. As the square in Edwin Abbott's *Flatland* realizes, for creatures who think by analogy and empathy, it is almost impossible to understand something utterly different from anything they know (like the existence of a third dimension in a two-dimensional world). Abbott's square begins to reflect on the possibility of a third dimension only after he encounters a sphere. This supposedly is the role of revelation—to add new dimensions to our understanding of existence. But this only goes a rather limited way. The data of revelation are sense data. Worse, most of them could quite easily be produced by human hands. What did the Israelites see on Mount Sinai? They saw smoke and lightening—pyrotechnics. What did the apostles see on Mount Tabor during the Transfiguration? A luminous figure of Christ, His face shining as the sun, and His garments white as the light? Two figures they identified as Moses and Elijah—nothing a good special effects department could not produce. And even if what witnesses experienced were impossible to duplicate (for now) by humans, it remains sense data. Of course, sense data were not *all* that the witnesses experienced. Quite often, what they sensed was accompanied by powerful inner feelings of conviction and awe, of mental and emotional transformation, that were as important as, or probably more important than, anything they saw or heard with their sense organs. Yet, unlike sense data that could be shared by many, these inner sensations are both private and subjective. They have to be transmitted by words, a medium easier to falsify than special effects.

All this might be unimportant. Faith, as Paul says so beautifully in his first letter to the Corinthians, is not a logical argument: "For Jews request a sign, and Greeks seek after wisdom; but we preach Christ crucified, to the Jews a stumbling block and to the Greeks foolishness, but to those who are called, both Jews and Greeks, Christ the power of God and the wisdom of God. Because the foolishness of God is wiser than men and the weakness of God is stronger than men" (1 Cor 1:22–25). What the apostle knows is the mysterious and, in human terms, absurd message of redemption. This has little to do with "Greek" wisdom.

And yet, some of the most significant things we "know" about divine knowledge, have very little to do with redemptive revelation. And they have much to do with Greek wisdom. "When the words [of Sacred Scriptures] taken literally," writes Augustine in his *On Christian Doctrine*, "convey an absurd sense (*sensus absurdus*), we must surely enquire whether it is spoken in this or that figurative sense which we do not understand, and thus much that lies hidden would be revealed."[2]

What makes the literal sense absurd? In book 12 of his *Confessions*, Augustine charts the limits of legitimate exegetical pluralism. The spiritual wealth of meaning of Scriptures makes it possible to interpret them in many ways. Indeed, Augustine argues, it is legitimate to disagree about the meaning of God's words even with their holy conveyor, Moses. What we *cannot* do is go beyond certain metaphysical (Neoplatonist) dogmata. *That* would be absurd:

> You will surely not assert to be false what the truth proclaims in a loud voice to my inner ear (*aurem interiorem*) concerning the true eternity of the creator, namely that his nature will never vary at different times, and his will is not external to his nature. It follows that he does not will one thing at one time and another thing at another time. Once and for all and simultaneously, he wills everything that he wills. He does

not need to renew his resolution. He does not want this now and that then, nor does he later come to will what formerly he did not will, or reject what previously he wished. For such a will is mutable and nothing mutable is eternal. "But our God is eternal" (Ps 47:15).[3]

Augustine, it seems, hears all this with his "inner ear," just as he sees with his "inner eye" (*interiori oculo*) a series of metaphysical "truths" that serve as the preconditions for all legitimate interpretation.[4] It is by these unrevealed truths that the words of revelation must be weighed and the content of revelation interpreted. When thinking about material things, one relies on the carnal senses. When thinking about spiritual things, one needs "spiritual senses."

What are the "spiritual" senses? In theological terms, they are special powers of understanding granted to the human soul by the Holy Spirit. Through them, the human mind becomes immediately present to the activity of divine grace. "To sense is to know a thing as present," writes Bonaventure.[5] It is this immediacy that makes sense perception so attractive for theologians.

But what started as a powerful metaphor soon acquired a life of its own. Spiritual knowledge has become akin to sensory knowledge. The soul sees, hears, smells, tastes, and feels truth. When, with the aid of grace, the calamitous effects of the Fall on the soul are reversed, our spiritual organs become once again open to the visual and auditory beauty of God, to His sweet taste and fragrant smell, to the pleasantness of His contact.

In his popular *Elucidarium*, the twelfth-century theologian Honorius Augustodunensis describes the experience of the blessed in heaven when their senses have been spiritualized:

> O what joy of sight, [they experience], whose eyes were closed and now see with open eyes, whose every member has become like the sun's eye, seeing the King of Glory in his splendor, observing all the angels and all the saints internally and externally. They see the glory of God, the glory of the angels, the glory of the patriarchs, the glory of the prophets, the glory of the apostles, the glory of the martyrs, the glory of the confessors, the glory of the virgins and the glory of all the saints—their eyes, their faces, all of their members, internally and externally; they behold the thoughts of each and every one of them; they see all there is in the new heaven and the new earth. They see

the enemies who have once tormented them perpetually in hell, and they are ineffably gladdened by all this. O how great is the joy of the blessed's hearing, for whom the harmonies of heaven, the choirs of the angels and the sweet-sounding organs of the saints resonate incessantly. What smell they sense who draw the most pleasant smell from God, the very source of pleasantness, and perceive the odor of the angels and all the saints. O what joy of taste [they sense] when they feast and rejoice in the sight of God and are satiated with the appearance of the glory of God; inebriated by the abundance of his house! What joy of touch, where all things hard and rough are gone and all things become smiling, soft, and agreeable![6]

Honorius uses terms like "externally and internally." He speaks about seeing thoughts and, more vaguely, of an undefined softness and of a mysterious "joy of taste." What is the meaning of these sensory experiences? Honorius does not explain. In his mystical masterpiece, *The Mind's Journey Into God*, St. Bonaventure tries to be more precise:

When the soul by faith believes in Christ as in the uncreated Word, who is the word and splendor of the Father, she recovers her spiritual hearing and sight: hearing to receive the words of Christ and sight to consider the splendors of that light. When the soul longs with hope (*spe*) to receive the inspired Word, she recovers, through her desire and affection, the spiritual sense of smell. When she embraces with love (*caritate*) the incarnate Word inasmuch as she receives delight from him and passes over (*transiens*) to him in ecstatic love, she recovers [the senses] of taste and touch. Having recovered these senses, the soul now sees, hears, smells and embraces her bridegroom, and can sing as his bride the Song of Songs, which was composed for the exercise of contemplation according to this fourth step. No one reaches this except him who receives it, for it consists more in affective experience than in rational consideration. It is at this step, where the interior senses have been restored to see what is most beautiful, to hear what is most harmonious, to smell what is most fragrant, to taste what is most sweet and to hold what is most delectable, that the soul is prepared for mental transports (*excessus*) through devotion, admiration and exaltation according to the three exclamations of the Song of Songs.[7]

Why call the newly received powers of the spirit "senses"? In what sense can the understanding brought about by faith in Christ be likened to smelling or tasting? Certainly, if we wanted to define those two senses in the way they are commonly used, there would be very little in common between them and the spiritual understanding described by St. Bonaventure. What is a "spiritual sense of smell"? In what sense is the *consideration* of the splendors of divine "light" (a problematic term in itself) akin to what we normally call "sight"? Spiritual sight and "hearing" make more sense to us than "smell," "taste," and "touch," but that is not because sight and hearing are in any way less corporeal than the other three senses, but because seeing and hearing are more common metaphors of perceiving God. For the term "senses" to work in the expression "the spiritual senses," it must be thoroughly metaphorized, and any real relation between it and the physical senses removed.[8]

The "spiritual senses" are an attempt to sneak sensuality into the halls of God-language without paying the price of corporeality. They allow the sensual language of the Bible an intermediate status—somewhere between the metaphorical and the literal. From a strictly logical point of view, this intermediate status offers nothing but confusion; but emotionally, it opens vast possibilities.

Before we turn to a discussion of some of the less-than-spiritual ways of sensing God, I would like to cite another passage that comes, like the opening quotation of this chapter, from the sermons of St. Bernard of Clairvaux on the Song of Songs:

> "Behold, there He stands behind our wall, gazing at the windows, looking through the lattices" (Cant 2:9). . . . He drew near the wall, therefore, when He joined himself to our flesh. Our flesh is the wall, and the bridegroom's approach is the incarnation of the Word. The windows and lattices through which He is said to gaze can be understood, I think, as the bodily senses (*sensus carnis*) and human feelings by which He began to experience our human needs. For "He has borne our griefs and carried our sorrows" (Is 53:4). On being made man, therefore, He has used our bodily feelings and senses as openings and windows, so that He would know by experience (*expreimento sciret*) the miseries of man and might become merciful. These were

things He already knew, but in a different way. As Lord of the virtues He knew the virtue of obedience, and yet the apostle bears witness that "He learned obedience through what He suffered" (Heb 5:8). By this means He also learned mercy, although the mercy of the Lord is from eternity (Ps 102:17). This same teacher of the Gentiles teaches this again when He states that He was tempted in all things as we are without sin, in order to become merciful (Heb 4:15). Do you see Him becoming what He was and learning what He knew, seeking in our midst openings and windows by which to search more attentively into our misfortunes? He found as many openings in our tumbling down and fissured wall as He experienced proofs of our weakness and corruption in His own body (*nostrae infirmitatis et corruptionis in suo corpore sensit experimenta*).[9]

This is a very subtle and bold statement on knowledge and experience. Practical knowledge is very different from theoretical knowledge. In theory, God already knows everything; in practice, there is much He can learn. The Incarnation, then, is not just a sacrifice, nor is it just a teaching process whereby Christ delivers the good news of the kingdom to humans; it is also a learning process. For the first time, God experiences the world the way *we* experience it—sensually, through the senses. He does not simply "bear" our sinful flesh in an act of self-sacrifice; He learns something. Not new data—he already knows everything there is to know—but a new way of experiencing, a sudden, new, and very different awareness of what it means to be limited and corruptible. God learns to know as we do—by empathy and analogy.

Jeremiah's statement "death has climbed in through the windows" (Jer 21:9) has been traditionally interpreted as signifying the infiltration of the soul by sense images seeking to detract it from its true path. "What scripture calls windows," writes Gregory of Nyssa in his commentary on the Lord's Prayer, "are the senses that make an entrance for death."[10] The door of the soul too is a dangerous place. Without self-control, writes Clement of Alexandria, "we may reopen the door of the soul, without being aware of it, through the senses as through doors, to the very dissipation we have put to flight."[11] Bernard's bridegroom opens the doors and windows of his newly acquired senses to make sense of our, and his, human experience.

CHAPTER EIGHT

Invisible

And God spoke all these words:

> I am Jehovah your God who brought you out of Egypt, out of the house of slavery. You shall have no other gods but me. You shall not make for yourself an effigy or a likeness in heaven above or on the earth beneath or in the water beneath the earth. You shall not bow down to them or worship them; for I, Jehovah your God, am a jealous God, punishing the children for the sin of the fathers to the third and fourth generation of those who hate me, but showing mercy to a thousand generations of those who love me and of those who keep my commandments. You shall not bear the name of Jehovah your God in vain, for Jehovah will not hold anyone guiltless who bears his name in vain (Ex 20:1–6).

From time to time, it is good to go back to the Bible and read it in a very literal translation. First, one must get rid of the habit of translating Jehovah as "the LORD." Jehovah is not a title, but a proper name.[1] The first six verses of the Decalogue form a single unit. This unit has little to do with metaphysical and ethical principles. It does not even proclaim the oneness of God (the existence of Jehovah's rivals and competitors is not denied). Rather, it is a warning that Jehovah is a jealous God who will tolerate no disloyalty or disrespect. The Israelites must have "no other gods." (English makes a distinction between the one true God with a capital G and the other gods who are written with a small g; there is no such distinction in Hebrew.) What does "not having other gods" mean? It means not worshiping any of them lest Jehovah wreak His vengeance upon the culprits and upon their descendants. Does the prohibition on making an effigy (*pesel*, a free-standing image) and a likeness (*temuna*, a drawn image) refer to Jehovah? The text is not clear, but it is unlikely.[2] The Israelites are warned, so it seems, against making and worshiping images of gods who dwell in the heavens, on earth, or under earth level, in the water. And yet it is clear that since seeing Jehovah's "face" is lethal (Moses, Aaron, Nadab, Abihu, and the seventy elders see the feet of the God of Israel),[3] neither can he be depicted. The Israelites are finally warned against bearing Jehovah's terrible name in vain.[4] This may give us a clue about the reasons for the prohibition on seeing Jehovah. Just like pronouncing his name, seeing is a risky seizure of the persona of the observed. Only the priests in the Temple precincts are allowed to pronounce the name of Jehovah, in very specific and highly ritualized circumstances.[5] Looking at Jehovah is more dangerous than pronouncing his name. When looking at the great, eyes should be lowered. Images teach people disrespect. They trivialize the presence. They are therefore prohibited.

What matters, however, is not what the original intention of the text was, but what tradition read into it (although in the last generation biblical scholars and archeologists have drawn a radically different image of Israelite religion than the one the purely monotheistic image held in the past).[6] The prohibition on making "graven images" was reinterpreted to fit "the LORD," the Hellenized divinity who, as we saw, was losing its wilder aspects and becoming ever more philosophical. The thing with the LORD was not that His shape and form were lethal to humans, as He warns, but that He was beyond shape and form, *aperigraphos* (uncircumscribed), as Proclus described the One. He could not be seen and of course His image could not be "captured" in stone or pigment. Those who did create images of Him were worshiping a false god, a golden calf.

They were both foolish and sinful. And though Jehovah is no longer there to smite them in *this* world, they are certainly not going to go unpunished in the next.

But what exactly is the problem with representing not other gods, but *the* God in pictures and statues? If we forget for a moment the magical explanation (a portrayal is a magic means of gaining a measure of control over the entity portrayed), the answer is far from simple. It is clear that any plastic depiction does not do God justice. No depiction can do justice to the absolute Supreme and most Perfect Being. But neither can words. Human understanding and expression are always partial and inaccurate. Why is this particular form of inaccurate depiction of God so offensive?

The issue was not restricted to monotheists. In his "Twelfth, or Olympic, Discourse," Dio Chrysostom (ca. 40–ca. 120), a Greek orator, writer, philosopher, and historian, dealt with the problems raised by representing the sublime. He begins with the sculptor Pheidias who produced the enormous statue of Zeus in Olympia, considered one of the Seven Wonders of the World. The statue, says Dio, had a problematic effect. Until it was created, men had only a vague idea about the Supreme Being; previous works were never seen as a true likeness, but Pheidias's Zeus changed all that: "you, by the power of your art, first conquered and united Hellas and then all others by means of this wondrous presentment, showing forth so marvelous and dazzling a conception, that none of those who have beheld it could any longer easily form a different one."[7] Can anyone think that Iphitus, Lycurgus, and the Eleans of that time, wonders Dio, who spent so much money reestablishing the Olympic Games, simply failed to find a statue of Zeus out of negligence, or was it rather "because they feared that they would never be able adequately to portray by human art the Supreme and most Perfect Being"?[8]

Pheidias offers a series of explanations for the decision to erect the statue despite such reservations. Men, he says, need something palpable through which to express their gratitude to the gods. They are like children stretching out their hands to their absent parents in their dreams. Representations have a psychological function. And why is Zeus portrayed in human form? It is not because he looks like a human being, but because the human form symbolizes reason:

For mind and intelligence in and of themselves no statuary or painter will ever be able to represent; for all men are utterly incapable of observing such attributes with their eyes or of learning of them by inquiry. But as for that in which this intelligence manifests itself, men, having no mere inkling thereof but actual knowledge, fly to it for refuge, attributing to God a human body as a vessel to contain intelligence and rationality, in their lack of a better illustration, and in their perplexity seeking to indicate that which is invisible and unportrayable by means of something portrayable and visible, using the function of a symbol.[9]

Pheidias's Zeus, then, is a symbolic expression of certain attributes of the "real" Zeus, but that is all. At no point does the sculptor forget its limitations:

As for these attributes, then, I [Pheideas] have represented them in so far as it was possible to do so, since I was not able to name them. But the god who continually sends the lightning's flash, portending war and the destruction of many or a mighty downpour of rain, or of hail or of snow, or who stretches the dark blue rainbow across the sky, the symbol of war, or who sends a shooting star, which hurls forth a stream of sparks, a dread portent to sailors or soldiers, or who sends grievous strife upon Greeks and barbarians so as to inspire tired and despairing men with unceasing love for war and battle, and the god who weighed in the balance the fates of the godlike men or of whole armies to be decided by its spontaneous inclination—that god, I say, it was not possible to represent by my art; nor assuredly should I ever have desired to do so even had it been possible.[10]

Pheidias's Zeus, according to Dio, is not an essential copy of the divine. It is a conventional symbolic expression of certain of its attributes. The artist adds his own interpretation. That interpretation cannot stray too far from the norm, lest the "representation" cease to produce the desired affect—that of inspiring awe and gratitude in the beholders. Religious art, in other words, is not a metaphysical statement, but a devotional mechanism.

This attitude is not unlike Augustine's discussion of visualization in *On the Trinity*. When we read Holy Scriptures, he writes,

The mind frames for itself bodily images with certain outlines and forms, as occurs in [the process] of thinking. Whether [these images] are false, or even if they are true, which rarely happens, this [image in its specificity] is of no benefit to our faith; but it is useful for some other purpose, which is suggested by means of it. For reading or hearing what the Apostle Paul has written, or what has been written of him, who does not create to himself a mental image of the face of the apostle himself, and of all those whose names are there mentioned? And since, among such a multitude of men to whom these books are known, each imagines in a different way those bodily outlines and forms, it is uncertain who imagines them more accurately and closer to reality. Nor, indeed, should our faith be busied with the bodily countenance of those men, but only with the fact that by the grace of God they have lived and acted as Scripture witnesses. . . . For even the countenance of our Lord Himself in the flesh is variously imagined by the diversity of countless imaginations, although, whatever it was, it was one. Nor in the faith which we have in our Lord Jesus Christ, does that which the mind imagines for itself—and is perhaps very different from reality—bring salvation, but that which we think of man according to his species [that is, that God became man, and hence looked like a man, whatever the peculiar aspects of that specific man were].[11]

For Augustine, the mind instinctively paints pictures of corporeal things. These pictures, he thinks, are harmless in themselves. Depicting Christ as a man reminds us that He became man. It is either a reflection of our familiarity with the dogma of the Incarnation or an indicator of it. As long as Christ is portrayed as a man, it does not matter whether we portray him as tall or short, dark or fair, blue or brown eyed. The depictions of Christ and his saints may be realistic, but they are not real. They are conventional icons.

As signs of sacred things, icons deserve respect. But what happens when they are treated as if they were not just conventional signs worthy of respect, but cultic objects? Do they not become harmful "idols"? No Christian thinker accepted for one minute Dio's apologetics. Worshiping Zeus's statue was idolatry. So should the faithful avoid *all* representation of the divine? The answer to this question stands behind one of the great controversies of Eastern Christianity.

Between about 726, when Emperor Leo III, "the Isaurian," began the "Iconoclast" campaign, and the "Triumph of Orthodoxy" in 843, when Empress Theodora reestablished the veneration of icons, a dispute over the boundaries of the legitimate use of imagery in the worship of the Christian God tore Eastern Christianity. In one camp stood the "iconoclasts" who denounced the veneration of icons as idolatry and in the other "iconodules" (icon venerators) who declared it Christian and orthodox.

The iconodule position was more complicated than Dio's. Iconodules agreed with their opponents that the Supreme and Most Perfect God, being incommensurable and uncircumscribable, could not be depicted. Such depiction is a gross misrepresentation of the divine nature and should be prohibited. However, with the Incarnation, God broke out of His ineffability and could now be depicted, just as He could, in the person of Jesus of Nazareth, be seen, heard, smelled, touched, and even tasted. If God is incommensurable, Jesus is not—He was in possession of specific weight, specific height, a specific tone of voice, a specific eye color, and so on. He was not everyman, but a male born in specific circumstances, speaking a specific language. He was a Hypostatic Union, both man and God: "truly divine and truly human." It is not absurd to depict the incarnate God, for strictly speaking it is not the divinity, but only the humanity that is being depicted. In his defense of icon veneration, John of Damascus argued,

> As the Word became flesh immutably remaining what it was, so also the flesh became the Word, without losing what it was, being rather made equal to the Word hypostatically. Therefore I am emboldened to depict the invisible God, not as invisible, but as he became visible for our sake, by participation in flesh and blood. I do not depict the invisible divinity, but I depict God made visible in the flesh. For if it is impossible to depict the soul, how much more God, who gives the soul its immateriality.[12]

John contended that icons receive "veneration" (*proskynesis*), not "worship" (*latreia*). They are "memorials honored not as gods, but as leading to a recollection of divine activities."[13]

But this was more complicated. The problem was not the act of paying homage to a material symbol. The iconoclasts did not object to the veneration of crosses or sacred books. They contended that depictions of Christ were not symbols of God in the same way that a fish, say, is the symbol of Christ. Nobody would mistake Christ for a fish, but the portrait of Christ can indeed be conceived as a "true image." Icons, then, were fake replicas. People treat them as true copies of the prototype, just as they would the image of the emperor on a coin. It is true, they conceded, that the Son's flesh was "circumscribable," but depicting *only* the flesh of Christ is not *part* of the truth; it is a total lie. The whole point of the Incarnation was that the Word incarnate could not be separated into its constituent elements, but formed an indivisible unity.[14] As one of the most ardent defenders of icons, Theodore the Studite, admitted, "There is a mixture of the immiscible, a compound of the uncombinable, that is of the uncircumscribable with the circumscribed, of the boundless with the bounded, of the limitless with the limited, of the formless with the well formed which is indeed paradoxical."[15] It is true that humans who saw or heard Jesus preach and perform miracles did not "see" or "hear" His divinity, but that was simply because the divine cannot be grasped by the senses. Yet divinity was ever present in the incarnate Word. In ways only partly understood by human reason, they formed an inseparable aspect of the experience of the living Christ. An icon, in contrast, cannot replicate that divine presence. It can only communicate (in a partial and inaccurate way) Christ's humanity. But that dedivinized Christ, the iconoclasts would argue, is not the cosmic savior. It is a caricature. One could try to remind people that it is only half the story, but, not unlike with Pheidias's Olympic Zeus, there's a risk that they would become too impressed with the fineness of the icon to remember fine points of theology. If we allow the humanity of the incarnate Son to stand for the divinity, which is inseparable from it, we might as well have allowed from the outset the depiction of the nonincarnate persons of the Trinity or even the godhead. And with time, as we know, this iconoclast outrage is exactly what happened. In the first millennium, iconodule churches did not allow depicting the Father, the Holy Spirit, or the Holy Trinity. Only the incarnate Son could be "circumscribed." But beginning in the eleventh century, and increasingly from then on, the Father, the Holy Spirit, and the entire Trinity were depicted (usually showing the Father as a bearded old man holding the crucified Son, with the Holy Spirit hovering in the form of a dove between them).[16] This became the norm, without serious theological debate; it was a "natural" outcome, one could argue, of iconodule unrestraint. The iconoclasts' fears, then, were not groundless.

Why were the limits of licit representation expanded? Is this yet another indication of the natural tendency toward idolatry that reformers always detect in "popular" religion? Maimonides, for example, thought that idolatry is natural to man, whereas monotheism is *contra naturam*. Humans, he claimed, always slide back to doing what comes naturally to them. Or is it, on the contrary, a return to the coherence of the "Pheidian" attitude that sees nothing wrong with the depiction of the Perfect and Supreme Being as long as the image's limitations are comprehended?

Perhaps we need to pause and reflect on the unique place allotted to visual imagery in theological thought. Why is it so important not to portray God in visual terms? Why is it important not to imagine him in pictures? Because they distort his true nature, we are told. But don't words do the same? Haven't we been told by theologians that words fail to do justice to the Supreme Being? Isn't human speech as bad (if not worse) than the visual arts? What is more likely to mislead us: an icon (think of an "unrealistic" Byzantine icon, drawn according to the rigid conventions of icon drawing) or a dogmatic statement? Theoretically, both convey a false impression of precision where precision is impossible, but surely the icon would fool very few, whereas the dogmatic statement with its many fine nuances could fool everyone.

"The father and maker of all this universe is past finding out; and even if we found him, to tell of him to all men would be impossible," declares Plato in an oft-quoted line of the *Timaeus*.[17] Even if the "father and maker of the universe" is not beyond our mind's grasp ("finding"), it is impossible to communicate this knowledge to others through words. Much more than images, words trigger chains of extremely complicated associations in listeners. The word "father," for example, elicits certain connotations, even when we "know" that its "meaning," when used to describe the first person in the Trinity, is very different from "normal" usage. The process of transmitting through words the nature of a being who, as we saw, is beyond lexical definitions and discursive modes of thought leads inevitably to illicit "misunderstandings." Though we know that certain connotations are "false," we cannot detach them from the "true," or "orthodox," connotations. The linguistic construct "God" is a Hypostatic Union of true and false. If we try to do more than mark (that is, point to the existence of that which is beyond words, and which we call "God"), then we will try more to elaborate, and problematic notions will attach themselves more to the "true" notion. The iconoclasts argued that "no depiction" is always more accurate than the most careful depiction.

But iconoclasts did not advocate silence about God, nor were they satisfied with using only verbal expressions that were obviously symbolic (like the cross or the fish). They assumed instinctively that images are more misleading than words.

As I tried to argue, this is less obvious than it might seem at first glance. At least certain forms of knowledge are nonverbal. We "feel" or we "sense" things that we cannot quite put into words. Once we are forced to pour our experience into words, we have no alternative but to use the vocabulary made available to us by our semantic environment. Even if we try to invent new terms, new "signs," for God, the signified would remain—for others with whom I try to communicate—part of a particular cultural repertoire that gives words, even new words, their meaning. More devious than words are syntaxes—the possible relationships permissible between parts of speech. It is exactly this hidden set of mental rules that apophatic theology was trying to destabilize.

The second person of the Trinity is also a Word, but it is obviously radically different from human words. The divine Word communicates, not as a sign of a "thing," but as an immediate presence. The Son is more an image of the Father than a "word" in the ordinary sense of the term. This image is not a symbol, but the "thing" itself—both signified and signifier. The Word of God cannot convey a specific meaning to all men, but He could be experienced. This experience would inevitably be falsified when translated into words, but as an immediate presence it is true, at least truer than anything human words can produce.

The iconoclasts argued that the only "image" we need is the Eucharist, because the Eucharist is not a sign. It is the "true" Christ in whose presence we experience both the human and the divine natures of the incarnate Word, whether we are aware of it or not.[18] The problem remains that most people do not "feel" the presence of the God-Man in the host.

Even though theologians tell them that He is "truly" there. One could argue that *awareness* of the presence is not important. It is a secondary process whereby the mind makes sense of what it experienced. Why do we need inaccurate and distorted representations of the Son, why do we need verbalizations when He is there for us to experience and incorporate by Communion? Because, as Dio told us, only very few people are capable of maintaining the state of mind we call "faith" without seeing. Christ allows Doubting Thomas to see, and then to verbalize.

But the old questions return, uncalled for: what is this "firsthand experience" *about*? What Thomas saw (the circumscribable flesh of the risen Christ) had nothing to do with what he said as a result of seeing—"my Lord and my *God*." The feeling of confidence that led to what we would consider an irrational act of faith was achieved through sight (and possibly, as we shall see, touch). The final aim of the veneration of images is not circumscribing the uncircumscribable—that is only the means. The aim is to achieve psychological certainty. This has been acknowledged by numerous theologians. Whether legitimate or not, images are effective mnemonic devices (we remember images much more easily than we remember words and ideas, hence their universal use in *artes memoriae*), and they are good for arousing emotions.[19] Pictures can create a powerful emotional reaction, even when they are not fully understood—"a picture is worth a thousand words."

The importance of visual imagery was universally understood in both East and West. It is too often dismissed as a concession to the unlettered (images are the "Bible of the poor"), but this is by no means restricted to the unlettered. In Ignatius of Loyola's *Spiritual Exercises*, written for the Jesuit elite, for example, Ignatius makes a subtle and bold use of images. When the exercitant is to consider his sins, he must not limit himself to words and ideas: "When a contemplation or meditation is about something abstract and invisible . . . the composition will be to see in imagination and to consider the soul as imprisoned in this corruptible body, and my whole compound self [body and soul], as an exile in this vale [of tears] among brute animals."[20] When contemplating Christ's redemptive message, the exercitant is to imagine the court of a great king who summons his men to holy war against the infidel, asking for their total commitment and identification with his cause.[21] When the exercitant is to think of the

Nativity, he should visualize "the road from Nazareth to Bethlehem. Consider its length and breadth, whether it is level or winds through valleys and hills. . . . Similarly look at the place or cave of the Nativity: How big is it, or small? How low or high? And how is it furnished?"[22]

The exercitant is to add details that are not supplied by Scriptures, enhancing what in literary theory is called the "reality effect." Quite often, he is expected to step *into* the picture, as a minor player in the sacred drama. Thus, in the Nativity scene, he must see himself as "a poor little unworthy slave, gazing at them, contemplating them, and serving them in their needs, just as if I were there, with all possible respect and reverence."[23] Standing before Christ on the cross, he should speak to him in this way: "How is it that he, although he is the creator, has come to make himself a man? How is it that he has passed from eternal life to death here in time, and to die in this way for my sins? . . . The colloquy is made, properly speaking, in the way one friend speaks to another, or a servant to one in authority—now begging for favor, now accusing oneself for some misdeed, now telling one's concerns and asking for advice about them."[24]

But Ignatius, as noted, was not directing his *Exercises* to the illiterate or the poor.[25] They were written for the highly educated elite of the Jesuit order. The Jesuits that went through the *Exercises* knew their Bible and their theology. Visualization was not ersatz theology; it was an indispensable mechanism of internalization. The *Spiritual Exercises* were meant to transform ideas and words into something intimate and personal. Sight is not the only sense used. In the "Fifth Exercise," dedicated to hell, Ignatius asks the exercitant to use all his senses—sight, hearing, smell, taste, and touch.[26] But this is exceptional. But sight predominates the *Exercises* as it predominates (either as actual visions or as visual metaphors) much of the Christian thought about God.

Why? There is a long tradition of treating sight as the primary sense. Both Plato and Aristotle share this view:

All men naturally desire knowledge. An indication of this is our esteem for the senses; for apart from their use, we esteem them for their own sake, and most of all the sense of sight. Not only with a view to action, but even when no action is contemplated, we prefer sight, generally speaking, to all the other senses. The reason of this is that of all the senses sight best helps us to know things, and reveals many distinctions.[27]

Sight is related to light, the most pure and noble of all physical phenomena, God's first creation, and the most fitting metaphor for God. Seeing God (the *visio beatifica*) is the ultimate reward for the righteous in heaven. Light, hence sight, is also considered the most fitting metaphor for man's intellectual ability (the "light of reason"). Augustine writes that "in a certain way sight can be seen as the 'generic' sense" (*generalis quodammodo sensus est visum*).[28]

But if images are to trigger emotional reactions, shouldn't they be as realistic as possible? Yet most Byzantine icons were portraits of Christ, his mother, and the saints, usually detached from the historical context they were supposed to invoke. They were highly conventional and their emotional effect, it was felt in the West, was limited. And indeed, the West has gone after effect, since the twelfth century, seeking to portray Christ in increasingly realistic ways consciously intended to provoke emotional reaction. It is enough to look at a late-medieval or Renaissance crucifixion and at a Byzantine icon, or at the work of later artists working within the Byzantine tradition to be struck by the difference. If the West seeks to make the image accessible, experience near, in Kohutuian terms (Ignatius inserts the exercitant into the holy scenes to break the distance and with it the emotional barrier between them), the Byzantine icon does not.[29]

What, then, does the Byzantine icon do? What is it really good for? It seems that the most important thing the icon does is capture not a true likeness of the thing portrayed, but the very presence that a sensual object can retain or even manufacture. It is quite clear that while the debate on images was raging in theological terms, a major influence on the understanding and function of icons was found in the cult of relics. The cult involved physical objects (fragments of saints' bodies or objects suffused with their presence). The theory behind the cult, first expounded by a rather minor ecclesiastic, Victricius of Rouen, was that relics, no matter how small, are not inanimate objects, nor are they body parts:

> In the holy relics there is nothing imperfect . . . the parts of the flesh are connected together and supported by the blood; and the spirit, which has its home in the blood, partakes of the igneous quality that

Scripture attributes to the divine Word. We can therefore have no doubt that the apostles and martyrs whose relics have been brought to us came here with all the efficacy of the power proper to them. We have proof in the benefits they now shower upon us. In fact, since we know that it was by their consent that a portion of their relics was transferred here, it is easy to see that in scattering themselves of their own accord, as it were, they are not impoverished in any way; but they only multiply their benefits, while preserving all their integrity. A flame disperses its light and preserves it in full. In the same way, the saints, enjoying a plenitude incapable of increase, lose nothing by their largesse, just as they felt no fatigue or unpleasantness from the journey that brought them here.[30]

Because the saint is not really dead, and because his excess energy allows him to be present in many places at the same time, the whole saint—body and soul—is present in each relic. The presence of the saint is manifested by the numerous miracles that his relics perform. In a sense, relics are like Aladdin's lamp. If you hold them, you have a certain hard-to-define hold on the saint.

Between the sixth and the eighth centuries, icons were increasingly acquiring the qualities of relics. Not only were they seen as worthy of veneration—an act that, though theologically different from worship, looked dangerously similar to it—and not only were they working miracles, but it became clear that in some way they were not just representations. "Material things on their own," states John of Damascus, "are not worthy of veneration, but if the one depicted is full of grace, then they become participants of grace, on the analogy of faith."[31] The prototype depicted is in a way not-fully-understood present in the depiction. This does not mean that the supernatural being "trapped" in the icon is thereby forced to obey the devotees venerating it. It is not. Miraculous icons, like miracle-working relics, have a will of their own and can at times be negative forces, threatening and punishing their venerators. But, whether benevolent or malevolent, the presence is there, and in the case of icons, in sharp distinction from relics, it is artificial and technical. While the painter may be a holy man, he does not have to be. An icon operates like the Eucharist and other sacraments. In both cases, material objects arranged in a specific way according to certain conventional rules become the "home" of the deity.

But the Eucharist, while being the perfect image (an image that is identical with the prototype), had its disadvantages. It was part of the ritual that was totally controlled and jealously supervised by the hierarchy. More importantly, it did not satisfy the sense of sight. Whatever the Church was saying, the host continued to *look* like bread (in the East) or a wafer (in the West).[32] There were many attempts to fill in this gap. People had elaborate visions of Christ appearing in the Host, either as a Child or as a grown man. Thus, the great defender of images, Pope Gregory the Great himself, was repeatedly presented as celebrating a mass in which Christ suddenly appeared in the host as the incarnate Word. And yet the host remained unsatisfying to the eye. For God and his Mother, icons functioned as primary relics. The icons' miracles were the visual "proof," not of their historical shape and form, but of their elusive presence. "Authentic images," notes Hans Belting, "seemed capable of action, seemed to possess *dynamis*, or supernatural power. God and the saints took their abode in them. People looked to such images with the expectation of beneficence which was often more important to the believers than were God and the afterlife."[33] Or at least more important than the theologians' God and afterlife.

Jehovah's fears were justified. Sacred images are metaphysical traps. The reverence shown to them could become a substitute instead of a sign. The medium is sometimes as strong as the message. The Israelites, waiting impatiently before Mount Sinai, wanted a visual representation, an icon, of the God who brought them out of Egypt. Pretty soon, they forgot about Jehovah and were dancing madly around the Golden Calf. They wanted to *see* God and soon what they saw became God for them. Seeing is believing. In time, he gave in to their desperate need to see, sending his circumscribable Son to them. The invisible God must be seen, ergo He is.

CHAPTER NINE

Tasteless

One might have expected the idea of the Trinity to be the hardest to comprehend for non-Christians. The idea of the three persons, each somehow separate and distinct from the other two, sharing one substance, seems to defy logic—at least the logic of the faithless. But while infidels have had their share of irreverent mirth with the Holy Trinity, it is not this idea that they found most offensive. Logical incoherence does not bother most people and Christian thinkers have long, complex, and extremely sophisticated explanations that make sense of what might seem senseless to the untrained eye. Moreover as far as Jewish infidels are concerned, it turns out that they have their own problems with the unity of God. The one God of Jews is divided into ten Sephirot—the exact nature of which remains unclear—and that are no less problematic for a strict monist than the three persons of the Trinity.

For non-Christians, the idea hardest to digest is not the Trinity, then, but the Incarnation. Greco-Roman philosophers found the idea of defiling the Absolute Spirit with human matter unthinkable. And even if it were thinkable, what good could come out of it? Even for those less committed to the hierarchies of metaphysics, the Incarnation seemed to involve inexplicable redundancies. It is not the claim that God could occasionally adopt human form or even that we are in some particular way made in His image and shape that gives offense. What most nonbelievers find hard to believe is that God chose manhood as a second career, so to speak: that He did not simply appear as a human being to deliver a specific message, but that He was carried in a woman's womb and born as all humans are born (we saw how appalled Marcion was by this idea), that He lived a fairly full human life, which consisted not only of the highlights of redemptive words and acts, but also of the drudgery of everyday existence, of simply moving from place A to place B, providing banal information in answer to banal questions, standing in line to buy eggs and fish, eating badly cooked food, and looking for a private spot to answer the call of (human) nature. For about thirty years, according to the Gospels—from His miraculous birth in Bethlehem to the beginning of his preaching mission—this was mostly what God made Man did. Thirty years where direct contact with the Absolute was "wasted" on learning carpentry and directing non-Galilean travelers to the nearest hostel between Nazareth and Capernaum. Even the evangelists find these years *non dignai memoriae* (not worthy of memory) and pass over them in silence. What did Jesus do when He turned twenty-six? What did He think of Joseph, the man who raised him? Was He a good carpenter? We have no idea.

It is those many dull, unheroic moments, rather than what St. Paul calls "the scandal of the cross," that non-Christians find scandalous. The cross is a metaphysical cavalry charge on the defense lines of conventional logic. Metaphysical cavalry charges are awe-inspiring. They may not breach the logical defense lines, but they certainly capture the imagination. As the French general Pierre François Joseph Bosquet remarked after the charge of the Light Brigade at Balaclava, "It is magnificent, but it is not war." Perhaps not; but it can undoubtedly make very fine religion. Metaphysical cavalry charges are sudden, short, and exciting. By contrast, the many lowlights of the Incarnation are more like a very long military drill. It serves some unknown purpose, but it's quite boring to watch. The unfaithful observe it with puzzlement. It isn't clear what the purpose of these seemingly pointless movements was. It's probably a good thing that we were not given a detailed account of the missing years.

Even more shocking is the undisputed highlight of Christian (or at least Catholic and Orthodox) ritual—the Lord's Supper. In the descriptions recorded in the synoptic Gospels (but strangely absent from John),[1] Christ, celebrating His last supper with his disciples, offered them bread and wine. According to Matthew, he said: "Take, eat; this is my body." Then, when he offered them the cup of wine he said: "Drink ye all of it; for this is my blood of the new testament, which is shed for many for the remission of sins" (Mt 26:26–27). In Mark (14:22–24), Christ says, more ambiguously, that his blood is shed "for many," and in Luke he is quoted as saying, "This is my body which is given for you. Do this in remembrance of me." Luke also has a different version of Christ's reference to the wine: "This cup is the new testament in my blood, which is shed for you" (Lk 22:19–20).

Paul, who must have heard of it from the disciples present at the Last Supper, has a version that—not surprisingly—resembles that of his companion Luke: "and when He had given thanks, He broke it and said, 'Take, eat; this is My body which is broken for you: do this in remembrance of me. In the same manner also He took the cup when He had supped, saying: This cup is the new testament in my blood: do ye this, as oft as ye drink it, in remembrance of me'" (1 Cor 11:24–25).

We do not know for certain what Jesus's exact (Hebrew or Aramaic) words were, or what He meant by them. Is the blood shed for the disciples to confirm the new covenant (as could be understood from Luke) or for "many"? And who are the "many"? What does Christ mean by "do this in remembrance of me"? Do *what* exactly? Most important, what did He mean when He said (in all three Gospels), "Take, eat; this is my body"? How literal was he? Tough questions. But tough questions do not obstruct the flow of religious sentiment. Theologians are often summoned *post factum* to explain what others, usually far less trained theologically, have established as creedal "facts." From early on, Christian communities repeated Christ's words to His disciples in their communal ceremonies, believing not just that this repetition is a "remembrance," but that Christ somehow becomes present in the Eucharistic elements. *How* was He present? Theologians tended to disagree. By the eighth century, it was commonly believed in the West that what was present in the Eucharistic elements was the flesh and blood of the historical Jesus who was born in Bethlehem, who lived in Nazareth, and who was crucified in Jerusalem.

This was not easy to believe. Miracles were needed. According to local tradition, the first Eucharistic miracle took place in Lanciano around 750 in the church of Saints Legontian and Domitian. A Basilian priest who had fled Byzantium during the Iconoclastic persecutions was celebrating mass when he was seized with doubts about the real presence of Christ in the Eucharist. All of a sudden, the consecrated bread and wine became accessible to all the senses in their usually hidden nature as flesh and blood.[2]

This miracle did not end theological debates. In the ninth century, Ratramanus of Corbie asserted that Christ is only present in the Eucharist *in figura* and in the eleventh century Berengar of Tours argued that the flesh and blood present in the Holy Eucharist are spiritual and not material.[3] Their position was flatly rejected by the established Church. Berengar was condemned by no less than fourteen synods.[4] In 1059, in Rome, he was made to sign a declaration of faith denying that "the bread and the wine placed on the altar are, after consecration, only a sacrament [a visible sign of an invisible thing], and not the real body and blood of our Lord Jesus Christ, and that these cannot be handled and broken by the hands of priests, and crushed by the teeth of the faithful sensually (*sensualiter*), but only as sacrament."[5] Ironically, the technical term for the process of the bread and the wine becoming Christ's flesh and blood—"transubstantiation"—was apparently first used by a pupil of Berengar, Hildebert of Lavardin (or of Tours).[6] "Transubstantiation" reflects Aristotelian metaphysics. It is the process whereby one substance (the substance of bread and wine) is replaced with another (the substance of Christ's flesh and the blood), leaving the sensory appearances of bread and wine (the "accidents") unaltered. After consecration, the Eucharistic elements continued to look, taste, feel, smell, and sound like ordinary bread and wine. The consecrated bread quells hunger just like unconsecrated bread; the consecrated wine lost none of its inebriating qualities just like unconsecrated wine. The senses can detect nothing to distinguish a consecrated host from an unconsecrated one. And yet, the most momentous change has occurred. Those modest pieces of baked flour and water are now the entire body of the Man-God, present simultaneously in numerous locations; the fermented juice of grapes is now the blood of the Savior "shed for many for the remission of sins."

"Transubstantiation" became the commonly used term, after being used in 1215 in the canons of the Fourth Lateran Council presided over by Pope Innocent III (who reigned from 1198 to 1216) and in the first official collection of canon law, the *Decretales Gregorii IX*.[7] In what follows, I shall have a lot to say about the consequences of transubstantiation and about Pope Innocent III, but first let me return for a moment to the infidel's point of view. All infidels are shocked by the Christian idea of the "Real Presence." It makes the sensuality of the ineffable God particularly flagrant and his passivity particularly embarrassing. As metaphors, eating and being eaten are very powerful—they convey a sense of a truly intimate mixing of substances. But one (one infidel, that is) finds the idea that this is *not* a metaphor shocking. Why would God want to be eaten in his human form? Why is this a good way to make humans more *spiritual*? Again, it is the endless repetition of the act in the most mundane circumstances that the infidel finds hardest to swallow. For the eating of God is not a singular, liberating act of law-breaking, but a repetitive ritual that is by necessity abused by overuse, devalued until its earth-shattering and mind-boggling aspects fade into bored familiarity. When you cause God to re-reincarnate on a daily basis, when you feed on God every day, you become fed up. Familiarity breeds contempt. Healing miracles and weeping Madonnas become more exciting than the most stunning miracle that has ever occurred on the face of this earth.

Whatever non-Christians thought about the Eucharist, the faithful in the High and Late Middle Ages accepted it as a simple fact—Christ is really (whatever "really" means) present in the consecrated host and wine. But for theologians, nothing is simple. They have been, and still are, struggling to explain the inexplicable. Before we turn to some of their more interesting discussions, one more clarification needs to be made. In spite of the fact that the Christian God is edible, we have no reports describing what he tastes like. From a theological point of view, this should not come as a surprise. We are not supposed to know how he "really" tastes, since the elements retain their accidental qualities even after their substance is annihilated. But we are also not supposed to know how the Father looks and yet numerous attempts have been made—by visionaries and artists—

to give him shape and form. It is true that we are supposed to have *faith* in the newly acquired nature of the Eucharistic elements. If the body of Christ were accessible to the senses after consecration, even unbelievers would believe. This point is often made by theologians: "The [elements do not change their form] so that they [the faithful] shall have the merit of faith in those things that are unseen."[8]

And yet numerous Eucharistic miracles do exactly that—they demonstrate that the presence is real, by making various doubting Thomases *see* what they should have accepted by faith.[9] The miracle of Lanciano was the first, but certainly not the most famous, account of mystical demystification. A more famous miracle was recounted by Paul the Deacon in his *Life of Gregory the Great*, written around 775. In one of its episodes, Paul recounts that when the pope was saying mass, a certain woman present started laughing at the moment of Communion, saying to a companion that she could not believe the bread was Christ, as she had herself baked it. Gregory prayed for a sign, and the host turned into a bleeding finger.[10] In later representations, it is not just a finger, but the whole Christ, portrayed as the "Man of Sorrows," that appears on the altar. Often the blood pouring from his side is shown filling up the chalice placed on the altar.[11]

These descriptions strive to show that even though Christ's real presence requires faith, it is not simply a subjective experience of the believer. Every once in a while, God reveals what is hidden, thus providing skeptics with what remains the ultimate proof—sensory data. It should be noted that the miracles often display rather dubious theology. From a correct theological perspective, the Christ who inheres in the consecrated host and wine is not a piece of meat (as he appears in the Lanciano host) or drops of blood, but the whole, undivided body of Christ as he is now, in heaven. The miracle of transubstantiation does not produce some past phase of Christ's life, but the living savior as he is *now*. He is not the Man of Sorrows or the bleeding baby that appears in some Eucharistic miracles. As Marilyn McCord Adams notes, it is the theological consensus that "the risen and ascended Body of Christ is glorified and hence impassible."[12]

There is no separation of body parts in the Eucharist (no bloody fingers then). Pope Innocent III emphasizes this in his hugely influential work *On the Sacred Mystery of the Altar*, written shortly before his accession to the Throne of Saint Peter:

It is not [to be thought] that because he is eaten, he is divided into parts, nor that he is cut into pieces as sacrament, like the meat they sell at the butcher's shop. He is consumed unharmed and eaten whole. He is eaten alive, since he rose from the dead after he has been killed. And when he is eaten he does not die, for he was resurrected and will not die....

The entire bread is transformed into the entire body (*quod totalis panis in totale corpus convertitur*) so that no part [of the bread] is transformed into a [particular] part of the body (*nulla pars transit in aliquam partem corporis*).... For in as many parts as the elements may be divided, in each of the individual parts Christ is whole: whole in every big part, whole in every small part, whole in the entire [host] and whole in the fraction.[13]

In the fifteenth century, Cardinal Nicholas of Cusa was quite emphatic in his reaction to reports about the miraculous bloodstained hosts of Andechs: "We cannot permit it [the adoration of the miraculous hosts] without damage to God, for our Catholic Faith teaches us that the glorified body of Christ has glorified blood, completely un-seeable, in glorified veins."[14]

But visionaries are not deterred by theological qualms. The theologians' Real Presence does not have a distinct taste, or any other quality detectable by the senses (it is his substance that is present in the Eucharist, not accidents like smell and taste), but the visionaries' Christ-in-the-host, theological reservations notwithstanding, should, at least theoretically, taste like something—milk and honey, human flesh, manna. Yet, while people often described Christ's look and feel and smell, while they described the sound of His voice, they did not describe His taste. The fleshy hosts of Lanciano, of Trani, and of Alatri remain uneaten, the blood of Christ in Ferrara, in Firenze, and in Bolsena undrunk,[15] the finger of St. Gregory's Mass untouched. In the eleventh century, Guitmund, Bishop of Aversa and adversary of Berengar of Tours, recounted a Eucharistic miracle that he had heard personally from Bishop Lanfranc of Bec (1005–1089):

The Lord Lanfranc told me that this happened when he was a boy in Italy. When a certain priest was celebrating mass, he found on the altar the true flesh, and in the chalice the true blood, under their proper species of flesh and blood. As he was afraid to consume them, he immediately revealed the matter to his bishop asking for his advice. The bishop, with many other bishops convened for this, carefully closed and sealed that chalice with that flesh and blood of the Lord, and placed it in the altar to be kept there as the most important relics.[16]

Why not eat the flesh as flesh, drink the blood as blood? In the thirteenth century, St. Albert the Great writes, without offering an explanation, that "if it [the host] is transformed in the sight of all, then it seems that it should not be consumed, but rather kept as relics and another [host] consecrated."[17] But wouldn't consuming the host be the ultimate confirmation of religious devotion, now that doubts have been removed? Shouldn't those whose faith is strongest eat and drink the flesh and blood of Christ? In their visions, mystics often recount drinking Christ's blood. They do *not* drink the miraculous blood. And if it is argued that the unveiling of the Eucharistic elements is a concession for those of little faith, a concession that the truly faithful do not need: why adore them more than any "ordinary" host? The substance, after all, is the same, and the merit of adoring an "ordinary" host is, as Innocent III (and many others) suggested, greater.[18]

Of course, one could offer a pragmatic explanation—the miraculous hosts were not consumed, because they were quickly made objects of veneration for the many. Their consumption would deprive others of benefiting from the miracle. This is not the explanation offered, though, in our sources. There must be another explanation: perhaps even for those of strong faith, the idea of eating human flesh was hard to stomach. Why is it, asks St. Ambrose of Milan (an early exponent of the doctrine of the Real Presence), that we do not see Christ's flesh and blood as they are? According to Ambrose, the apostles (with the exception of Peter) were horrified when Christ offered them his flesh and blood: "Lest therefore many should say this, shrinking in horror from the blood (*horror cruris*), as it were, and in order that they receive the grace of redemption, you receive the sacrament in likeness (*in similitudine*), but truly obtain the grace of its nature."[19] Petrus Comestor, agreeing with Ambrose (that the true nature is hidden "lest the soul be horrified by what the eye perceives"), introduces the faithless into the picture: "lest the Christian religion be despised (*insultaretur*) by the incredulous, if they see [the faithful] eating raw meat."[20] Believers (even the apostles themselves) would be horrified. Nonbelievers would be scandalized—no matter how firmly theologians affirm that no "raw meat" is involved in eating the body—for, as we said, eating Christ is a totally different from eating ordinary meat.[21] And yet even by association it is (too) horrible.[22] Jews accused of consuming the blood of innocent Christian children (though not, interestingly, of drinking the blood of hosts they have desecrated) are not fully human.[23]

When they did not have to contend with the less palatable aspects of theophagy, theologians were not beyond dealing with some very practical sides of eating the flesh of Christ. What, wonders William of Middleton, happened in the Last Supper, when Jesus offered His flesh and blood to the apostles? He too ate the consecrated elements. Did He eat His own body then? He did, says William. The discussion is worth quoting in full:

1. It is asked about Christ whether He ate His own body in the Last Supper. It seems that He did, for see the gloss on Ruth 3:7: "Boaz ate and drank." The Ordinary Gloss says: "Christ ate and drank in the Last Super, and gave the sacrament of His body and blood to the apostles. When the disciples have shared (*communicaverunt*) His body and blood, He too participated (*participavit*) in them."

2. Likewise, Leviticus 8:24: "of the blood of the ram." The Gloss of Heschius says: "First the priest was anointed by the blood and then his sons, because in the Last Supper, Christ first accepted the blood and then gave the disciples." Another gloss says: "When He drank and gave the others to drink, it refers to the blood that he spilled over the altar—that is to His body."

3. Likewise, the hymn says: "The king sat in supper, surrounded by a crowd of twelve; he held himself in his [own] hands, he ate himself as food."

4. Likewise, in the Old Testament the greatest sacrament was circumcision; in the New Testament it was baptism. Christ has received both. Why not also *this* sacrament?

5. Contra: If Christ had eaten His own body, then He had eaten only sacramentally like a bad priest who [does not gain spiritual advantage from the sacrament, but] receives the sacrament for his dam-

nation, which is impossible. Furthermore, then He would have given himself less than he gave the others. He could not have eaten spiritually, because then grace would have been added to Him, which cannot be. Thus in no way could He have eaten.

6. Likewise, in the Ordinary Gloss to 1 Corinthians 11:25 sacramental eating signifies the union of the members with the head, and if a person had properly (*digne*) eaten, it would have been effected. But such an effect could not occur in Christ, because [in Him] the union has already occurred.

7. Likewise, nothing superfluous was done by Him. But sacramental eating was ordained for the spiritual; He had not eaten sacramentally, since He had eaten spiritually. But in spiritual eating the eater is united with the eaten. Christ, however, could not be united with Himself.

8. Likewise, Christ was not divided within Himself; hence He could not be the eater and the eaten.

9. Likewise, the glorified body does not need nutrition or food. Only the mortal and corruptible body does. Hence, since the relation between the glorious soul and the soul still in this world (*animam viatoris*) is like the relation between the glorified body and the unglorified body, in the same way the glorious soul does not lack (*non indiget*) spiritual food. Since the soul of Christ was glorious, he needed no such food or eating.

I answer that according to many authorities, Christ had eaten Himself (*seipsum*) in the Last Supper when He gave himself to the disciples. It should be said then that just as Christ received the sacrament of Baptism not because He needed purgation, but with the intention of informing us, that is, to serve as an example for others and a source of information to them, in the same way, I say, He did not receive his own body, because of any effect achieved by that consumption, but to give others an example of consuming. Whence Chrysostom says on Matthew 26:27: "He drank of it so that those hearing Him would not say: 'What? Do I drink blood and eat flesh?' He drank his blood first, so they would not be perturbed, as they were when [after the Eucharistic sermon in Capernaum] many went away [horrified], according to John 6:67.[24]

According to the scholastics, the sacrament of the Eucharist can be eaten "carnally," "sacramentally," and "spiritually." It is eaten "carnally" when eaters (human or inhuman) are not aware of what they are eating. It is eaten "sacramentally" when eaters believe the bread and the wine to be the flesh and blood of Christ or at least believe that others believe so. The highest form of eating is "spiritual." It occurs when the eater is inflamed with the love of Christ and seeks to unite Himself spiritually with his Mystical Body, through Communion.[25] The spiritual effects of the three kinds of eating are very different. Carnal eaters simply turn the accidents into physical nourishment. Spiritual eaters gain the highest promise of the sacrament, which is unification with God through love and adoration. Rather than making what they eat part of themselves, they succeed—with God's grace—in making themselves part of what they eat. "Sacramental" eaters of good intention (which includes most ordinary partakers) may not achieve the highest aims of the sacrament, but *are* getting certain spiritual benefits. Christ, according to William, must have eaten himself in the highest fashion—spiritually. Of course the benefits of spiritual eating were "wasted" on him, since He did not need to be unified with himself. He ate, then, not for his own good, but for the good of others. More important perhaps, Christ ate His own flesh and blood purely for psychological reasons. Nothing metaphysical was gained by His eating His body. The only gain was emotional. This tells us something about the depth of the taboo on cannibalism.

There were others who do not benefit from the sacrament, for very different reasons. People who take communion believing by association (they believe that others believe) or those who have faith in the reality of the sacrament without having faith in its salvific effects, or those who are separated from the mystical body of Christ by their mortal sins, gain nothing by eating. Indeed, their eating is a spiritual outrage for which they deserve to be punished. And yet, although, like Christ, they do not receive the spiritual benefits of the Eucharist, the sacrament is as present for them as it is for their more spiritual brethren. Unlike the other sacraments that exist only when there is a receiver (there is no baptism unless someone is baptized, no absolution unless someone is absolved, and so on), the Eucharist exists per se. Once the words of consecration have been pronounced in a canonical manner and in the appropriate setting, the flesh and blood are there, even if nobody partakes of them, even if nobody knows of them. Christ's eating may have been quite unique, but what He was eating was exactly the same as what sinners were eating when they deliberately or accidentally consumed the Eucharistic elements.

Theologians were quite concerned about the natural vicissitudes of the species. Though they were nothing but "accidents" lacking substance, whose only role was to veil the Lord's flesh and blood from horrified believers, they were the way Christ was venerated. Unfortunately, they wouldn't always go away gracefully. Things happened to them, undignified things. Consecrated hosts behaving like simple material objects— eaten, spat, vomited, allowed to go bad, simply digested—were hard for theologians to accept. What, for example, if an insect fell into the consecrated wine? In his *Jewel of the Church (Gemma ecclesiastica)*, written around 1197, Gerald of Wales discusses this unpleasant possibility:

> There is nothing defined in the Decretals or in theological books concerning the question of a fly or some other impurity falling into the consecrated blood. However, I have personally heard Master Peter Comestor speak about this matter. He said that if this happened to him, he would not drink the blood, but would pour it into the *sacrarium.* He also said he had heard about certain monks at Tours who, when their abbot was celebrating mass, mixed poison with the wine in the chalice. One of the monks, however, told the abbot just as he was about to drink from the chalice. The abbot drank it nevertheless and he died. He also told of another priest who drank the sacred blood with a spider in it and was not harmed; in fact the spider afterwards came out through his arm, alive and well.[26]

Spiders were considered poisonous and swallowing them life-threatening. The problem with the insect in the communion wine was not only that it was drenched with Christ's blood, but that it probably also swallowed some of it. The celebrant had to decide whether to allow the sacred blood to be degraded by waste or whether, overcoming revulsion and fear, he would consume it together with the insect, thus depositing it in the proper vessel.

But what if the host were eaten by a larger animal that could not be swallowed whole? Do irrational creatures really consume the body of Christ when they eat the consecrated host or drink the consecrated wine?

Some say [writes Petrus Comestor] that the body of Christ is eaten by a mouse just as it is eaten by a man. [After all,] the mouth of a mouse is cleaner than the mouth of Judas Iscariot [who ate with the other apostles at the Last Supper]. Others say that only the species [that is, the bread] is nibbled and that anything less dignified that seems to be done to this sacrament is done [only] to the species of bread and wine and not to the real body of Christ.[27]

This was not enough for Guitmund of Aversa. He claimed that, appearances notwithstanding, nothing unseemly *ever* happens to the Eucharistic elements:

In truth, it seems to me that these sacraments can never be nibbled by mice or other brute animals. When it seems as if they are corrupted, one could answer as was said concerning the gardener, the wayfarer, and the leper [all appearances taken by Christ]—that they cannot be corrupted, but can appear in such a manner to punish and correct the negligence of ministers or to test the faith of those who see this. As for those who say that they can be eaten by brute animals, we can respond that it is for the said reasons—testing faith, punishing and correcting the negligence of guardians—that brute animals can only approach the body of Christ to the point where human vision can reach. After that [the body of Christ] is immediately and invisibly snatched away and carried to heaven either by the angels who are always attending it or by some virtue that inheres in it.[28]

Later theologians were unhappy with this explanation. They tended to limit unphilosophical miraculous explanations—an expression of a philosophical cul de sac—to a minimum. Innocent III has a more philosophically acceptable (though equally miraculous) explanation:

If indeed it is asked what is eaten by a mouse when the sacrament is nibbled or what turns to ashes when it is burned, the answer would be that just as the substance of the bread is miraculously transformed when the body of the Lord begins to be under the sacrament [that is, the moment of transubstantiation] so in some manner it is reversed (*qodammodo miraculose revertitur*) when He ceases to be there—it is not the substance of the bread that had become flesh that returns, but something [else] miraculously created in its stead (although the accidents could be corrupted and eaten [even] without a subject).[29]

Note that Guitmund solves the problem by summoning either God or the angels ex machina. Comestor is willing to allow that mice do eat the real body of Christ, or attributes, happening, everything undignified to the species alone. Innocent, however, suggests the possibility of something more radical—a reversal of transubstantiation.

This reversed miracle is essential for saving the body of Christ not only from voracious animals, but from the fate of all food consumed by humans—excretion. The idea that the Body may end up in the latrine is naturally abominable to believers. This ultimate sacrilege is sometimes attributed to Jews keen on desecrating the host in all kinds of abominable ways. Thus, in a letter written in 1205 Pope Innocent III wrote to the archbishop of Sens and to the bishop of Paris, ordering them to use their influence with the secular authorities to prohibit the employment of Christian wet nurses by Jews. "Whenever it happens," writes the pope, "that on the day of the Lord's resurrection Christian women who are wet-nurses for the children of Jews receive the body and blood of Jesus Christ, the Jews make these women pour their milk into the latrine for three days before they can nurse again."[30] In Chaucer's "Prioress's Tale," the little Christlike victim of the Jews' ritual murder is thrown into the latrine where he continues to sing the *Alma redemptoris mater* until his tormentors are caught and punished.

It is hard to believe that this horror could be committed by faithful Christians simply by digesting the host. What, then, is the fate of the Eucharist after it has been eaten by a faithful recipient? Answers vary, but all authorities insist that at some point in the digestive system a process of *de*-transubstantiation occurs. When exactly? It is hard to say. Gratian offers a cautious answer in his *Decretum*, in the treatise dedicated to the Eucharist (*De Consecratione*):

It [the Eucharist] is not incorporated like other foods that are digested in the stomach. Either it does not descend into the stomach like other foods, or it does not turn like them into the sustenance of the body, [for] it is the food of the soul, not of the body. . . . The species, however, do indeed go there, but is it the sacrament? No, because the Body of

Christ is no longer there. The sacrament is there [only] as long as the body of Christ is there. But when [exactly] does this occur—until what place does it descend from the throat? I do not know.[31]

Like Gratian, Petrus Comestor is uncomfortable with the question and equally vague in his answer:

> It is asked what happens to the body of Christ after it has been taken and eaten, although this should not be asked. But such is human thought that it seeks answers on the very things that should not be asked.
>
> Solution: In the past, when He had assumed the Virgin's flesh, Christ invited us to venerate his bodily presence. Later, when His mission was accomplished, He ascended in his body to heaven, not thereby removing His spiritual presence from us. Whence He Himself said: "Lo, I am with you always even to the end of the age" [Mt 28:20]. Thus, every day He is with us in body in his sacrament, so that through his corporeal presence He stimulates us to the spiritual. Hence, when the priest holds the sacrament in his hands, Christ is with him bodily; when he raises Him to his mouth, He is with him bodily, when he eats Him and tastes Him, He is with him bodily, and as long as it is perceived by the bodily senses, His bodily presence is not removed. Afterward, when sensual bodily perception ceases, ask not where Christ is. If you wish to ask, ask in heaven—Christ is there at the right hand of the Father. Ask there, where He was first, whence He did not depart when He came to you. After that, one should ask not about his bodily, but about his spiritual presence. When its mission is accomplished, the sacrament is brought to completion (*perfectum est sacramentum*). Christ passes from the mouth to the heart. It is better for you that He passes to the soul than to the belly (*in mentem quam in ventrem*). He is food for the soul not for the body. He came to you to be eaten, not to be consumed, to be tasted, not to be incorporated [that is, to become part of the body of the eater through digestion].[32]

It might have been better not to ask about the mechanism of de-transubstantiation, but Comestor realizes that the unpleasant question cannot be avoided. His solution consists of two parts. First, he makes an analogy between the Incarnation and the Eucharist. In both,

Christ removes his physical presence from us once his mission has been accomplished. The heart of the Eucharist is the act of eating, not of digesting. Once eaten, Christ can remove his physical presence and return to heaven, where he sits at the right hand of his Father. The puzzling question remains: how this miracle—in theory just as amazing as transubstantiation—happens and, more confusing still, when. If the appearance of Christ's substance in lieu of the substance of bread and wine occurs at an exact moment (when the formula of consecration is pronounced by a canonically ordained priest), the moment of reversal is hard to pinpoint. It seems to depend on the eater's subjective sensations—when he or she no longer senses it, when he or she can no longer see, feel, smell, and taste it, it ceases to be the body of Christ.

For Comestor, the Eucharist never actually reaches the stomach. Others were less certain. In his commentary on the *Sentences*, Bonaventure answers those who feel it is unfitting that Christ be chewed by the faithful during Communion:

> It should be said that in eating there are these three: chewing, passing to the stomach, and incorporation. These three correspond to three aspects of the sacrament. Chewing relates only to the species, incorporation relates [only] to the mystical body of Christ; passing to the stomach relates not only to the species, but also to the true body of Christ. It is there, as long as the species of bread is there. But the body of Christ cannot be said to be truly eaten corporeally, because it is chewed corporeally. Just as it is not broken [corporeally], it is not chewed [corporeally].[33]

Why is it important for Bonaventure to insist that the body of Christ really passes to the stomach, although not in bodily fashion? Perhaps because "eating" for him consists not merely of chewing and swallowing but also of digesting something that at least looks like bread (the exact moment of reverse transubstantiation is not given) is there.

Bonaventure's Dominican contemporary Simon of Hinton offers a more detailed discussion:

> To the second, namely, whether the body of Christ passes into the stomach, some say that it is present under the species as long as it is in

the mouth, but as soon as it is swallowed, the body of Christ passes into the mind and the species of bread and wine into the stomach. Others, who are more to be trusted, say that it enters the stomach, and remains there as long as the species remain uncorrupted, and when they cease to be the species of bread and wine, they cease to be the body and blood of Christ. The same sometimes happens when the [consecrated host] is kept too long in a pyx and becomes corrupted. Nor is this contrary to that text of Augustine relied on by those who hold the prior position, namely: "As long as it is in the mouth, it is in you; it does not go down to the cesspool, but up in rapture [of the mind] (*non ducitur in secessum sed rapitur in excessum*)." Augustine does not here deny that it passes into the stomach, but he does deny that it becomes food for the body, that it is digested in the stomach, and that part of it is carried to the liver where it turns into blood with which the body's losses are restored, while the less pure part passes on and is excreted. Such an idea is horrible to utter, and should not even be thought with assent.[34]

And what if the host has reached the stomach and was then vomited whole? Does it maintain its nature as the Lord's body, a nature supposedly lost only when the species become corrupted? What if it is excreted whole, undigested? Such a "polluted" host is an ambiguous object. "It is to be venerated" (*cum veneratione est servandum*) not because [it is a sacrament], but because it *was* a sacrament."[35] The polluted host is declared "corrupted" merely by being covered with corrupt matter and not because corruption has occurred in the species themselves. On the other hand, even though they are no longer different from the digested species—that, like them, *were* the sacrament— they deserve veneration. It is the appearance of things, once more, that determines our reactions. And why not? After all, God Himself was not indifferent to our sensibilities, when He hid the "horror" of his flesh and blood under the soothing appearance of bread and wine.

Psychology, human psychology that is, played an important role, as we have seen, in confusing Eucharistic matters. Humans care deeply about things that have little significance in the grand scheme of things. Humans are horrified by the idea of eating human flesh, be it the glorified flesh of the Man-God. They are offended by the idea that something revolting might happen to the "species," no matter how often theologians tell them that what matters is not what they *can* see but what they can't, the substance and not the appearances. People see Christ in the Eucharist as pieces of flesh or as drops of blood or as a bleeding baby. In theory this is wrong; and yet theologians tend not to dismiss it out of hand. Human sentiments were important enough to make Christ eat his own flesh at the Last Supper; they are not to be slighted by the experts even if they require some particularly complicated explanatory acrobatics.

*   *   *

This chapter has dealt with one of the most strikingly corporeal epiphanies of God. The icon may embody a mystical presence, but it remains a sign. The Eucharist is not a sign. It is God incarnate. Popular devotions paid great attention to the visual aspects of the Eucharist. The Elevation of the Host during mass was for many of the faithful more important than Communion itself and was experienced with much greater frequency. But what is being seen when the host is elevated is nothing but an empty shell. Vision is totally unimportant in this sacrament. What you see are the accidents. You may believe in the Real Presence, but to experience it you must eat the host and drink the wine. Only then does it happen. It is a spiritual experience—the highest possible spiritual experience—that can be communicated only orally. We do not know what God tastes like, but we do know how it feels to taste God. If you believe, then your lips, mouth, tongue, teeth, and throat sense the presence of the Lord, hidden underneath the species, in the most intimate way our human bodies can feel the divine.

CHAPTER TEN

Untouchable

Aristotle considered touch and taste the basest of the five senses.[1] Unlike sight, hearing, and smell, taste and touch require direct contact between bodies. In a culture that puts the spiritual above the material, this unmitigated materiality is a distinct sign of metaphysical inferiority and ethical danger. We derive nobler pleasures from the nobler senses. In that sense, taste is slightly better than touch. The Philosopher perceives certain aspects of gustatory pleasures that are peculiar to humans. The pleasures of touch seem to be the same for man and brute. Maimonides, ever the faithful Aristotelian, finds touch "shameful."[2]

And yet emotionally, touch is a privileged source of information. The psychologist Thomas Ogden has argued that we realize only gradually that we are receptors of knowledge about the world. Our primal sensation is the fairly simple binary mechanism that distinguishes between the pleasant and the unpleasant. Our skins are the substratum upon which all else (including the notion of selfhood) is inscribed:

> The nature of one's relationships to one's objects is determined to a large degree by the nature of the subjectivity (the form of "I-ness")

that constitutes the context for those object relations. In the autistic-contiguous position, the relationship to objects is one in which the organization of a rudimentary sense of "I-ness" arises from relationships of sensory contiguity (i.e., .touching) that over time generates the sense of a bounded sensory surface on which one's experience occurs (the beginnings of the feeling of "a place where one lives").[3]

Humans derive pleasure and epistemological certainty from their skins. It is instinctively felt that tactile information is more "real" than other sensory data. But since touching requires contact between two bodies, and since God has no body, it would be impossible to touch Him. When the Word became flesh, however, it became accessible to touch, as to all other senses. Jesus's flesh was touched by many. Indeed, His willingness to allow almost free access to His body (especially by sinful women) raised criticism even among His followers. These contacts were not metaphysical "proofs." They were part of the everyday commerce of humans or attempts to benefit from the power that Jesus's body emitted. At the end of the Gospel of John, however, Thomas the Apostle seeks tactile assurance of the risen Lord's true identity:

> But Thomas, called Didymus, one of the twelve, was not with them when Jesus came. The other disciples therefore said to him, "We have seen the Lord." But he said to them, "Unless I see in His hands the print of the nails, and put my finger into His side, I will not believe." And after eight days His disciples were again inside, and Thomas with them. Jesus came, the doors being shut, and stood in the midst and said, "Peace to you!" Then He said to Thomas, "Reach your finger here, and look at my hands, and reach your hand here and put it into my side. Do not be unbelieving but believing." And Thomas answered and said to Him, "My Lord and my God!" Jesus said to him, "Thomas, because you have seen me, you have believed; blessed are those who have not seen and yet have believed." (Jn 20:24–29)

Did Thomas accept Jesus's invitation and use his sense of touch to establish the veracity of the Lord's resurrection? Generations of artists portraying the scene answered in the affirmative. The depicted Thomas does touch Jesus. This seems unwarranted by the text. Not only does the Gospel not mention touching, but Jesus declares that the transformation of Thomas from doubting to believing was achieved through sight and not through touch.[4] Still some exegetes were willing to read the ultimate act of verification in the silence of the Gospel.

In his commentary on the Gospel of John, Augustine seeks to show that touching, though not explicitly mentioned, may have occurred:

> He did not say, "you have touched me," but "you have seen me," because in a certain way sight is used to indicate the senses in general, for it is often used to refer to the other four senses, as when we say: "listen and see how good it sounds, smell and see how good it smells, taste and see how good it tastes, touch and see how warm it feels. [The verb] "See" is always used, even though in the strict sense one cannot deny that it properly belongs to the eyes. When He said, "Reach your finger here and see my hands," what was He saying but "touch and see"? Surely, he [Thomas] did not have eyes in his finger. Hence, by reason either of seeing or even of touching, [Christ] said, "because you have seen me, you have believed." Although it could also be said that the disciple did not dare to touch him, when he offered himself to be touched, for it is not written, "And Thomas touched [him]." But whether only by looking or also by touching, he saw and believed; that which follows proclaimed and commended better the faith of the nations: "blessed are those who have not seen and yet have believed."[5]

Augustine does not consider touching the risen Christ as unthinkable (he could easily have said that it did not occur). The problem for him is the very need for sensory proof. Both seeing and touching are sensual, and both, as Christ himself states, are signs of weak faith, an indication of a still-too-Jewish seeking of signs (1 Cor 1:22). True faith needs no signs: "for the things which are seen are temporary, but the things which are not seen are eternal" (2 Cor 4:18). Blessed are those who have not seen (or touched, for that matter) and yet have believed.

But there is more than just touching in Christ's encounter with Thomas. Christ invites Thomas to move beyond the surface of the skin into his sacred flesh: "reach your hand here and put it *into* my side" (*affer manum tuam et mitte in latus meum*).[6] Although the scriptural text seems to suggest, as we have seen, that Thomas did not in fact put his hand into Christ's side, generations of Christian artists chose to depict a human penetration of Christ's body—the one and only incident where a human organ breaks through the skin into the inner layers of the Man-God's flesh. The relationship between humans and God, it must be remembered, is not symmetric. God is the penetrator, not the penetrated. He enters humans in a variety of mystical ways. He even enters them physically (as the Eucharist). But humans do not penetrate God. No human organ is allowed such sacrilegious breach of boundaries. Except Thomas's finger.

The yearning to touch God, to receive the ultimate assurance of His presence, was always there. Christian mystics imagined themselves touching the God-Man, Christ. In the late twelfth century, the New Mysticism, using the idiom of the Song of Songs, describes Christ, the Bridegroom, in amorous terms. God is not just touched; He is held, embraced, and kissed. The dividing line between the spiritual and the physical senses is often extremely hard to detect. The New Mysticism sought to find ways to express the divine presence while not erasing the Self. The Neoplatonic-Dionysian model of mystical union requires the abandonment of everything that is distinctly human. At its climactic moment, the mystic "disappears" into God. His human desires vanish; his "accidents" lose their power of pulling him down and away from God. He becomes "oblivious of himself," "transcends himself," ceases to be himself, and becomes one with God. This always involves a radical decarnation. The Neoplatonic mystic must abandon his or her body if he or she wants to ascend the divine heights.

The "New Mysticism" refuses to decarnate the human seeker of God. Instead, it projects human carnality ever more boldly onto God. While the transcendent aspects of God are not written off, they now exist side by side with an "enfleshed" God that is thoroughly humanized by the mystics. His physical and emotional aspects are acknowledged and extended by the mystics and the act of union is described as the result of a spiritually sensual courtship. Rather than a gradual shedding off of human error, the erotic mystical union is the ecstatic result of lovemaking. And although this lovemaking is carefully distinguished from carnal lovemaking (it is the union of spirits, not of bodies), it is not just a metaphor. The mystic is not quietly meditating. He or she shows a range of psychosomatic symptoms (palpitation, blushing, tears, pain, pleasure), suggesting a mirror effect in the Beloved.

In the erotic mystical union, there isn't a total blurring of boundaries. Gender roles do not disappear, nor are they interchangeable. Humans remain those penetrated by God, not those who penetrate him. This is true not only for female mystics. Caroline Bynum has studied male mystics and showed that when mystical lovemaking occurs, the male mystic becomes female. For it is deeply rooted in many world cultures that penetration is an act of taking over, of possession (Michel Foucault has discussed the implication of this view in Greco-Roman culture). Christ must be the Bridegroom, in the Song of Songs or out of it. He can even be the *virgin* mother giving birth (a birth means pushing out, not taking in); what He *cannot* be is the Bride.[7]

But there was another way of achieving radical contact with God—of penetrating the divine flesh while being penetrated by it—making the human *body* divine.

Conformis Christi: Personal Real Presence

From a distance of eight hundred years, the stigmatization of St. Francis of Assisi has lost much of the shocking effect it had on contemporaries. We tend to group it with other paranormal phenomena related to mysticism.[8] Within that group, it is not even particularly impressive. There are, after all, saints who can be in two places at the same time, saints who are immune to fire, saints whose bodies exude oil, saints who levitate, saints who survive without food, and saints who can elongate and shrink their members. There were (and perhaps still are) saints who walk on water, heal the sick, restore severed limbs, and raise the dead. The appearance of four fairly superficial wounds (or of protruding bits of flesh) on a saint's hands and feet and of a slightly deeper bleeding wound in his side pales in comparison with some of the more flamboyant physical manifestations of saints just mentioned.

But the relatively minor infringement of the laws of nature is not what gave the stigmata of St. Francis their tantalizing effect. When the stigmatic wounds began to appear on Francis's flesh (the traditional date is

September 14, 1224),[9] a new and, in the views of many of his followers, singular wonder was being added to the Catholic repertoire of miracles. The wounds of Jesus Christ have miraculously appeared on the flesh of a man. This has never happened before. Why did it happen? Francis's first followers were convinced that it was a message from God, a message of crucial importance.

We shall return to the attempts to make sense of the stigmata, but first it is worth noting that for a miracle of such momentous importance, we have surprisingly few eyewitness descriptions of the actual wounds.[10] The details of *what* the witnesses saw—how the wounds looked, for example—were not recorded. Even Brother Leo, Francis's travel-companion and secretary, who was with the saint when the wounds appeared on La Verna, offers a frustratingly vague account. Leo added a short note on the reverse side of a piece of parchment on which the saint wrote the praises of God shortly after his mystical experience:

> Two years before his death, blessed Francis observed a forty-day fast La Verna in honor of the Blessed Virgin Mary and Blessed Michael the Archangel, from the Feast of the Assumption of the holy Virgin Mary to the Feast of St. Michael in September. The hand of God was upon him. After seeing and hearing the Seraph and the impression of the stigmata of Christ on his body, he composed with his own hand these praises that appear on the opposite side of this parchment giving thanks to God for the favor conferred upon him.[11]

The list of eyewitnesses who saw the wounds *after* the saint's death is longer,[12] but surprisingly, given the immense importance of the miracle, we do not have a single testimony in which the witness speaks in his or her own words about the appearance of the stigmatic wounds. A document found in the communal archives of Assisi lists four witnesses who supposedly saw the stigmata while the saint was still alive and nine who saw it after he died. The document was produced sometime between 1237 and 1250, eleven to twenty-four years after the saint's death. It is obvious that the commune's authorities were eager to supply reliable evidence in the face of growing doubts. Unfortunately, no individual accounts are recorded and the brief description of the stigmata at the end of the document is Thomas of Celano's account in the *First Life*. The witnesses simply concur.[13]

It is to Thomas of Celano's *First Life*, then, that we must turn to learn of the exact appearance of the stigmata, and also of the vision that preceded their appearance. The *First Life* is the earliest and most reliable account we have of the miracle. We may assume that the source of the account was Francis himself. He was alone when the vision took place. Who did he tell about it? Who was Thomas's immediate source? Was it Brother Leo? Brother Elias? We do not know. Here is Thomas's account of the miracle:

> He saw in a vision from God a man standing above him, like a seraph with six wings, his hands extended and his feet joined together and fixed to a cross. Two of the wings were extended above the head, two were extended as if for flight, and two were wrapped around the whole body. When the blessed servant of the most high saw these things, he was filled with the greatest wonder, but he could not understand what this vision should mean. Still, he was filled with happiness and rejoiced greatly, because of the kind and gracious look with which the seraph, whose beauty was beyond estimation, looked at him. But the fact that the seraph was fixed to a cross and the harshness of his suffering filled Francis with fear. And so he arose, sorrowful and joyful, if I may so say, with joy and grief alternating within him. He wondered anxiously what this vision could mean and his soul was greatly anxious to understand it. Unable to come to any understanding of it [his vision] and with his heart entirely preoccupied with it, the marks of the nails began to appear in his feet just as he had seen them earlier in the crucified man above him. His hands and feet appeared to be pierced in the center by nails whose heads were visible on the inner side of his hands and on the upper sides of his feet, while the pointed ends protruded from the opposite sides. The marks on his hands were round on the inner side and elongated on the outer, and small pieces of flesh looked like the ends of the nails, bent and beaten back and rising above the rest of the flesh. In the same way the marks of the nails were impressed on his feet, and raised above the rest of his flesh. His right side was also pierced as if with a lance and covered over with a scar, and it often bled, and his tunic and undergarments were often splattered with his sacred blood.[14]

Francis's seraph is different from the seraphs of theology, who have no bodies and who are incapable of suffering.[15] Indeed, the Seraphic Christ may be more problematic theologically than the imprinting of Christ's wounds on Francis's flesh. It is not clear what brought this image to the saint's mind, but it was destined to have a huge importance among the interpreters of the stigmata.

What was the meaning of the seraphic vision and the unusual grace that followed it? The stigmata were not a miraculous fixing of something broken. Francis needed no healing (if anything, the stigmata made him sick), nor were they the infringement of natural laws to achieve a clearly defined goal (crossing a natural obstacle, feeding a multitude, stopping a storm). Francis did his best to hide the wounds, and, during his lifetime at least, they did not help the saint work miracles. The miracle of the stigmata was the stigmata themselves.

There were two interpretive strategies for deciphering the code left on Francis's flesh. One focused on the angelic aspect of the vision, the other on the Christological aspect of it. For many of his contemporaries and successors, Francis was to be identified as the Angel of the Sixth Seal of Revelation 7:2 ("And I saw another angel ascending from the east, having the seal of the living God"). He was the embodiment of Joachim of Fiore's hugely influential interpretation of this mysterious figure, as a messenger of the approaching third age of sacred history, the age of the Spirit.[16] In 1224, when Francis received the stigmata, the arrival of the Angel was seen not as something that will occur at the end of days, but as an event due within years or decades at the most. While the Christological aspects were not disregarded (the angel bears "the seal," the stigmata, of the living God, Christ), this line of interpretation saw Francis not as a second Christ, but as an angelic man, an eschatological herald.

The other possibility, more daring, was that the wounds of Christ were not the insignia of the master borne by the servant, but the marks of a profound transformation that turned Francis into a Christlike figure. How Christlike? That was the question. If Francis's body has somehow become the body of Christ, then the body was not an obstacle to be discarded, but a means to achieve contact, physical contact, with God. That seems to be the option that some key figures among Francis's followers came to adopt. They did not reject the "seraphic" aspect of the vision of La Verna. Francis was, for them, the harbinger of the messianic age, but he was also one of its most important manifestations—the divinization of man through psychophysical rebirth. The stigmatization was not like any other miracle. It was the mark of a turning point in the economy of salvation.

One more point needs to be made before we continue. There is no indication that Francis thought of himself either as the Angel of the Sixth Seal or as a reborn Christ. He never discussed the vision at La Verna. In all his public expressions, Francis's Christology was very conservative. He had a special devotion to the Eucharist and never in word or action did he display any messianic vision of himself. There is no trace of Joachism in anything that he wrote or was reported to say. The ideas I shall discuss presently were not his. They would probably have shocked him. Francis's own radicalism (and he was much more radical than a new generation of conservative historians make him to be) was not centered on himself, but on his interpretation of the apostolic life. But for many of his admirers, who Francis *was* mattered much more than anything Francis said.

A New Thing

The first thing we note in the Franciscan sources is the bold language of spiritual renewal. Here is a passage from the *First Life*, which precedes the account of the stigmatization:

> For when the teachings of the Gospel, not indeed in this or that respect, but generally, had everywhere ceased to be put into practice, this man was sent by God to bear witness to the truth throughout the whole world (*universaliter*) in accordance with the example of the apostles. And thus it came to pass that his teaching showed that the wisdom of this world is most evidently turned into foolishness, and within a little while he brought it under the guidance of Christ to the true wisdom of God by the foolishness of his preaching. For in this newest of times (*novissimo tempore*), this new evangelist, like one of the rivers that flowed out of paradise, diffused the waters of the Gospel over the whole world (*in toto terrarium orbe*) by his pious

watering, and preached by his deeds the way of the Son of God and the doctrine of truth. Accordingly in him and through him (*in eo et per eum*) there arose throughout the world (*orbis terrarum*) an unexpected happiness (*insperata exultatio*), and a holy newness (*sancta novitas*), and a shoot of the ancient religion suddenly brought a great renewal (*multum subito innovabit*) to those who had grown calloused and to the very old. A new spirit was born in the hearts of the elect, and a saving unction was poured out in their midst, when the servant and saint of Christ, like one of the lights of heaven, shone brilliantly with a new rite and with new signs. Through him the miracles of ancient times were renewed (*renovata*), while there was planted in the desert of the world, by a new order (*ordine novo*), but in an ancient way, a fruitful vine bearing flowers of sweetness unto the odor of holy virtues by extending everywhere the branches of a sacred religion.[17]

Francis, we must remind ourselves, lived in a world where the Church Militant has been most triumphant—the Church was thriving, the Eastern Church had been returned (albeit forcibly) to the fold after the conquest of Constantinople in 1204, the Fourth Lateran Council of 1215 could claim true ecumenical status, and its canons were to be the new foundation for Church theology and practice. While heretics were still a problem, the Albigensian Crusade of 1208 dealt them a severe blow. The man by whose fiat the Franciscan order was authorized was Innocent III, perhaps the greatest pope of the Middle Ages. And yet the images used by Celano describe a desert, a religiously desiccated and spiritually dehydrated world. Francis appears in this spiritually arid world suddenly (*insperata*, *subito*) and brings with him rebirth. He is presented as a cosmic savior that does not simply reform the monastic way of life in the Latin world, but renews a decaying world in which the teaching of the Gospel has all but ceased to be practiced. Celano hyperventilates: he uses a flood of words denoting renovation: in this "newest of times," a "new evangelist," "holy newness," a "great renewal," a "new spirit," "new rite," "new signs," "renewed miracles," a "new order."[18]

Celano repeatedly describes Francis in terms of radical innovation; sometimes even when referring to occurrences that would not strike contemporaries as particularly new. Thus after the crucifix in the church of

San Damiano spoke to Francis and ordered him to "repair his house," Celano writes:

> A wonderful thing, a thing unheard of in our times. Who would not be astonished at this? Who had ever known like things? Who would doubt that Francis, returning now to his native city, appeared crucified when, though he had not yet outwardly completely renounced the world, Christ had spoken to him from the wood of the cross in a new and unheard of miracle (*novo et inaudito miraculo*). From that hour on, his soul was melted when his beloved spoke to him. A little later, the love of his heart made itself manifest by the wounds of his body.[19]

For Celano, Francis's entire life is to be examined in light of the "new miracle" par excellence—the stigmatization. Summarizing the saint's life, Celano describes the stigmata and its relation to Francis life thus:

> But an unheard joy tempered their grief, and the newness of a miracle (*miraculi novitas*) threw their minds into great amazement. . . . For they have never heard or read in the Scriptures what was set before their eyes, what they could hardly be persuaded to believe, had it not been proved to them by such evident testimony. For in truth there appeared in him the image of the cross and of the passion (*forma crucis et passionis*) of the immaculate lamb who washed away the sins of the world, for he seemed as though (*quasi*) he had been recently taken down from the cross, his hands and feet were pierced as though by nails and his side wounded as though by a lance. . . .
>
> O Singular gift and mark of special love that a soldier should be adorned with the same arms of glory suitable for the son of the king by reason of their most excellent dignity! O miracle worthy of everlasting memory, and memorable sacrament worthy of admirable and unceasing reverence, which represents (*repraesentat*) to the eye of faith that mystery in which the blood of the Immaculate Lamb flowed from five outlets to wash away the sins of the world. . . . He loved you much whom you adorned so very gloriously. Glory and blessing be to the one wise God who renews signs and works new miracles that He might console the minds of the weak with new revelations. . . . O wonderful and lovable disposition of God, which, that no suspicion

might arise concerning this new miracle, first mercifully displayed in Him who descended from heaven what a little later was to be wonderfully wrought in Him who dwelt upon earth.[20]

The stigmatization is a singular *new* miracle. Celano is not a Joachite. He identifies Francis as a seraph, not as the Angel of the Sixth Seal. He says that Francis "bore the image and form of a seraph, and persevering upon the cross, merited to rise to the ranks of the heavenly spirits."[21] It is significant that the all-important theme of *Imitatio Christi* is not invoked in this context. The stigmata are not the result of a metaphysical transformation in Francis. They are a divine reward for a life of love and total commitment. Francis is not a second Christ, but a servant deemed worthy of bearing his lord's arms. The stigmata are a "representation," not a reincarnation.

And yet in his *Second Life*, Celano recounts an episode that seems to hint at something different:

> The glorious father appeared, on the night and at the hour of his death, dressed in a purple dalmatic, to another brother of praiseworthy life who was absorbed in prayer at the time. He was accompanied by a great crowd of men. A large group then separated itself from the crowd, and said to the brother: "Is not this Christ, brother?" And he said: "It is he himself." But the others asked again: Is not this St. Francis?" The brother answered in the same way—[that it is indeed Francis]." Truly it seemed to the brother and to all those who were there that Christ and the blessed Francis were one and the same person (*quod Christi et beati Francisci una persona foret*). This is not considered at all a rash (*temerarium*) judgment by people of understanding, for "he who cleaves to God is made one spirit with him" (1 Cor 6:17).[22]

Note that Francis's turning into a Christ figure in this vision is not related to what others have come to see as the clearest proof of this blending of persons—the stigmata. Celano may see Francis as a cosmic renovator and his stigmatization as the ultimate sign of divine approval, but the melding together of the *poverello* and Christ is, as the quotation from Corinthians indicates, spiritual. The stigmatization is surely a new and impressive miracle, but the real act of renewal is related to the rebirth of the apostolic spirit, to corrective actions that bring to life a way of life.

But the idea that the miracle of La Verna was just a sign did not satisfy many Franciscan thinkers. As André Vauchez points out, from the second half of the thirteenth century the Franciscans developed a theology focused on the stigmata.[23] This is related to a fundamental idea of Francis himself—that the surest way to reach spiritual perfection is not contemplation, but active imitation. While Francis did go through periods of contemplation (the vision of La Verna came at the end of such a period), it is significant that he says absolutely nothing in his writing not only about the Seraphic vision, but about other visions as well. For him, the path to salvation goes through action. In his later years, he has made his entire life an *exemplum*:

> We who have been with him cannot count the necessities he denied his body in food and clothing to set a good example for the brothers, and so that they would bear their necessities more patiently. The blessed Francis's chief and supreme wish was always—especially once the brothers began to grow in number and he gave up his role as leader—to teach the brothers what they should do and what they should refrain from doing, by acts rather than words.[24]

Francis expected to be imitated—to the letter. This meant that he expected the closest attention to be given to his *actions*. The saint's writings are, with the exception of the rules and the testament, conservative texts. They play a rather minor role in the history of the order compared with the saint's biographies. If you wished to learn from St. Francis, you did not read his texts; you listened to stories about him. It was the saint as a person that mattered.

Franciscans thought that Francis was not just another great saint; they thought that he was categorically different from all others. What made him greater than other founders of religious orders and even the apostles themselves? For many Franciscans, the answer was related to the stigmata. The stigmata were the crucial clue—they meant that Francis's imitation of Christ had succeeded to such a degree that the two became "one and the same person" (we shall return to this later) both in spirit and in body.

Celano's description of religious rebirth is still deeply rooted in the twelfth-century notion of *renovatio*—of the return to the ideals of the *primitiva ecclesia* and the *vita apostolica*. His Francis is not related to the future, but to the past. He is a renovation and his "new order" resuscitates ancient times. When more and more intellectuals were joining the order, especially after the deposition of Brother Elias as minister general, in 1239, the cosmic and eschatological aspects of Francis were emphasized. Franciscans trained in scholastic theology needed a *theological* explanation for the Francis phenomenon.

The most important exponent of this conceptual shift was St. Bonaventure, minister general of the Franciscan Order, between 1257 and 1274, and a major theologian. Bonaventure was also the writer of the official biography of St. Francis, *Legenda major*, published in 1263, and by decree of the general chapter of Paris in 1266, the sole biography allowed in the order. Upon election, the young minister general found himself amid a political storm raging between "Spirituals" and "Conventuals." The former upheld a literal interpretation of Francis's message and sought to impose strict poverty and "simplicity" on the entire order. The latter believed in mitigating the strictness of the original ideal in the name of pragmatism and the interest of the Church. Both parties based their claims on a specific image of the founder of the order that each party insisted was the "true" Francis.

In the Franciscan Order, a biography of the founder was not simply an act of piety; it was an important political instrument. The decision to destroy all earlier biographies by the general chapter of 1266 was an attempt to establish a single authoritative narrative. Some historians, eager to defend this drastic act at all costs, presented it as a mere liturgical "tidying up." This is nonsense. In the Franciscan Order, unlike, for example, the Dominican Order, the founder's biography was not simply a devotional tool of relatively minor importance. It was a spiritual plan of action, and it was exactly this implicit plan of action—a too "Spiritual" plan of action in the early biographies—that Bonaventure's hagiographical masterpiece sought to deactivate.

As I have shown in another work, *Bonaventure's* Francis is not a man of action nor does he order his disciples to follow his example. He is more *admirandus* (to be admired) than *imitandus* (to be imitated).[25] Bonaventure's saint is a contemplative who offers a model so elevated that one should not attempt to emulate him *ad litteram*.[26] But while Bonaventure wants his order to be moderate, his concept of the founder's spiritual status is surprisingly radical. While Bonaventure "deactivates" the political aspects of Francis, he activates a new theological bomb. Francis, for him, is not just a precursor. In the very prologue of the *Legenda major* the stigmata are defined as a seal of *similitude* or true likeness to the living God, that is, Christ crucified (*signaculum similitudinis Dei viventis, Christi videlicet crucifixi*).[27]

The theme of similitude recurs in Bonaventure's description of the stigmatization on Mount La Verna: "He realized from this, by divine revelation, that God has shown him this vision in His providence, to let him know, as Christ's lover, that not by physical martyrdom, but by the fire of the spirit will he be wholly transformed into a true likeness of Christ crucified (*totum in Christi crucifixi similitudinem transformandum*)."[28] True likeness is the result of a total (*totum, totaliter*) transformation. It is important to note that while spiritual transformation is certainly not unique to Francis, the completion of the transformative process—making transformation "total"—is. Thus, in the prologue of his *Mind's Journey Into God* Bonaventure writes:

> The road to this peace is through nothing else than the most ardent love of the Crucified, the love which so transformed Paul into Christ (*transformavit in Christum*) when he was rapt to the third heaven that declared: "With Christ I am nailed to the Cross. It is now no longer I that live, but Christ lives in me" [2 Cor 12:2]. And this love so absorbed the soul of Francis too that his spirit was manifested in his flesh (*mens in carne patuit*) the last two years of his life, when he bore the most holy marks of the Passion in his body (*in corpore*).[29]

The stigmata are not something external added to the saint's body as a coat of arms, but a radical change—both internal and external—brought about by the fire of love. A little later, Bonaventure repeats this same expression: "the love of Christ has now transformed his lover into his image (*Christi amor in eamdem imaginem transformavit amantem*)." The transformed creature is a copy—someone re-created, like Adam, to bear the image and likeness of God. But if the image and likeness of God are borne by all sons of Adam, the image and likeness of Christ are borne by Francis alone. The Franciscan theologian Pierre Jean Olivi (1248–1298) reports that he heard Bonaventure offer a more explicit version of these positions in a sermon preached in Paris. According to Olivi, he said,

It is established by the indubitable testimony of St. Francis's ineffable sanctity and innumerable miracles, and most of all by the most glorious stigmata impressed upon him by Christ, that he was truly the Angel of the Sixth Seal of Revelation, having the sign of the living God, the sign, that is, of the wounds of the crucified Christ, which is also the sign of his total transformation and configuration to Christ and into Christ (*totalis transformationis et configurationis ipsius ad Christum et in Christum*). And this was established by a clear and trustworthy revelation according to what Brother Bonaventure, a most respectable master of theology and once minister general of our order, said in a sermon, as I have heard with my own ears.[30]

In a sermon dedicated to St. Francis, Matthew of Aquasparta, who was a student of St. Bonaventure and one of his successors as minister general of the Franciscans, also refers to the stigmatization as a redemptive rebirth and to Francis as a second Adam, a role usually reserved to Christ: "And just as in the beginning of the world God made the First Man in his image, so in the end of days he formed that man singularly in true-likeness of the Crucified one, so that the image of God, almost abolished, obfuscated, and deformed in the first man, was in some way repaired and reformed in Francis."[31]

Surprisingly, these statements did not raise as much opposition as one might have expected. The practical aspects of Francis's teaching, especially in relation to poverty, seemed much more pressing than the speculations of theologians, even if what they were speculating was theoretically very problematic. Bonaventure and Matthew are implying that a "total" transformation made Francis a second Christ, but they are also calling for political obedience and conformity. The authorities were willing to live with it. The Franciscan veneration of the founder was excessive perhaps, but it was not dangerous, especially since it had no practical implications.

An interesting example of the extent to which ecclesiastical authorities were willing to allow individual Franciscan theologians to speculate about Francis and Christ is the publication (in 1399) of Bartholomew of Pisa's *De conformitate vitae Beati Francisci ad vitam Domini Iesu Christi* (On the Conformity of the Life of the Blessed Francis to the Life of Our Lord Jesus Christ).[32] Bartholomew's work deals at great length with what was discussed in more general terms in the works of his predecessors. He counts forty points of similarity between the lives of Christ and Francis, which he likens to a tree with twenty branches, each bearing four fruits— half involving Christ and half Francis. Bartholomew always begins with a relatively short discussion of each particular fruit in relation to Christ, followed by a much longer discussion of the life of St. Francis. Some of the chapters are very long, since Bartholomew uses them to recount the numerous miracles attributed to Francis and to present the many Franciscan communities around the world.

Bartholomew presented his book to the general chapter of the Franciscans in Assisi in 1399, presided by the minister general Enrico Alfieri. The text was enthusiastically endorsed by the chapter. It enjoyed impressive success,[33] at least until the Reformation, when, in 1542, Erasmus Alber published a scathing attack on the book under the title *Der Barfusser Monche Eulenspiegel und Alkoran* (The Mendicants' Distorted Mirror and Koran), with a postscript by Martin Luther himself.

The reformers accused Bartholomew of making Francis Christ's equal, if not his superior, and of spreading ridiculous and sacrilegious tales about the founder of the Franciscan Order. In the strict sense, the accusations are false. Bartholomew is not the gullible fool he is made out to be by his critics. He is, in fact, a learned and in many ways sober thinker. Like his predecessors, Bartholomew does not make a god out of Francis. Francis is the servant and Christ the master. The conformity between the two is not complete, since no creature can ever be equal to the God-Man Jesus Christ. But one has to concede that Bartholomew goes further than his predecessors in his discussion of the similarities between the two. He is certainly more explicit in his claim that Francis is not just an imitator of Christ, but similar to him.

Like Matthew of Aquasparta, Bartholomew begins his prologue with a comparison between the creation of First Man and the "creation" of the Perfect Man—Francis:

> If creating man in this fashion was prodigious and marvelous, it is still greater to make a man similar to Himself [*sibi simile*] in holiness and virtue; for natural similitude compared with perfecting [similitude] is of little or no worth in matters of salvation; for it is not by natural

causes, but by grace that eternal life is gained. The greatest and most miraculous act, above all others, is when God makes a man similar and comparable (*simile et conformem*) to Him in soul and body, as He did to the blessed Francis, above all other saints. For such similitude includes all other [similitudes]—natural and perfecting—to which are added imitative in all things, and transformative.[34]

Bartholomew stresses the fact that Francis was similar to Christ not only in will but also in body: "This transformation dignifies the body in such a way that by it a man is transformed into Christ and becomes similar to him, and is called 'a type' of Christ . . . by this transformation a man becomes similar to God in the highest possible manner (*ultima similitudine possibili*)."[35] In his long discussion of the stigmata, Bartholomew offers an interesting discussion of psychosomatic phenomena, where the mind causes changes in the body. He dismisses the possibility that the stigmata were such a phenomenon. Not only did the wounds not suffer infection (as natural wounds, whether psychosomatic or not, would have), but Francis's stigmata were not simply a bleeding. Bleeding is related to soft and pliable matter (blood vessels), and could result from powerful emotion, but fleshy growths, such as Francis displayed on both hands and feet, could not have occurred in response to mental change.[36] Furthermore, if strong identification with the suffering of Christ were enough, then surely the Blessed Virgin Mary would have displayed the stigmata, as her pain at her son's crucifixion (and apparently that of St. John the Evangelist) was greater even than Francis's. Why wasn't the Mother of God worthy of the stigmata? Bartholomew explains that a woman could not physically conform to Christ. As for the apostles, and especially St. John, they simply lived in the wrong era. They may have been worthy of the great honor that befell St. Francis, but the time for the emergence of the Perfect Man (the time of the Angel of the Sixth Seal) had not yet come. Francis was the right man at just the right time.[37]

Having had all the needed qualities and having been born at the right time, Francis precedes *all* other saints (*prae aliis sanctis*) in dignity. He is both *alter Christus* and the herald. *All* others must follow:

Christ in his compassion and solely through his grace, since he is the maker of saints and the king of kings, wished there to be, in both the

Church Militant and the Church Triumphant, one sign-bearer, standard-bearer, treasurer, and chancellor to carry the signs of his victory and whom all must and can follow. That man was St. Francis whom he has marked with the stigmata and signs of his Passion.[38]

But the most radical theological point is not made by Bartholomew while extolling St. Francis's merits. Bartholomew sees Francis prefigured (*figuratus*) in the Old Testament. Many of the "classical" prefigurations of Jesus are seen by him as prophecies alluding to the "perfect copy," Francis, as well. But Bartholomew is willing to see the New Testament too as *figura*. Indeed, Christ himself becomes a prefiguration in the *Liber de conformitate*. Thus, Francis's sending of brothers to baptize the sultan is *prefigured* by Christ's sending of two of the disciples to bring him an ass and the foal of an ass in Matthew 21:1–7.[39]

In orthodox thinking, Christ is never the sign. He is the ultimate signified—that which signs refer to. In the deep sense, all things are mere signs of God, who is the being that signifies only itself. Making Christ a prefiguration of Francis implies a reversal of natural roles or at least a dangerous equality. The copy has acquired the metaphysical status of the original.

REINCARNATION

There are two striking elements about the idea of Francis as an *alter Christus*. One is the notion of a soteriological restart. This idea goes against the grain of Christological thinking and Augustine's famous refutation of cyclical time in the *City of God* (book 12, chapter 13): "for Christ died once for our sins and rising from the dead he dies no more." The crucifixion was a singular event. It never happened before, nor will it ever happen again. But then, in the eyes of his admirers, so was Francis's recrucifixion. It was another singular event. This second crucifixion did not replace the first one. It reignited the crucifixion when its energies seemed to have waned. This idea would not have been possible without the Joachite foundation upon which it was built. The Joachite idea of time has a spiral aspect built in it. The three ages, of Father, Son, and Holy Spirit, display recurring structures. But this recurrence in not a simple repetition; it is an evolution. The world is moving toward greater spirituality and each age surpasses the age that preceded it. Each age is restarted by an "epochal" event—the Creation began the age of the Father, the Incarnation launched the age of the Son. For the less radical Franciscan thinkers, it was enough to think of Francis as the leader of the spiritual avant-garde, the Angel of the Sixth Seal. The real launching of the third age was hidden in the (near) future. But for the more radical thinkers, the momentous "new miracle" was more than a prophetic sign. It was the fulfillment of prophecies that was the starting point of the new age. If Christ was the Second Adam, couldn't Francis be the Third?

The second element that needs our attention is *how* this soteriological copy expressed itself. Even though it was to launch the Age of the Spirit, the redemptive tipping point was the moment the stigmata appeared on the saint's *flesh*. Much has been written about the enfleshment of God in the twelfth and thirteenth centuries. Francis himself was one of the driving forces of this new "carnal" spirituality. But the stigmatization was not the humanization of God; it was the divinization of man. And paradoxically, the most radical expression of the divinization of man was, just as it was in the Age of the Son, carnal. Of the Hypostatic Union, Francis reproduced only the divinized *flesh* of the Man-God. As a created being, his spirit could cling to God, but not become God. His body, however, could become "similar" to Christ's.

The reproduced body had a unique feature in it, a feature that made it different from the original. All contemporaries noted something that years of misleading art made us forget. Francis's stigmata were not just the marks of perforation left by the nails. They reproduced the nails themselves. This was a foreign element that had no place in Christ's resurrected body. But it was there in the copy, and it was not foreign. The "nails" were not divine flesh; they were human flesh lodged boldly and irremovably inside Christ's body. The intimate contact with the divine that Thomas sought but was afraid to attempt was finally achieved.

CHAPTER ELEVEN

Inaudible

The Bible is full of references to God speaking. God's first recorded action is speech—"Let there be light!" As noted, seeing God is either impossible or lethal for humans. And even though sound is as sensual as sight, hearing Him seems to pose no problem to the writers of the Bible. God's voice often comes out of heaven and it is never allegorized. In Deuteronomy, the distinction between forbidden sight and permissible hearing is clearly made: "And Jehovah spoke to you out of the fire. You heard the sound of words; you saw no image (*tmuna*), but only [heard] a voice [or sound, *qol*]" (Deut 4:12).

In this chapter, I will focus on one particular manifestation of God's voice—the giving of the Law at Mount Sinai. This miraculous occurrence was not simply the moment when the religion of Jehovah became the national creed of the Israelites. It was a collective revelation made not to a few religious virtuosi, but to the entire nation, a fact that was to play an important role in Jewish apologetics in the future. The Israelite nation as a whole experienced at Mount Sinai not only manifestations of God's power in the form of the many miracles worked for the entire nation, but a direct revelation of God. The book of Exodus stresses the importance of God's vocal manifestation: "Behold I come to you in the thick cloud that the people may hear when I speak with you and believe you forever" (Ex 19:9). Moses speaks to Jehovah "face to face, as a man speaks to his friend" (Ex 33:11), whereas the people only see a thick cloud. And while God hides "His face" from them, His voice is clearly and distinctly heard by every member of the people waiting at the foot of the mountain.

Before we turn to an examination of the nature of God's voice in post-biblical Jewish thought, it is important to examine the account of the giving of the Law in Deuteronomy. In Deuteronomy, a text intimately associated with King Josiah's Yahwistic reform (insisting that Yahweh-Jehovah is not just the most important god but the only god) of the seventh century BC, the voice of Jehovah acquires added importance:

> These words Jehovah spoke to all your assembly in the mountain from the midst of the fire, the cloud, and the thick darkness, with a loud voice, and He added no more. And He wrote them on two tablets of stone, and gave them to me. And when you heard the voice out of the darkness and the mountain burning with fire, you came near to me, all the heads of your tribes, and your elders. And you said: Behold, Jehovah our God has shown us His glory and His greatness, and we have heard His voice out of the fire. We have seen this day that God speaks with man, and he lives. Now therefore why should we die? For this great fire will consume us; if we hear the voice of Jehovah our God any more, then we shall die. For who is there of all flesh who has heard the voice of the living God speaking from the midst of the fire, as we have, and lived? You go near, and hear all that Jehovah our God shall say: and tell us all that Jehovah our God says to you; and we will hear it, and do it. And Jehovah heard the voice of your words, when you spoke to me; and Jehovah said to me: I have heard the voice of the words of this people, which they have spoken to you. They have well said all that they have spoken . . . Go and say to them, Return to your tents. But as for you, stand here by me, and I will speak to you all the commandments, the statutes, and the judgments, which you shall teach them, that they may observe them in the land which I am giving them to possess. (Deut 5:22–31)

It is clear from this text that what the people heard was the terrible and life-threatening voice of Jehovah, the living God. Hearing Jehovah's voice is not as lethal as seeing Him, but even this lesser form of presence is not something that ordinary humans can bear for long. The voice of Jehovah is like a great fire and the people fear that staying too close will consume them: "if we hear the voice of Jehovah our God any more, then we shall die." Now that God's presence and Moses's veracity have been conclusively established, God should speak only to Moses, who will transfer His messages to the people.

In the Midrash on the Song of Songs (*Shir hashirim rabbah*), we are told that hearing the *voice* did in fact kill listeners lacking the spiritual resilience of Moses. The Midrash explains that the Israelites died upon listening to just the word "I [am Jehovah your God]" with which the first commandment begins and had to be miraculously resurrected:

> When the people of Israel heard "I" at Mount Sinai, their spirit left them. This is the meaning of that which is written [in Deuteronomy 5], "if we hear the voice [of Jehovah] any more [then we shall die]," and this is what [Song of Songs 5:6] refers to in, "my soul has left me when He spoke." The [first] Commandment then turned to God and said: "Master of the Universe, you are a living [God] and your Torah is living [law], why do you send me to the dead—for lo, they are all dead. Then God sweetened his voice[1] . . . Rabbi Shimon bar Yochai said: God's Torah brought them back to life, for it is said [in Psalms 19:8]: "the Torah of Jehovah is perfect, reviving the soul" (*Shir hashirim rabbah* to 5:16).[2]

There can be no doubt that the voice the people heard at Mount Sinai was of an entirely different order from the other paranormal phenomena they experienced. Only the true God kills by His very presence. The people of Israel have heard the *unmediated* voice of God. It may have cost them their lives, but it brought the ultimate certainty that only a direct contact with God can bring.

We have already seen that the rabbis of the Talmud are often bolder than the Bible in referring to God's physicality. Their "vocal" stories are a case in point. In tractate *Berakhot* (59a) of the Babylonian Talmud, Rabbi Qatina says that the sound of thunder is caused by God's clapping His hands and Rabbi Nathan says that it is God emitting a sigh.[3] In an earlier discussion in the same tractate (*Berakhot* 3a), God's voice is overheard by Rabbi Jose, and the prophet Elijah happens to be there to provide further information about God's sighs:

Rabbi Jose says: I was once traveling on the road, and I entered into one of the ruins of Jerusalem to pray. Elijah of blessed memory appeared and waited for me at the door till I finished my prayer. After I finished praying, he said to me: "Peace be with you, rabbi!" And I replied: "Peace be with you, my rabbi and teacher!" And he said to me: "My son, why did you go into this ruin?" I replied: "To pray." He said to me: "You ought to have prayed on the road." I replied: "I feared lest passersby interrupt me." He said to me: "You ought to have said a shortened prayer." ... He further said to me: "My son, what sound [or voice] did you hear in this ruin?" I replied: "I heard a heavenly voice (*bat qol*) cooing like a dove, saying, 'woe to the children, on account of whose sins I destroyed my house and burnt my temple and exiled them among the nations of the world!'" And he said to me: "By your life and by your head! Not in that moment alone does it [the voice] so exclaim, but thrice each day does it exclaim thus! And more than that, whenever the Israelites go into the synagogues and schoolhouses and respond [to the cantor]: 'May His great name be blessed!' the Holy One, blessed be He, shakes His head and says: 'Happy is the king who is thus praised in this house! Woe to the father who had to banish his children, and woe to the children who had to be banished from the table of their father!'"

While the story is often discussed as a demonstration of the rabbis' belief in divine emotion and fallibility (God regrets and laments His actions), it has been generally overlooked as evidence of human beings' ability to hear God's *actual* voice. The important thing about Rabbi Jose's story is that the voice of God is *overheard* by him. This is not God delivering a message (for the purpose of which He might have created a "voice"), but a private expression of grief, not intended for human ears at all. Rabbi Jose's God has a voice that He uses for His own purposes, a voice that others can hear, apparently without God being aware of it.

For thinkers influenced by Greek philosophy, however, this idea was unacceptable. To be considered the true voice of the speaker, speech must be produced by the corporeal vocal mechanism of the speaker. The sounds produced by Stephen Hawking's voice generator are not *his* voice, even though these sounds are an exact expression of what he wants to say. Since God does not have a vocal mechanism, there must be a way to detach the divine voice from its source; it must not be a "natural" production of God's body, but a "voice generator" created by God for communicating His ideas and wishes to human recipients.

The earliest Jewish thinker to address this problem was Philo of Alexandria and his solution later became the standard explanation for Christian theologians (Philo had miniscule influence on Jewish thought). In his work on the Decalogue, Philo writes:

> Did he then do so—uttering *himself* some kind of voice? Away! let not such an idea ever enter your mind; for God is not like a man, in need of a mouth, and of a tongue, and of a windpipe, but as it seems to me, he at that time wrought a most conspicuous and evidently holy miracle, commanding an invisible sound to be created in the air, more marvelous than all the instruments that ever existed, attuned to perfect harmonies; and that not an inanimate one, nor yet, on the other hand, one that at all resembled any nature composed of soul and body; but rather it was a rational soul filled with clearness and distinctness, which fashioned the air and stretched it out and changed it into a kind of flaming fire, and so sounded forth so loud and articulate a voice like a breath passing through a trumpet, so that those who were at a great distance appeared to hear equally with those who were nearest to it. For the voices of men, when they are spread over a very long distance, do naturally become weaker and weaker, so that those who are at a distance from them cannot arrive at a clear comprehension of them, but their understanding is gradually dimmed by the extension of the sound over a larger space, since the organs also by which it is extended are perishable. But the power of God, breathing forth vigorously, aroused and excited a new kind of miraculous voice, and diffusing its sound in every direction, made the end more conspicuous at a distance than the beginning, implanting in the soul of each individual another hearing much superior to that which exists through the medium of the ears. For the one, being in some degree a

slower kind of external sense, remains in a state of inactivity until it is struck by the air, and so put in motion. But the sense of the inspired mind outstrips that, going forth with the most rapid motion to meet what is said.[4]

For Philo, the voice that the Israelites heard was unlike any other created voice, but it *was* a created voice, not God's voice in the sense that voices of created beings are theirs. This is not simply because God does not have a body and the organs required for producing an audible voice, but because it is not a "natural" manifestation of the divine wish to deliver a message. Just as God can create images that represent Him, yet are not in any sense *His* images, so can He create an auditory phenomenon that expresses his wishes without being "Him."[5]

But if the voice created *by* God is not *God's* voice, then the revelation at Mount Sinai ceases to serve as the unprecedented firsthand proof of the existence of God. It is no different from the thunder and burning fire that the people saw before the giving of the commandments, or from the miraculous creation of a dry passage in the Red Sea. These are impressive supernatural phenomena, but it is God revealing his *power*, not himself. Now, this may not be a serious problem for Christians. For them, the founding moment of revelation is the Incarnation of the Word. The giving of the Torah, important though it may be, is but a preparation for the Real Presence, which makes many of the commandments, and indeed the whole concept of a covenant based on the commandments, obsolete. This is not the case for Jews. For them, the founding moment of the relationship between God and His chosen people is the giving of the eternal, never-to-be-replaced Torah. It is a collective sticking of human fingers in the side of God. God made his terrible and life-threatening voice heard by the entire nation, as proof of the veracity of the messages transmitted to the people by Moses. It is only after they experienced the unmediated presence of God that they were willing to believe fully and unquestioningly in the Law that Moses brought to them. If we hold that it was God's voice that the people heard, we compromise his immateriality; if we hold that what they heard was just another miracle, we lose the experiential proof upon which the whole edifice of faith is built. Either way we have a problem.

The problem was dealt with by the Spanish philosopher and poet Ye-huda Halevi (1075–1141) in his philosophical work *The Kuzari*—an imaginary dialogue between a Jewish sage and the soon-to-be converted king of the Khazars. Halevi places great importance on the communal nature of the divine revelation at Mount Sinai. For him, Judaism is based not on the faith of many unseers believing the few seers, as with other religions, but on a zero point, the giving of the Torah at Mount Sinai, at which the entire community—old and young, wise and foolish, righteous and sinful—experienced the unmediated presence of God. Judaism for him is a religion of recollection and tradition, not merely of faith. The divine revelation at Mount Sinai would be practically impossible to fabricate, since each and every Israelite has experienced it and not just a single prophet or a small, privileged group. According to Halevi,

> Although the people believed in the message of Moses, they retained, even after the performance of the miracles, some doubt as to whether God really spoke to mortals, and whether the Law was not of human origin, and only later on supported by divine inspiration. They could not associate speech with a divine being, since it is something tangible. God however desired to remove this doubt and commanded them [at Mount Sinai] to prepare themselves morally, as well as physically, enjoining them to keep aloof from their wives, and to be ready to hear the word of God. They prepared and became fitted to receive the divine afflatus [inspiration], and even to hear publicly the words of God.
>
> This came to pass three days later, being introduced by overwhelming phenomena, lightning, thunder, earthquake and fire surrounded Mount Sinai. . . . The people then distinctly heard the Ten Commandments which are the essence and foundation of the Torah. . . . The people did not receive these Ten Commandments from single individuals, nor from a prophet, but from God, only they did not possess the strength of Moses to bear the grandeur of the scene [for long]. Henceforth the people believed that Moses held direct communication with God, [and] that his words were not creations of his own mind, that prophecy did not (as philosophers assume), burst forth in a pure soul become united with the Active Intellect, (also termed

Holy Spirit, or Gabriel) and be then inspired. They did not believe Moses had seen a vision in sleep or that someone had spoken with him between sleeping and waking, so that he only heard the words in fancy, but not with his ears, that he saw a phantom, and afterwards pretended that God had spoken with him. Before such an impressive scene, all ideas of jugglery vanished.[6]

Note that the Israelites consider God's miracles insufficient. According to Halevi, they had no problem believing "philosophically." Moses might have been an inspired man whose ideas and imaginings were worthy of divine acceptance and support. Even before the revelation at Mount Sinai, they did not suspect him of being a false prophet. The miracles were enough to convince them of that. Moses was undoubtedly acting under God's guidance. What they lacked was proof that the very *origin* of the Torah was divine, that the source of faith came directly from God. Such proof could be provided only by an unmediated divine revelation. Still in a philosophical mood, the Israelites had doubts whether such proof was possible ("they could not associate speech with a divine being, since it is something tangible"). God did not offer a logical solution to this dilemma. He "desired to remove this doubt from their hearts," not by argument, but by experience. Halevi does not explain how God's speech was truly His and yet not physical. It just was; all doubts vanished before "such an impressive scene." Halevi mentions both hearing the voice and the miraculous appearance of the commandments on the tablets, but it is obvious that the miraculous writing was a mediated phenomenon, whereas the voice was not.

Halevi's discussion of the voice of God does not end here. If the Israelites' doubts were removed, the Khazar king's were not:

The Khazari said: Should anyone hear you relate that God spoke with your assembled multitude, and wrote tablets for you etc., he would not be blamed for accusing you of holding the theory of personification [anthropomorphism]. You, on the other hand, are free from blame, because this grand and lofty spectacle, seen by thousands, cannot be denied. You are justified in rejecting reasoning and speculation. . . .

[The rabbi denies ascribing physicality to God, saying:]

We must not however endeavor to reject the conclusions to be drawn from revelation. We say, then, that we do not know how the [divine] intention became corporalized and the speech evolved which struck our ear, nor what new thing God created from naught, nor what existing thing he employed. [For] he does not lack power. [The speaker lists a series of divine miracles.] . . . As the water [of the Red Sea] stood at his command and shaped itself at his will, so the air which touched the prophet's ear assumed the form of sounds which conveyed the matters to be communicated by God to the prophet and the people.[7]

The "Khazari" rightly notes, as we have, that the revelation at Mount Sinai may have had a deep emotional effect on those who witnessed it, but it hardly solves the dilemma of physicality. He is willing to admit that while the divine revelation at Mount Sinai may not make sense, it cannot be denied, because it was experienced by so many earwitnesses whose doubts have all been removed as the result. But "the rabbi" feels uneasy with the king's concession. True, what happened at Mount Sinai cannot be rejected, but he is not willing to rely on faith alone. He feels constrained to offer a satisfactory philosophical explanation: the words heard by the assembled people were somehow created for the occasion, either ex nihilo or out of existing sounds that God brought together to form words: "the air which touched the prophet's ear assumed the form of sounds which conveyed the matters to be communicated by God to the prophet and the people." This seems very close to Philo's explanation of the voice being a mediated phenomenon. If this is so, however, the very problem that Halevi was trying to solve in the first place again raises its head. Why should we consider the voice any different from numerous other manifestations of God's creative power? Surely, creating a thunderous voice is no different from making the earth tremble or producing "thick darkness" at daytime.

Unlike the philosophers of the Kalam, who believed that divine voices came from within the soul of the prophet and did not exist in the outside world,[8] Halevi believes that the voice of Mount Sinai was heard, in the real world, but hearing by itself, impressive though it may have been, is not the unparalleled contact with the divine essence that could alone constitute the "proof" he was seeking. Only God's voice could constitute such proof.

The collective hearing of the voice of God at Mount Sinai is a source of puzzlement and anxiety for Maimonides, a more systematic thinker than Halevi and a very strict opponent of the idea that any direct contact between God and creatures is possible. Like the Kalam, Maimonides holds that divine revelation is not an external phenomenon. For him, the visions and voices that a prophet sees and hears are in the eyes and ears of the beholders. What the Bible refers to as divine speech is in most cases simply inspired indications of God's will.[9] The prophet's imaginative faculty expresses in physical terms abstract truths received from the Active Intellect. Divine revelations are not occurrences in the physical world. They are in most cases subjective events that need correct interpretation to make them conform to the truth of faith.

This is true for "normal" prophetic revelations. But then there is the voice of God at Mount Sinai. Maimonides begins his short and rather obscure discussion of the voice with a double reduction. What the people heard at the mountain was only the first two commandments. He relies on the midrashic interpretation of Deuteronomy already examined: the divine voice was too much for the people to take; they asked that communication with God be made through an intermediary, Moses.[10] But according to Maimonides, the assembled people never heard a single recognizable word. What they heard was an inarticulate "voice."

This voice, however, was more than just an inarticulate indication of divine presence. Maimonides argues that the first two commandments, concerning the existence and oneness of God, were the part of revelation that did not require mediation by Moses. Moses may have put them in articulate words, but as concepts they were accessible to all those who "heard" the voice. The existence and oneness of God can be grasped according to Maimonides by human intellect alone, and do not require external knowledge that only prophetic revelation can provide. Hence, the first two commandments were grasped by the entire people without mediation, in just the same way that they were grasped by Moses.[11] The "hearing" was in fact a confirmation of existing knowledge. This is the meaning of the "voice":

Taking into consideration whatever else they had said about this, the texts [of the Bible] and the dicta of the sages permit considering as admissible that all Israel only heard at that gathering one voice one single time—the voice through which Moses and all Israel apprehended "I" and "Thou shalt not," which commandments Moses made them hear again as spoken in his own speech and with an articulation of syllables that were heard. The sages said this, quoting in support of this assertion the dictum: "God hath spoken once, twice have I heard this" [Ps 62:12]. And they made it clear at the beginning of *Midrash Hazit* that they had not heard another voice coming from Him, may He be exalted. Thus too says the Torah: "A great voice and no more" [Deut 5:19]. It was after they had heard that first voice that they, as is written, were terrified of it and felt great fear, and that they, as is reported, said: "And you said, Behold the Lord [our God] has shown us" and so on, "Now therefore why should we die" and so on. "You go near and hear" and so on.[12]

Why would an intellectual understanding that could be, and often is, reached without recourse to any supernatural phenomena inspire such deep fear in the hearts of the assembled Israelites? Surely, the miraculous phenomena that preceded it were not in themselves different from the great miracles wrought by God during earlier stages of the Exodus. What was special about it? One gets the impression that for Maimonides the whole audiovisual display at Mount Sinai smacks of crass materialism, which he seeks to reduce to the absolute minimum. He is reluctantly willing to concede that the first two commandments were apprehended through an "objective" physical occurrence of unclear nature. The sources are unfortunately too clear about this. Still, it was brief and incomprehensible. Like the Israelites at Mount Sinai, though for very different reasons, Maimonides cannot bear the voice of God. At the most, he is willing to concede that the people heard an indistinct voice; and they heard it once only:

> As for the voice of the Lord, I mean the created voice from which the speech [of God] was understood, they heard it once only, according to what the text of the Torah states and according to what the sages make clear in the passage to which I drew your attention. This is the voice on hearing which their soul left them and through which the first two commandments were apprehended.[13]

Earlier in the *Guide of the Perplexed*, Maimonides dwells a little longer on the "created voice"—something he would have preferred to do without. Discussing instances where God is said "to pass," Maimonides argues that it is never God who passes but rather the "glory" of God or the "word" of God or the "voice" of God—that is, "a thing related to God not His essence."[14] And what is the voice? There are different interpretations:

> You should not consider as blameworthy the fact that this profound subject, which is remote from our apprehension, should be subject to many different interpretations.... You may believe that the great station attained by [Moses] was indubitably, in its entirety, a vision of prophecy and that he [Moses] solely desired intellectual apprehension—everything, namely that which he had demanded, that which was denied to him, and that which he apprehended,[15] being intellectual and admitting no recourse to the senses, as we had interpreted in the first place.

This is the interpretation that Maimonides prefers. It is clean, intellectual, and free of messy materialism. There are those, however, who insist on involving the senses, and Maimonides feels constrained to allow it under certain conditions:

> Or you may believe that there was, in addition to this intellectual apprehension, an apprehension due to the sense of sight, which, however, had for its object a created thing, through seeing which the perfection of intellectual apprehension might be achieved. This would be the interpretation of this passage by Onqelos,[16] unless one assumes that this ocular apprehension also occurred in the vision of prophecy.... Or again you may believe that there was in addition an apprehension due to the sense of hearing—that which "passed by before his face"[17] being the voice, which is likewise indubitably a created thing. Choose whatever opinion you wish, inasmuch as our only purpose is that you should not believe that when Scripture says, in the verse we are discussing, "He passed by," the phrase is analogous to "pass before the people" (Ex 17:5).[18] For God ... is not a body and it is not permitted to ascribe motion to him.[19]

Once again, the created voice is mentioned without explanation. Maimonides could certainly do without it. For the first time, however, he assigns to sensual phenomena (the voice, visions) a role that is more than divine accommodation to the crass human tendency to cling to concrete objects, real or imaginary. Divine epiphanies somehow help perfect intellectual apprehension. How? It is not quite clear. As we saw, Maimonides holds that even the apprehension of the first two commandments somehow communicated by "the voice" to the entire people required Moses's verbalization.

Although at the beginning of his discussion Maimonides argues that "the existence of the deity and His being one are knowable by human speculation alone," and that "with regard to everything that can be known by demonstration the status of the prophet and that of everyone else who knows it are equal . . . [and] there is no superiority of one over the other,"[20] by the end of the discussion he states that "with regard to that voice too their rank was *not* equal to the rank of Moses our Master."[21] Indeed, the whole thing is a mystery that cannot be fully expounded and perhaps not fully understood. It is at one and the same time just another example of "Scripture speaking the language of men"—an exegetical problem that the expert should have no problem dealing with—and a metaphysical *unicum*. For all his distaste for materializing God, Maimonides seems to feel—or at least this is what I read in Maimonides's unusually confused text—that something happened at Mount Sinai that defies his Aristotelian logic: "It is impossible to expound the Gathering at Mount Sinai to a greater extent than they spoke about it, for it is one of the mysteries of the Torah. The true reality of that apprehension and its modality are quite hidden from us, for nothing like it happened before and will not happen after. Know this."[22]

If the voice of God heard at Mount Sinai was just a mediated epiphany, it might be argued that there were others that were more impressive. The midrashic traditions referring to the collective revelation at the crossing of the Red Sea are exceptionally bold:

> *"This is my God [and I will glorify Him]" etc.* (Ex 15:2). Rabbi Eliezer says: How does one know that [every] female slave saw by the sea what [even] Ezekiel and the rest of the prophets have not seen? For it says in Scripture: " . . . and spoke parables through the prophets" (Hos 12:11) and " . . . the heavens opened and I saw visions of God"

(Ez 1:1). This is like a king of flesh and blood who entered a city with an entourage of guards surrounding him and soldiers before and after him, and warriors on his right and left. Everyone asks which one is the king, because he is flesh and blood like them. But when the Holy One blessed He be appeared by the sea, not one of them had to ask who the king is. They all recognized Him on sight and they all sang [together]: "This is my God and I will glorify him."[23]

Another Midrash offers a daring explanation for this recognition. According to *Deuteronomy Rabbah*, when the Egyptians sought to kill all newborn Hebrew males, Israelite women gave birth in the field and left their babies there to be cared for by God. According to Rabbi Resh Laqish, they were tended to by two angels, but according to Rabbi Hiyya, it was God Himself who took care of them. They grew like plants in the field, and when they were grown enough to return home, God Himself would take each to his parents' home:

> Then the boy would say to his mother: Don't you remember giving birth to me in a certain field on a certain day, five months ago? And when she would ask, who raised him, he would answer: A certain incomparable young man with lovely locks of hair [cf. Sg 5:11]. He is outside. It is he who brought me here. And she would say: Show him to me. But when they would go out to search for him in the streets and all other places they would not find him. When they arrived at the [Red] Sea and saw Him, they pointed at him with their fingers to their mothers and said to them: He is the one who raised me. "This is my God and I will glorify Him."[24]

The Midrashim relating to the crossing of the Red Sea are more daring than the Midrashim relating to the giving of the Torah. Rabbi Eliezer thinks that the revelation of God to the entire people (female slaves included) at the crossing of the Red Sea was greater than what the prophet Ezekiel (who provides the most plastic description of God) and the other prophets saw. Rabbi Hiyya offers an outrageous Midrash that describes an incarnate God choosing to perform tasks easily performed by others (one is reminded of God's shaving the king of Assyria). The Israelites see not just the effects of God's will and God's power, but his physical appearance.

To the young males, He appears as the young and handsome man with locks of hair who took care of them.

At this point, none of this should be surprising to the reader. The God of Israel (and of the Talmudic rabbis) is not the abstract God of the philosophers, but a psychosomatic being. It is exactly with traditions such as these that rabbis, like Halevi and Maimonides, living in a cultural environment that valued Aristotelian philosophy, had to cope with. It was easy to dismiss the Crossing-of-the-Sea Midrashim as mere fables. What the people saw was an anthropomorphic image that they, being sensually conditioned like all illiterati, recognized not as a created sign in need of literate interpretation, but as God. Obviously, this was not *really* God. The *Mekhilta of Rabbi Ishmael* itself offers a Midrash that would support such an interpretation. For it states that God appeared to the people in different shapes on different occasions. In the crossing of the sea, He appeared as a man of war, at Mount Sinai he appeared as a merciful old man, and finally "like the very heavens in its clarity" (Ex 24:10). God is neither a man nor clear skies, though He sometimes looks this way.

But the hearing of the voice of God at Mount Sinai is not like any other miracle, nor is it like the Midrashim of the crossing of the Red Sea. It is, as Maimonides reluctantly concedes, an event that never happened before and will never happen again. The detailed description of Deuteronomy 5 makes it more than just a Midrash. Midrashim, just like "authority," as Alan of Lille noted, "have noses of wax."[25] One can pull them whichever way one chooses, and one can simply ignore them. Of course, the scriptural text could also be interpreted in ways that give it a radically new meaning, but this particular scriptural text is different. It touches the very core of Jewish religious experience—the giving of the Torah. Whether or not God revealed Himself at the crossing of the Red Sea is of little importance. Judaism is not about miracles but about obeying the commandments. But the giving of the Torah at Mount Sinai is the foundation upon which the Jewish way of life is built. At that unique moment in cosmic history, the revelation of God was not the creation of the imaginative faculty, but the "real" thing—a solid ontological foundation upon which the elaborate edifice of faith and authority could be built.

The voice of God at Mount Sinai is the Jewish Incarnation, the moment when the barrier between creator and creature collapsed—at least momentarily. To handle such a moment, one needs a willingness to abandon the logic of either-or and believe in hypostatic unions. This is exactly what Christianity has done. Judaism has a problem with this moment of dual logic. It functions well either in the mythological mode or in the logico-theological mode, but it cannot be both simultaneously.

The rabbis of the Talmud are quite comfortable with a carnal God, as we saw, and care little about what Greek philosophers would say about this. Jewish philosophers, however, care a great deal about the Philosopher. They would like to dematerialize God to make Him presentable in mixed society. But then there's the voice at Mount Sinai. What is a committed rationalist like Maimonides to do with it? He could have said that there are certain moments in sacred history where "normal" categories have to be breached and logical explanations must fail. Halevi, a less committed Aristotelian than Maimonides, can live with it quite comfortably. Maimonides can't. The only sound we hear in his confusion is the sound of teeth gnashing and categories clashing. For rationalists like Maimonides, that too is an epiphany of sorts.

CHAPTER TWELVE

Scentless

In the Epic of Gilgamesh, we find one of the earliest versions of a cosmic flood story. The Sumerian Noah, Utnapishtim, tells Gilgamesh how he sailed in his boat on the water covering the world. When the rain stopped, he sent a swallow and a raven to see if the water has subsided. As the raven failed to return, he realized that the surface of the ground was dry, and opened the doors of his boat to the four winds. He made a sacrifice and poured out a libation on the mountaintop. He set up fourteen cauldrons on their stands and heaped up wood and cane and cedar and myrtle. When the gods smelled the sweet odor, they gathered "like flies."[1] This description is notoriously close to the biblical flood story. When Noah leaves the ark, after sending forth a raven and a dove, he builds an altar to Jehovah and sacrifices on it every clean animal and every clean bird. "And Jehovah smelled the pleasing smell, and Jehovah said in His heart, I will not again curse the land because of man" (8:21). The smell of sacrifices had a soothing effect on Jehovah. It succeeded in abating his anger, something that the horrendous scenes of human and animal suffering failed to achieve.

Jehovah seems very fond of the smell of roasted meat, but also of incense, an indispensable part his cult.[2] The term "soothing [or pleasing] smell" (*reach nichoach*) is used systematically in relation to the sacrifices, sometimes by Jehovah himself. The subject of this book, however, is not the way God senses, but the way humans sense Him. The sources offer us very little information on God's smell. This is not because smell was considered more "carnal" than the other senses. As we saw in chapter 10, Aristotle thought that sight, hearing, and smell are in fact nobler than taste and touch. And even if it were carnal, one would have expected the Incarnation to provide us with a reference to the way the Word incarnate became accessible to this sense as well as to the other three.[3] People saw, heard, and touched Jesus. They must have smelled Him too, but we are not told about it. When He was born, He was given frankincense and myrrh by the wise men from the East (Mt 2:11). Did He smell of precious perfume? We do not know.

This may have less to do with olfactory timidity and more with the nature of the sense of smell. Smell might be the oldest sense in mammals, and until recently it was the least studied. Olfactory data are transmitted directly to the most primitive ("paleo-mammalian") part of the brain—the limbic system. This system is primarily responsible for our emotional life, and is involved with the formation of long-term memory.[4] When we smell something familiar, it is immediately associated with memories, quite often deeply buried memories, and with emotions that are not necessarily accessible to our conscious mind. Smell is the most important producer of our Madeleine cookies (especially since what we call "taste" relies heavily on our ability to smell). Smells trigger emotions—lust, nostalgia, love, revulsion, pain—that we often cannot explain. Moreover the sense of smell never shuts down. When we're unconscious or asleep, we continue to smell as effectively as when awake and fully conscious, and are as affected by olfactory data. As an ever-growing number of studies conducted in the last decades have shown, smell functions as our emotional invisible hand. Our brain can recognize a vast array of scents and, if recognized by us, associate them with an emotional response and a memory.

This highly sensitive mechanism has surprisingly poor verbal expression. Our vocabulary for olfactory data is very limited. As William Miller has noted, "Odor qualifiers, if not the names of things emitting the odor ['like roses,' 'like freshly baked bread,' 'like old leather'], are usually simple adjectives and nouns expressing either the pleasantness or unpleasantness of the smell, most of which are merely 'bad' or 'good' smell."[5] The lexical poverty may be explained by the way smell activates us. The limbic system deciphers olfactory data at such speed that the conscious brain is presented not with raw material but with a fait accompli. By the time consciousness kicks into action, it's too late. What we now need are not descriptions and classifications of the original data, but explanations and excuses for our unconscious responses. We shall return to this.

The dearth of scent terms does not mean that worshipers were uninterested in their deities' smell. In Greco-Roman, Persian, and Egyptian religions, the gods did smell. Their bodies, their hair, their garments, and their dwelling places exuded a fragrance that was sensible to humans (the Olympians smell of ambrosia, a sign of their immortality, the antithesis of the foul-smelling stench of mortality).[6] But even pagan deities, unfettered by the laws of ineffability, offer a limited vocabulary of olfactory description. They do not have a distinctive smell. They are simply fragrant. The God of Israel is no exception. He smells good. We know this because He often makes His presence known by smell. When the air suddenly fills with inexplicable perfumes, it is a sign that a god is present. In a famous passage in the *Antiquities*, Josephus relates that when Solomon's Temple was dedicated, the air was filled with fragrance. The sweetness reached even those who were far away and made known the arrival of God and His establishment in the place just consecrated to Him.[7] About four centuries later, Severus of Minorca describes a similar occurrence of the olfactory signs of God's presence. In his account of the conversion of the Jewish community of Minorca to Christianity, allegedly under the influence of the relics of St. Stephen (in 418), the decisive turning point is reached not when threats made the community lose heart, as a modern reader would suspect, but by a sudden perfumed rain filling the air with the odor of honey.[8]

The sweet odor is God's "tell." Mythically, it is a simple expression of His goodness. Good smells good; evil smell bad. Philosophically, things are more complicated. What exactly is the relation of these heavenly odors to the "true" essence of God? We have come upon this problem in the discussion of God's voice: Is the scent something He creates to make his presence known or is it a necessary product of His presence? We are not sure. And does God have a preference for any particular smell? Would it be possible to identify the divine odor, as distinct from any other, perhaps like the ambrosial scent of the Olympians? Again, one is not sure what to say. The ancients often recognized in the perfumes that they identified as indications of God's presence the precious perfumes of their times, the same scents used to produce incense, especially myrrh and frankincense. Sometimes they smelled flowers, the lily and the rose. Sometimes divine presence was indicated simply by olfactory pleasure. Scents beyond human words or even imagination filled the souls of human smellers.

Unlike with God's other sensual epiphanies, no fear accompanies scent. When God decides to make His presence known by olfactory means, it is always pleasing. God's image and sound can be terrible and life-threatening. Touching him may be too frightening to attempt. In contrast, the smells that accompany God (whatever we make of them metaphysically) are always soothing, refreshing, heavenly.

In real life, the good and the pleasant are often disassociated, but in the "primitive" areas of our brain they are not. Experience teaches us that beautiful people can be evil and good people ugly. It teaches us that the Sirens' song can be pleasing and maleficent, that poison can taste good. A significant part of our rational activity is dedicated to resisting the simplistic equations of the primitive brain. We contrast physical with spiritual beauty; we learn to refuse harmful pleasures. The problem with smell, as I noted, is that its effects are so subtle and yet so deep that we often become aware of them only in retrospect. This is also true for God. The smell of burnt offering and of incense has a soothing effect on God that is purely irrational and is totally unrelated to the nature of the offense and to the appropriateness of the offering in relation to it. This irrational "essentialism" (good equals pleasant) is projected on God's olfactory faculty. People can "wear" fake smells (the perfume industry is based on faking smells), but this is simply a disguise. The real "moral" smell of things cannot be changed; it can only be concealed. It is like the atomic mass of elements—if you change it, it won't be the same element. While the more "sophisticated" senses allow complexity and inner tensions (God can be compassionate and terrible, sweet and bitter), smell retains its fundamental simplicity. In olfactory terms, God is good-fragrant just as the Devil is evil-stinking. The Devil occasionally disguises his "natural" (foul) smell, but God doesn't.[9] When He becomes accessible to the sense of smell, He can only be what He is: his goodness cannot be anything but fragrant. What kind of fragrance? Good. The details depend on what those becoming aware of the divine presence consider good.[10]

God can fill the air with his fragrance, but He can also infuse humans with his olfactory attributes. Some people close to God, the saints notably, have the gift of an "odor of sanctity"—their living bodies, and at times their cadavers, exude a powerful supernatural perfume. Some saints exude this supernatural fragrance constantly; others display it at specific occasions (often related in one way or another to the Eucharist). Still others only display it only after death—either at the moment of dying or when the tomb is opened. Sometimes their incorrupt bodies or their relics ooze perfumed oil (such saints are called myroblites).[11] Unlike the fragrance of God, the heavenly odor of sanctity is not an expression of the bearers' essential holiness, but a reward for virtue. Losing the supernatural fragrance means losing the presence of God.

There are grades in goodness and evil. No human can smell as good as God or as bad as the Devil. But in a diminished fashion, smells denote the moral and religious status of *all* people. Thus, in a poem celebrating the conversion of the Jews of Clermont in 576, Venantius Fortunatus tells Gregory of Tours (to whom the poem was sent) how the evil smell of the Jews (*Judaeus odor amarus*) was washed away by baptism (*abluitur Judaeus odor baptismate divo*) and replaced by a heavenly sweet (Christian) smell (*vertice perfuso chrismatis efflat odor*).[12]

We find the idea that moral status has a smell in the *Chronicle of Zuqnin*, a Syriac work of the eighth century. The author describes the transformation of the Christians who converted to Islam: "They grew different from the faithful people in both person and name: in person, because their once happy personal appearance became repugnant in such a way that they were recognized by the intelligent ones through their persons, odor and the look of their eyes."[13] The change of religion changes not only a person's mental state and external appearance; it also changes body odor. This has often been alleged concerning Jews. In their unbaptized state, Jews stink as is only fitting for ministers of the Devil. Once they convert, however, all trace of the Jewish smell vanishes.[14]

Similar stories can be found in Jewish sources where stench naturally characterizes *non-Jews*. Thus, in *Avot de Rabbi Natan*, a collection of Midrashim published at roughly the same time as the *Chronicle of Zuqnin*, the following story is told about one of the heroes of the Talmud, Rabbi Akiva. When Akiva went to Rome, somebody informed the authorities of his arrival:

A certain official sent him two beautiful women. They bathed them and anointed them, and adorned them like brides for their bridegrooms. And the two women kept throwing themselves at him all night: the one saying, come to me, the other saying, no, come to *me*. And he was sitting between them and spitting, without looking at them. [In the morning] they went to the official and said to him: we would rather die than be given to this man. He sent [for Akiva] and said to him: "Why did you not treat these women as men do? Are they not beautiful? Are they not human like you? Were they not created by the one who created you?" "What can I do," answered Akiva, "their smell assaulted me (*ba alai*)[15] like the flesh of forbidden animals, carrion, and vermin."[16]

All humans were created by the same God, but there is a difference. And even when "they" look and sound and feel exactly like "us," their smell exposes them to be morally inferior. That smell is related (in saints in a major way, in all the faithful in a minor way) to the presence of God in the believer.

Smell then is both a reality (people claim to sense it physically) and a metaphor of presence. In the rest of this chapter, I would like to discuss a case where the metaphor becomes mixed.

DIABOLICAL MESS

The setting first. Toward the end of his book on the beginning of the Order of Preachers,[17] Jordan of Saxony, St. Dominic's successor as master general of the Order of Preachers, offers a short personal memoir. In 1221, he became the provincial of Lombardy. Arriving at the Dominican convent of Bologna, he discovered a community in crisis. A certain uneducated brother, Bernard, was possessed by a terrible demon. Day and night, the demon tormented him most horrendously (*furiis exagitaretur*). The unfortunate community suffered "beyond measure" (*supra modum*).[18] But the problem, Jordan soon realized, was not simply the nuisance of having to deal with a raving demoniac. It was a moral, indeed a theological quandary. What was uncanny about this particular demoniac was that when not raging like a madman, Bernard, unlettered and untrained, spoke most wonderfully about scriptures and theology. "His words could rightly be considered worthy even of Augustine," writes Jordan. For a fresh graduate of the University of Paris, as Jordan was, this is surely the highest compliment. Worse still, Bernard preached such marvelous sermons that, moved by the profundity and the piety of his words, listeners shed copious, sincere tears. Finally, and most importantly for us, the possessed brother's body gave off an odor "sweeter than anything humans could produce" (*super omnem humanam confectionem*).[19]

As I noted, the Devil can disguise himself. He can produce artificially the smells that God's presence produces authentically. The simplest way of distinguishing between false and authentic claims of divine presence is by a careful examination of the claimant's moral behavior. You know a tree by its fruit. The frontal lobe cortex is summoned to examine the morally suspicious data offered by the limbic system, exactly because it tends to push us in "irrational" directions. We need to ask whether a particular person possesses the virtues that make him or her a suitable carrier of the fragrance of divine presence. The answer in Bernard's case was not easy to give. On the one hand, it seems clear that Bernard's "ravings" should be diagnosed as demonic. Demonic intrusion (both positive, in the form of temptations, and negative, in the form of physical and spiritual assaults) did not rule him out as a candidate for sainthood. Like many saints, Bernard could have been suffering from periodic demonic attacks: demons are attracted to saints and attempt to assault them in a variety of ways. But Bernard's spiritual diagnosis as demoniac meant that he was seen not as a conquering hero but, at least temporarily, as a prisoner in the war against evil. This does not ipso facto make him evil. A possessed person is not responsible for what he says and does during his trances. Some saints have been possessed by demons (the most famous, traditionally, was Mary Magdalene). They broke out of the demonic prison and triumphed. The problem with Bernard was that the divine and demonic presences seemed to occur not in sequence but simultaneously. And the problem was also that both types of signals were exceptionally powerful. Bernard was a very annoying demoniac (screaming, cursing, and frothing at the mouth), and at the same time a great preacher, a profound theologian, and a subtle biblical exegete. Most confusing of all, there is no hint that there was anything wrong with Bernard's messages. They were not heretical or otherwise subversive. Bernard's words did not lead his listeners astray as one would expect from messages produced by the Father of Lies. On the contrary: when he was good, he was very good.

But not perfect. Bernard, Jordan tells us, was very proud of his intellectual and rhetorical achievements. Pride is diabolic, especially among the socially inferior. The first round in the battle between Jordan and Bernard was fought with traditional weapons. Jordan demanded obedience. Surely, if Bernard refused to obey, he did not possess the virtue of humility or respect his vow of obedience. When ordered by Jordan to cease from engaging in "positive" activities—his preaching, theologizing, and interpreting were all done without permission—Bernard offered his superior a tit for tat deal. He would if Jordan would. Jordan responded to this outrageous show of impudence with the righteous outrage of a young theologian: "God forbid that I should reach an agreement with death, or strike a deal with hell. Your temptations will, against your will, profit the brothers. They will lead them into the life of grace, for the life of man on earth is temptation." When the demon tried to reason with him, Jordan rejected him out of hand: "Why do you multiply your deceptions with us?" he asked. "We are not ignorant of your real thoughts."[20]

The Devil obviously did not like Jordan's attitude. In truly egalitarian spirit, he issued a threat and a challenge: "I too know you. Now you refuse and despise the deception offered to you, but with the aid of my cunning you will easily and willingly accept it." A little later, when Jordan was attending the possessed brother, he began to show signs of great distress and exclaimed: "Here is that smell! that smell! that smell!" Then the devil, speaking through Brother Bernard, explained to Jordan that it was the friar's angel that gave off the perfume to console the possessed man and to torment him (the Devil). The Devil's smell was very different. As a demonstration, he filled the air with the stench of sulfur, "hoping to conceal the false nature of the first odor's sweetness with the succession of smells (*intendens eorum successione precedentis illius suavitatis palliare fallaciam*)."[21]

It is exactly the "succession of smells" that baffles Jordan. The Devil (Bernard) offers Jordan an explanation he could theoretically live with. Good and evil cannot mix, but they *can* alternate, without intermingling. Instead of conceding that the odor was false, Bernard suggested that both odors (good and foul) were authentic. Bernard has the Devil *and* God (or an angel of God) in him. This should have solved Jordan's theological dilemma: the odor, the effective preaching, and the theological skill were angelic; the stench, the pride, the howling, and the contortions were demonic.

Jordan hesitated. This could be a solution. True, Bernard's virtues were apparently not sufficient to convince him that Bernard was a saint under demonic attack. But what if the fragrance occurred in someone more worthy than Bernard? All of a sudden, Jordan himself began to give off an immensely powerful odor, constantly immersed in a cloud of heavenly fragrance. He was afraid to take his hands out of his habit, for fear the smell would overwhelm him. When he had to raise his hands during mass, he was struck by joy so powerful and so sweet (*miri odoris suavitas, immensitate tante dulcedinis*) that he almost fainted.[22]

For a while, a truce was reached. In the Dominican house in Bologna, there were now two theologians and preachers, both exuding a marvelous fragrance (though the odor seems to have been discernible only by the two of them). One was the official head of the community, Jordan, exercising his authority by right; the other was Bernard, exercising authority by usurpation. Who was more authoritative? Did Jordan's sermons touch people to the heart and bring copious tears to their eyes? Who was the better theologian? Who was better at expounding Scripture? We are not told.

But the truce could not last. Jordan was undergoing an ever-deeper moral and theological crisis. He could not live with such ambivalence. He craved certainty. Was the odor divine or demonic? It could not be both. Jordan was displaying all the positive symptoms of divine presence with none of the negative ones. Why not see himself (as the Church later saw him) as one of God's saints? Still very young, he became in a very short time the leader of men in an up-and-coming religious elite; he was praised to high heaven by his peers and brought hordes of Parisian students to the Order of Preachers; and wasn't the odor of sanctity about him? A rash presumption of his own sainthood (*temerariam sanctitatem presumptionem*) was entering his heart.[23] Was this the odor of *his* sanctity? Was he a saint? What would that make of Bernard? If his odor was a mark of divine presence, as Bernard's Devil contended, shouldn't he (as part of an unspoken deal) be willing to concede that Bernard was indeed the locus of both God *and* the Devil? "I was bewildered by great ambiguity. I doubted my own merits and yet I hesitated, uncertain. Wherever I went, I was surrounded by a wonderful fragrance. I hardly dared to pull my hands [out of my habit] for fear of losing a sweetness [or sanctity—both readings are possible] of which I was not yet aware."[24]

Jordan's reaction to the miraculous odor is highly emotional, as is often the case with smell. His bewilderment reflects the fact that his intellect has difficulty following through. He is excited by the idea that this is the odor of his sanctity, yet he finds it hard to justify in rational terms—at least "not yet." Finally, he could take it no more:

Once, when I was about to celebrate Mass, I was praying with some fervor the psalm "Judge, O Lord, them that harm me" [35:1]—a psalm very effective for resisting temptation. When I reached the verse "all my bones shall say, Lord, who is like you?" [35:10], suddenly such an immensity of sweet smell poured over me that it truly seemed to suffuse the very marrow of my bones (*repente tanta super me effusa est odoriferi dulcoris immensitas, ut re vera viderentur omnes medulle meorum ossium irrigari*). Stupefied, and struck by the extreme unusualness of the phenomenon, I begged the Lord to reveal to me in His mercy if this was achieved by the wiles of the Devil and suffer not the weak, for whom there was no certain helper but Him, to be reviled by the powerful. As soon as I prayed thus to the Lord—for whose glory I tell this—I received such inner clarity of spirit and such unquestionable certainty through infused truth that I no longer had the slightest doubt (*omnino nihil ambigerem*) that all these were tricks of the deceiving enemy.[25]

Jordan's reason finally issued its verdict: the odor of sanctity was out of the question (yet). Furthermore, it came at too high a price. Implicitly at least, it meant accepting the Devil's deal of dividing power. Jordan was now confident, or at least this is what he felt in hindsight. The whole thing, he declared, was a delusion, a diabolical ruse. Good and evil were again clearly separated. Armed with his newly acquired certainty, Jordan rushed to Bernard and told him the news. Right away, Bernard's fragrance as well as all the other positive aspects of Bernard's possession stopped. Instead of preaching devout sermons, Bernard cursed and blasphemed like a proper devil:

Now that the secret of his iniquity had been revealed, I assured that brother of the diabolic nature of this temptation. The emission of smell now stopped in both of us. From then on, he, who previously used to speak to us in many words full of devotion, began to speak evil and depraved words (*ex tunc mala loqui cepit et turpia, qui prius sermones multos devotione plenos narrare consueverat*). When I said to him, "Where are your beautiful words now?" he replied: "Since my deceiving intent has been exposed, I wish to exercise my malice openly (*manifestam iam volo exercere nequitiam*)."[26]

It seems that, once "exposed," Bernard's devil, albeit a liar by nature and calling, developed a taste for consistency and transparency. The Church of the thirteenth century had little patience with ambiguities. The new, university-trained, Church leaders sought to put things in order. Are you with us or against us? You cannot be both.

We do not know what later happened to Bernard. Once the unfortunate matter of the confused smells was sorted out, Jordan lost interest in him. He was not particularly interested in demonic possession per se and he was certainly not interested in lay brothers with a scandalous penchant for theology. Had he not experienced the (fake?) odor of sanctity in his own person, he would probably not have bothered to mention Brother Bernard at all.[27] But then, it did happen. What did he make of it? The answer to his personal problem came ex machina without too many details. Smell was the easiest thing to explain. One could think of it as perfume—something added to your person by an external agent (be it God or the Devil); but the other positive aspects of Bernard's possession were not as easily explained. Were the orthodox theological insights, the deep understanding of Scriptures, and the effective preaching demonic? Was the heavenly perfume that suffused the devout Jordan as he prayed and celebrated Mass *just* a demonic ruse? For what purpose?

There are answers to these questions. Yes, the Devil can offer a very good imitation of God. He tempts God's elect in a thousand strange ways. But perhaps the most important conclusion we can draw from this episode is that one never knows. Even the most impressive, seemingly trustworthy indications of God's presence can be falsified. The age of the "Discernment of Spirits" was about to begin—a concentrated effort to tell the divine from the demonic.[28] In vain. After all these efforts—the desperate witch hunts, the burning of suspects, the many learned guides written by the greatest experts—the smells of God and the Devil remained, and still remain, intermixed.

POST SCRIPTUM

In his brilliant essay "Religion: If There Is No God . . . ," Leszek Kolakowski writes: "Religious ways of perceiving the world, institutions of worship, beliefs, are never born of analytical reasoning and need no 'proofs' of their veracity unless they are attacked on rational grounds. Logos in religion is a defensive mechanism."[1] Kolakowski argues that within its own sphere, "religion" makes just as much sense as "science." These two mental cows, one holy, the other profane, simply yield different types of milk. The scientific cow produces predictability and probability; the religious cow consolation and redemption. One can mix these very different liquids to a certain degree: secular reasoners can replace God with "human dignity" as their guiding principle; religious thinkers can build syllogistic structures on the dogmata of faith. But in the end, as Kolakowski says in the concluding words of his essay, "the real is what people crave for."[2] It is futile to look for a common denominator. All attempts to explain faith in logical terms are bound to fail, just as it is futile to understand the spiritual meaning of quarks. One can bat for both teams, as long as one remembers to play by the rules that govern each.

Sadly, as Kolakowski would be the first to admit, metaphysical pluralism is all too often diagnosed as schizophrenia. It works better in theory than in practice. In practice, people (especially people in positions of power) find the "Averroist" idea of Double-Truth irritating. They tend to define the "other team's" truth as a lie, and make those who adhere to it see the light in rather ungodly ways.

But while Kolakowski is aware of the intricacies of real life, he seems to believe that had it only been possible to separate the spiritually inclined from the materially inclined, each group would live happily ever after. Unfortunately, reasoners of the scientific (practical) and the religious (mythical) modes of explanation live in the same world. They are thus bound to collide, and form, willy-nilly, the *monde du mélange* in which we live.

Kolakowski's interpretation of the relations between "religious" and "scientific" ways of thinking is strangely reminiscent of Gnostic myths. In the utopian *Urwelt*, believers and nonbelievers lived in separate conceptual worlds. At some point, the forces of disbelief (Greek Philosophy, Science, the Enlightenment) invaded the realm of untarnished religion (the faithful were "attacked on rational grounds"), forcing it to defend itself by weapons that, in a deep sense, are alien to its very nature. It should be recognized that Kolakowski's explanatory model makes no ontological truth-claims. Like Hobbes's or Rousseau's "states of nature," it is a theoretical model, not a historical account of how thing "really" were. In real life, the two modes of thought were never neatly separated. But Kolakowski believes that his model enables us to better understand why people who could be perfectly happy in their "mythical" realm try to fix what he thinks ain't broke. They try to fix unbroken conceptual systems, because of the critical, sarcastic gaze of others. "L'enfer, c'est les autres."

There is something quite appealing about Kolakowski's dislike for mixed modes of explanation. Rationalists do not like hybrids. They find it easier to accept St. Paul's faith in Christ Crucified, "a stumbling block" to the Jews and "foolishness" to the Greeks, than the scholastics' hybrid of revelation and Aristotle. Pascal's God of Abraham, Isaac, and Jacob is more attractive to nonbelievers than the philosophers' God. One can move from realm to realm only by losing faith or by leaping toward it. As long as He remains in His sphere, Jehovah makes perfect sense. The trouble begins when He is given a metaphysical visa to nonbelievers' territory. There, alas, he is simply out of his element. The "logical" explanations that theologians produce on his behalf require a greater mental effort than the willingness to accept that some things just defy logic. There is a story about a very learned rabbi who, facing the endless intricacies of Talmudic debates, felt incapable of deciding what the law was in any particular instance. He asked his disciples to go to the town rabbi, a very simple man, and ask for his halachic rulings. But they were not to give him the rabbi's justifications for them. Authority, like irrational faith, is what it is. Once you try to mix it with reason, it becomes much harder to swallow.

But is unfaith always the aggressor? Are the faithful only using reason as a defensive mechanism? The analytical dualist is eager to answer these questions in the affirmative, but history seems to suggest otherwise. Reason is not an external aggressive force nor are the faithful adopting it as a last resort. The dualist division of the mythical and the scientific is the result of one particular moment in Western thinking (the marriage of the Enlightenment and experimental science). It tells us more about the post-Enlightenment rationalist's fears of impurity than about the religious frame of mind.

When Greek reason was introduced systematically into the religious thinking of the West in the twelfth century, there were no Greeks to impress or secular scientists to convince. The Church had a practical monopoly on learning. The challenge came from within. Even when it was supposedly aimed at outsiders, like in Thomas's *Summa contra gentiles*, for example, the real addressees were other members of the community, eager to ask all the difficult questions that we have encountered in this book, while at the same time committed to one particular type of answer—the "orthodox."

Reason and unreason cannot be separated, because human beings need both. The fault is not with Greek philosophy. Moments of reflection always follow the initial act of faith. The question, in other words, is not why we believe in "God"—we believe because we believe—but what it is that we believe *in*, what the *content* of our belief is. Very few people are capable of leaving faith in its pristine purity, as a mental attitude. Least of all are intellectuals capable of it. The mixing of realms is not an external addition to believers, not (just) a defensive weapon (though it can be that too), but an integral aspect of the human mind—of both the faithful and the faithless. Reason is an essential element in the development of religious systems. It is true that in the West the language of reflection was deeply influenced by Greek models, but reflection can exist in a great variety of ways, some of which are clearly unphilosophical. The Talmudic rabbis, for example, found Greek philosophy unappealing. They committed philosophical atrocities that would have shocked Plato and Aristotle with total equanimity. Against our "progressive" expectations, they often made God more, not less, human, more, not less, material.

And yet, even our nonphilosophical rabbis were not simply adding mythological and devotional elements to the God of revelation. They sought to make sense of a God that, according to Kolakowski, already made perfect sense. Making sense led them into trouble, logical trouble. This "trouble" is not the unfortunate result of sloppy thinking, as is too often suggested. On the contrary, the trouble they introduced into their belief system was sophisticated, complex, often ingenious. Religious reasoners were not adding a patch to a dysfunctional system. As we saw, difficulties were often introduced into the sacred corpus where a literal reading would have been quite unproblematic from both a believer's and a nonbeliever's point of view. Take transubstantiation, for example: surely, the Real Presence was simpler without it. And what about the bizarre story of God shaving the king of Assyria? Did we really need that? Making religious sense does not proceed by the simplest, shortest path. Riddles, contradictions, complications, and detours are not accidents; they are the flesh and blood of religious thinking in complex communities.

It is tempting to think that the experts are simply motivated by class interest—complexities make them indispensable—but that would not be the truth, or at least not the whole truth. Experts do gain social benefits from their mind games, but the main benefit is, for lack of another term, aesthetic. Complex systems are intellectually more pleasing, at least for intellectuals. Beautiful explanations are encouraged and rewarded. What makes them "beautiful"? Sometimes it is their ability to create a metaphysical Esperanto, a logical language that all can understand—the ultimate logical "proof" that even the most stubborn skeptic would find irresistible. But more often, this has nothing to do with convincing nonbelievers (foreign or domestic).

The dynamic nature of all societies forces them to change their aesthetics (sensual and intellectual) to correspond to changing circumstances and needs. But while new arguments are being produced, the old arguments cannot simply be forgotten. They continue to exist as layers of past tastes and preferences that must be dealt with in a way that will not destroy the all-important myth of continuity on which religious establishments are based. The coincidence of new with old solutions engenders new problems and requires new solutions, some more beautiful, others, sadly, less.

Many of the issues discussed in this book are beautiful explanations that ran into trouble. The idea that God is both transcendent (totally unlike us) and immanent (hence like us; hence sensual, if only "spiritually") is universal, as is, to varying degrees, the urge to offer explanations for this uneasy coexistence. In the historical ages discussed in this book, the existence of God was never seriously challenged. God was a constant—the ontological foundation of all else. But at the same time, the *content* of the idea, "God," was ever changing in an attempt to catch up with the flow of ideas produced by professional "explainers." The complex products of colliding trains of thought are constantly projected onto God—the "ontological substratum of everything"—so that speculation is reified and re-reified. God is that which theology asserts; hence, what theology asserts, within varying moments of the speculative process, is God. At any given moment, he is the *consensus theologorum*—a reification of past strata of theological thought, philosophical trends, and political, social, and cultural pressures. That is why, in spite of all efforts to make him a coherent set of ideas, he is a logical chimera. Absolute coherence exists only in the *fons et origo*—in the Hidden God whose coherence is without spot and blemish because he is an empty concept, because he is, in a deep sense, totally unknown, unknowable.

Does knowing this (assuming that a believer might concede that this is knowledge and not nonsense) change anything? Probably not. The news of God's death has proved, once again, premature. For those with a thirst for God, God, as Kolakowski (and Paul) observed, requires no proof. Cognitive, psychological, and sociocultural observations can merely scratch the surface of faith. That faith cannot be reconciled with the current philosophical dogma is unfortunate, but it is not critical. It is always possible to turn to the *ultima ratio fidelium*: *credo quia absurdum*. Indeed, under the combined assaults of Darwin and Freud, the faithful are more likely than in the past two millennia to use this ultimate weapon. One might even suspect that Kolakowski's argument—which would have been totally unacceptable to St. Thomas Aquinas and Maimonides—is itself just a symptom of a (temporary?) retreat of the religious reasoners to their last defense lines.

Too satisfied with itself, the present generation does not like the beautiful explanations of the past, but the next generation may again find pleasure in them, or produce others. As long as the need for the Ultimate exists, as long as people sense the urge to feel, to fear, and to understand a force profoundly greater than them and yet profoundly intimate, they will produce explanations full of tensions and internal contradictions, making *their* God in *their* image.

NOTES

Unless otherwise noted, all translations are mine.

1. Instability and Its Discontents

1. Augustine, *Confessiones* 11.20; Augustine, *Confessions*, trans. Henry Chadwick (Oxford: Oxford University Press, 1991), 232.

2. Augustine, *Confessiones* 10.13–14; *Confessions*, 186–187.

3. Plato, *Symposium* 207d–208b; Plato, *Symposium*, trans. A. Nehamas and P. Woodruff, in *Plato: Complete Works*, ed. J. M. Cooper (Indianapolis: Hackett, 1997), 490–491.

4. Eliot Deutsch and J. A. B. van Buitenen, eds., *A Source Book of Advaita Vedanta* (Honolulu: University of Hawaii Press, 1971), 151–153.

2. Loving God Like a Cow

1. Meister Eckhart, German Sermon 16b, in *Meister Eckhart: Teacher and Preacher*, ed. and trans. Bernard McGinn et al. (New York: Paulist, 1986), 278.

2. The last argument of philosophers. The phrase, *Ultima ratio regum* (the last argument of kings), was inscribed on the cannons of Louis XIV.

3. *Tikunei Zohar* 122.2.

3. Endless

1. John Chrysostom, *On the Incomprehensible Nature of God*, trans. P. W. Harkins, Fathers of the Church 72 (Washington, D.C.: Catholic University of America Press, 1984), ser. 3, p. 97.

2. *The Collection of the Middle Length Sayings*, trans. I. B. Horner, 3 vols. (London: Pali Text Society, 1954), 2:97–99.

3. *The Book of Kindred Sayings*, 5 vols., trans by Rhys Davids and Woodward (1917; Oxford: Oxford University, 1993), 5:354.

4. See the brilliant discussion of apophasis in Michael A. Sells, *Mystical Languages of Unsaying* (Chicago: University of Chicago Press, 1994), esp. 14–33.

5. Pseudo-Dionysius, *The Mystical Theology* 4; Pseudo Dionysius, *The Complete Works*, trans. C. Luibheid, Classics of Western Spirituality (New York: Paulist, 1987), 140–141.

6. Pseudo-Dionysius, *The Mystical Theology* 5; *The Complete Works*, 141 (emphasis mine).

7. *Zohar* 2:239a.

8. Marjorie Schuman, "The Psychophysiological Model of Meditation and Altered States of Consciousness: A Critical Review," in *The Psychobiology of Consciousness*, ed. J. M. Davidson and R. J. Davidson (New York: Plenum, 1980), 333–378.

9. Plotinus, *Enneads* 6.9.3.

10. Pseudo-Dionysius, *Mystical Theology* 3; *The Complete Works*, 137.

11. Plotinus, *Enneads* 6.9.3.

12. Martin Luther, *The Bondage of the Will*, trans. J. I. Packer and O. R. Johnston (Grand Rapids, Mich.: Revel, 1992), 232. For a discussion of Leibowitz's "Protestantism," see Avi Sagi, "Leibowitz: Jewish Thought vis-à-vis Modernity" [Hebrew], in *Yeshayahu Leibowitz: His World and Philosophy*, ed. A. Sagi (Jerusalem: Keter, 1995), 162–175.

4. Credo

1. Augustine, *De trinitate* 8.4.

2. Peter Abelard, *Historia calamitatum*, ed. J. Monfrin (Paris: Vrin, 1959), 82–83; Abelard, *The Story of Abelard's Adversities*, trans. J. T. Muckle (Toronto: Pontifical Institute of Mediaeval Studies, 1964), 42–43.

3. Innocent IV, *Commentaria in quinque libros decretalium* ad 1.1, s.v. *firmiter* (Frankfurt, 1570). I discussed this text in Kleinberg, *Flesh Made Word: Saints Stories and the Western Imagination*, trans. J. M. Todd (Cambridge, Mass.: Harvard University Press, 2008), 291–293.

4. Paul L. Gavrilyuk, *The Suffering of the Impassible God: The Dialectics of Patristic Thought* (Oxford: Oxford University Press, 2004), 148–149.

5. Maimonides, *The Guide of the Perplexed*, part 2, chap. 17; Maimonides, *The Guide of the Perplexed*, trans. Shlomo Pines (Chicago: University of Chicago Press, 1963), 295–296. Maimonides alludes to the famous philosophical parable of Ibn Tufail, *Hay ibn Yaqzan*, where the protagonist, raised by a deer on a desert island, succeeds in acquiring full knowledge of the world through the use of his natural reason.

5. Unimaginable

1. *Bab. Talmud, Yoma* 22b.

2. Immanuel Kant, *Conflict of the Faculties*, trans. Mary J. Gregor (New York: Abaris Books, 1979), 115.

6. Impossible

1. Maimonides, *Commentary on the Mishnah*. Sanhedrin 10.

2. *Bab. Talmud, Sanhedrin* 95b–96a.

3. www.sacred-texts.com/jud/talmud.htm.

4. Moshe Halbertal, "Ilmale mikra katuv i efshar le-omro" (Were It Not Written, It Would Be Impossible to Utter) [Hebrew], *Tarbiz* 68a (1999): 39–59.

5. *Lamentations Rabba* proem 24.

6. *Lamentations Rabba* 49.

7. For a short overview of biblical references to God's body, see Benjamin D. Sommer, *The Bodies of God and the World of Ancient Israel* (Cambridge: Cambridge University Press, 2009), 1–11; Howard Eilberg-Schwartz, *God's Phallus: And Other Problems for Men and Monotheism* (Boston: Beacon, 1994), 59–80.

8. This is the biblical etymology. The more likely etymology is "the power of God."

9. It is highly unlikely that this is a correct etymology.

10. See William T. Miller, *Mysterious Encounters at Mamre and Jabbok* (Chico, Calif.: Scholars Press, 1984). Miller points out that many of the ancient translations simply substitute God with an angel in the statement that Jacob has seen God face to face (98). This exegetical position has roots in the Bible itself. Thus Hosea states: "He [Jacob] has struggled with the angel and overcame him" (Hos 12:5).

11. Alon Goshen Gottstein, "The Body as Image of God in Rabbinic Literature," *Harvard Theological Review* 87, no. 2 (1994): 172.

12. For a very important essay on the corporeality of God, see Yehuda Liebes, "Natura Dei: The Jewish Myth and Its Transmutations," in *God's Story: Collected Essays on the Jewish Myth* [Hebrew] (Jerusalem: Carmel, 2008), 35–117. See also Daniel Boyarin, "The Eye in the Torah: Ocular Desire in Midrashic Hermeneutic," *Critical Inquiry* 16, no. 3 (1990): 532–550; Yair Lorberbaum, *Image of God: Halakha and Aggadah* [Hebrew] (Tel Aviv: Schocken, 2004), where the author discusses the projection of Maimonidean ideas of incorporeality on rabbinic literature.

13. *Bab. Talmud, Bava Metzia* 59b.

14. Christian readers were horrified by the blatant nature of Talmudic language on God. See Ch. Merchavia, *The Church Versus Talmudic and Midrashic Literature* [Hebrew] (Jerusalem: Bialik Institute, 1970), esp. 93–152, 227–290.

15. See *Bab. Talmud, Berachot* 68a.

16. *De genesi ad litteram* 12.9.20.

17. *Contra epistulam Fundamenti* 5, in CSEL 25:197.

18. Tertullian, *De carne Christi* 4; *Tertullian's Treatise on the Incarnation*, ed. and trans. E. Evans (London, 1956), 13–15.

19. Tertullian, *De carne Christi* 3; *Tertullian's Treatise on the Incarnation*, 11.

20. Tertullian, *De carne Christi* 5; *Tertullian's Treatise on the Incarnation*, 19.

21. The extent to which Marcion manipulated the text he had is still debated by scholars. See David Salter Williams, "Reconsidering Marcion's Gospel," *Journal of Biblical Literature* 108, no. 3 (1989): 477–496.

7. A SHORT DISCOURSE ON THE SPIRITUAL SENSES

1. Bernard of Clairvaux, *Sermones in cantica* 74, 5, in PL 183:1141.

2. Augustine, *De doctrina Christiana* 3.29.41.

3. Augustine, *Confessiones* 12.15.18; Augustine, *Confessions*, trans. Henry Chadwick (Oxford: Oxford University Press, 1991), 254.

4. Augustine, *Confessiones* 12.19.28–12.20.29. On Augustine's understanding of the spiritual senses, see Matthew R. Lootens's essay in Paul L. Gavrilyuk and

Sarah Coakley, eds., *The Spiritual Senses: Perceiving God in Western Christianity* (Cambridge: Cambridge University Press, 2012), 56–70.

5. Bonaventure, 3 *Sent.* D. 34, p. 1, a. 1, q. 1.

6. Honorius of Autun, *Elucidarium*, in PL 172:1172.

7. Bonaventure, *Itinerarium mentis in deum*, trans. P. Boehner (Saint Bonaventure, N.Y.: Franciscan Institute, 1956), 4.4, p. 74. See also Fabio Massimo Tedoldi, *La dottrina dei cinque sensi spirituali in San Bonaventura* (Rome: Pontificium Athenaeum Antonianum, 1999); Karl Rahner, "The Doctrine of the Spiritual Senses in the Middle Ages," in *Theological Investigations*, 23 vols. (New York: Crossroad, 1979), 16:104–134; William of Auxerre, *Summa Aurea* 4, cited by Boyd Taylor Coolman, *Knowing God by Experience: The Spiritual Senses in the Theology of William of Auxerre* (Washington, D.C.: Catholic University of America Press, 2004), 37–38; Susan Ashbrook Harvey, *Scenting Salvation: Ancient Christianity and the Olfactory Imagination* (Berkeley: University of California Press, 2006), 169–180.

8. Richard Cross argues very convincingly that Aquinas sees the whole idea of the spiritual senses as redundant and treats sense terminology as purely metaphorical: Gavrilyuk and Coakely, *The Spiritual Senses*, 174–189. On the problems involved in the "Beatific Vision," see Caroline Walker Bynum, *The Resurrection of the Body in Western Christianity, 200–1336* (New York: Columbia University Press, 1995), 279–317. For a discussion of sensual language in Jewish theology, see H. A. Wolfson, "Maimonides on the Unity and Incorporeality of God," *Jewish Quarterly Review* 56 (1965): 112–136; Moshe Halbertal, *Maimonides* [Hebrew] (Jerusalem: Zalman Shazar Center, 2009), 244–250.

9. Bernard of Clairvaux, *Sermones in cantica* 74, 5, in PL 183:1046–1047. See also Gordon Rudy, *Mystical Language of Sensation in the Later Middle Ages* (New York: Routledge, 2002), 45–65.

10. Gregory of Nyssa, "The Lord's Prayer," in PG 44:1185.

11. Clement of Alexandria, *Christ the Educator*, trans. S. P. Wood, Fathers of the Church 23 (New York: Catholic University of America Press, 1954), 2.8.66–67, pp. 150–151.

8. Invisible

1. This process began in the Septuagint where Jehovah is systematically rendered "kurios." See Joseph Dan, *History of Jewish Mysticism and Esotericism* [Hebrew] (Jerusalem: Shazar, 2009), 1:109–113.

2. In Deuteronomy 4:15–19, God specifies that the forbidden images are those of beast, bird, and fish, the sun, the moon, and the stars. It seems quite clear that

these are not attempts to portray Jehovah who is anthropomorphic in shape. The same argument is in fact made by John of Damascus. See John of Damascus, *Three Treatises on the Divine Images*, trans. A. Louth (Crestwood, N.Y.: St. Vladimir's Seminary Press, 2003), treatise 1.5–7, 22–23.

3. Exodus 24:9–11.

4. See George Foucart, "Names (Primitive)," in *Encyclopedia of Religion and Ethics* 9:130–136.

5. There is a great deal of mystery involving God's name. Jehovah or Yahweh—the One Who Is—is probably just a nom de guerre. The "real" name remains unknown.

6. See, for example, Neil A. Silberman and Israel Finkelstein, *The Bible Unearthed: Archeology's New Vision of Ancient Israel and the Origin of Its Sacred Texts* (New York: Touchstone, 2002).

7. Dio Chrysostom, *The Twelfth, or Olympic, Discourse* 53; Dio Chrysostom, *Discourses 12–30*, trans. J. W. Cohoon, Loeb Classical Library 339 (Cambridge, Mass.: Harvard University Press, 1939), 59.

8. Dio Chrysostom, *The Twelfth or Olympic Discourse* 54; Dio Chrysostom, *Discourses*, 59.

9. Dio Chrysostom, *The Twelfth or Olympic Discourse* 59; Dio Chrysostom, *Discourses*, 63.

10. Dio Chrysostom, *The Twelfth or Olympic Discourse* 78; Dio Chrysostom, *Discourses*, 81.

11. Augustine, *De trinitate* 8.4. See the interesting discussion in Gilbert Dagron, "Holy Images and Likeness," *Dumbarton Oaks Papers* 45 (1991): 23–33.

12. John of Damascus, "Defence Against Those Who Attack Holy Images," in *Three Treatises on the Divine Images*, 22.

13. Ibid., 17, 32.

14. See Jaroslav Pelikan, *Imago Dei: The Byzantine Apologia for Icons* (Princeton: Princeton University Press, 1990), 74–78; Herbert L. Kessler, *Spiritual Seeing: Picturing God's Invisibility in Medieval Art* (Philadelphia: University of Pennsylvania Press, 2000), 29–52.

15. Theodore the Studite, *On the Holy Icons*, trans. C. P. Roth (Crestwood, N.Y.: St. Vladimir's Seminary Press, 1981), 21.

16. See Robin Margaret Jensen, *Face to Face: Portraits of the Divine in Early Christianity* (Minneapolis: Fortress, 2005), 69–130; Steven Bigham, *The Image of God the Father in Orthodox Iconography* (Torrance, Calif.: Oakwood, 1995).

17. Plato, *Timaeus*, in *Plato: Complete Works*, ed. J. M. Cooper (Indianapolis: Hackett, 1997), 28C.

18. See Daniele Menozzi, *Les images l'Église et les arts visuels* (Paris: Cerf, 1991), 13–63. See also S. Gero, "The True Image of Christ: Eusebius's Letter to Constantia Reconsidered," *Journal of Theological Studies* 32 (1981): 460–470.

19. In the West, this is based on Gregory the Great's defense of images in his letter to Serenus (*Registrum* 11.13, in CCSL 140a:873–875) as the Bible of the poor, as memory aides, and as emotional triggers for the faithful. See Herbert L. Kessler, "Gregory the Great and Image Theory in Northern Europe During the Twelfth and Thirteenth Centuries," in *A Companion to Medieval Art: Romanesque and Gothic in Northern Europe*, ed. Conrad Rudolph (Malden, Mass.: Blackwell, 2006), 151–153.

20. Ignatius of Loyola, *Spiritual Exercises*, trans. G. E. Ganss, in *Ignatius of Loyola: The Spiritual Exercises and Selected Works*, ed. G. E. Ganss (New York: Paulist, 1991), 47, p. 136.

21. Ibid., 54, p. 138.

22. Ibid., 112, p. 150.

23. Ibid., 114, p. 150.

24. Ibid., 53–54, p. 138.

25. "For what writing presents to readers, this a picture presents to the unlearned who behold, since in it even the ignorant see what they ought to follow; in it the illiterate read." See note 14.

26. Ignatius, *Spiritual Exercises*, 66–70, p. 141.

27. Aristotle, *Metaphysics*, trans. Hugh Tredennick, Loeb Classical Library 271 and 287 (Cambridge, Mass.: Harvard University Press, 1933, 1935), 980a; Plato, *The Republic*, in Cooper, *Plato*, bk. 6, pp. 507–508.

28. Augustine, *In Johannis evangelium tractatus CXXIV*, 121.5, in CCSL 36:667.

29. On the difference between Catholic holy images and Orthodox icons, see G. Ostrogorskij, "Les décisions du 'Stoglav' concernant peinture d'images et les principes de l'iconographie Byzantine," in *L'art byzantine chez les Slaves* (Paris, 1930), 399. See also the two articles of Pierre Miquel in *Dictionnaire de spiritualité* 7, "théologie de l'icône" (1229–1239) and "Images, culte des" (1503–1519).

30. Victricius of Rouen, *De laude sanctorum* 9, in PL 20:451–452.

31. John of Damascus, *Three Treatises*, 1:36, p. 43.

32. See Symeon the New Theologian, *On the Mystical Life: The Ethical Discourses*, 3 vols., trans. A. Golitzin (Crestwood, N.Y.: St. Vladimir's Seminary Press, 1996), 1:130–135. Symeon strives to convince his skeptical congregation to believe in what they do not see.

33. Hans Belting, *Likeness and Presence: A History of the Image Before the Era of Art*, trans. E. Jephcott (Chicago: University of Chicago Press, 1994), 6. This is a

somewhat strange translation of the original title, *Bild und Kult: Eine Geschichte des Bildes vor dem Zeitalter der Kunst* (Image and Cult: A History of the Image Before the Era of Art). See also David Morgan, *The Sacred Gaze: Religious Visual Culture in Theory and Practice* (Berkeley: University of California Press, 2005), 1–21, 49–74.

9. Tasteless

1. Though John relates a "Eucharistic" sermon delivered by Jesus in the synagogue of Capernaum (Jn 6:41–59), he omits to mention an actual eating of the bread and drinking of the wine in the Last Supper.

2. See Stanislao Fioramonti's introduction to Innocent III, *Il sacrosanto mystero dell'altare (De sacro altaris mysterio)*, ed. and trans. S. Fioramonti (Vatican City: Libreria Editrice Vaticana, 2002), xv n.16.

3. For a discussion of the Eucharistic controversies, see Jean de Montclos, *Lanfranc et Bérenger: La controverse eucharistique du XIᵉ siècle* (Louvain, 1971); Nathan Mitchell, *Cult and Controversy: The Worship of the Eucharist Outside Mass* (Collegeville, Minn., Liturgical Press, 1990), 73–85; Jaroslav Pelikan, *The Growth of Medieval Theology (600–1300)*, vol. 3, *The Christian Tradition: A History of the Development of Doctrine* (Chicago: University of Chicago Press, 1978), 184–204.

4. On Berengar, see Brian Stock, *The Implications of Literacy: Written Language and Models of Interpretation in the Eleventh and Twelfth Centuries* (Princeton: Princeton University Press, 1983), 273–287.

5. Denzinger, *Enchiridion symbolorum* (Freiburg, 1911), n. 690. The declaration is presented somewhat misleadingly as an example of crass literalism by Marilyn McCord Adams in her interesting and lucid work on scholastic interpretations of the Eucharist. McCord Adams, *Some Later Medieval Theories of the Eucharist: Thomas Aquinas, Giles of Rome, Duns Scotus, and William Ockham* (Oxford: Oxford University Press, 2010), 260–262.

6. Hildebert of Lavardin, Ser. 93, in PL 171: 776. Some claim that it should be attributed to Petrus Comestor. See James T. O'Connor, *The Hidden Manna: A Theology of the Eucharist* (San Francisco: Ignatius Press, 1988), 182nn21, 22. Joseph Goering has published a text ascribed to William de Montibus or his circle where the invention of the term is attributed to Robert Pullan (who died in 1146). However, unless the attribution of sermon 93 is put in doubt, it would seem that Hildebert's usage is earlier. See Joseph Goering, "The Invention of Transubstantiation," *Traditio* 46 (1991): 147–170.

7. Denzinger, *Enchiridion symbolorum*, 802; *Liber Extra* 1.1.3 (*De summa trinitate et fide catholica*).

8. Petrus Comestor, *De corpore et sanguine domini* 8, in *De sacramentis*, ed. R. M. Martin (Louvain, 1937), 37.

9. See Miri Rubin, *Corpus Christi: The Eucharist in Late Medieval Culture* (Cambridge: Cambridge University Press, 1991), 118–129.

10. Ibid., 120–122. The story became hugely popular in the Later Middle Ages, in both art and literature.

11 See Caroline Walker Bynum, *Wonderful Blood: Theology and Practice in Late Medieval Northern Germany and Beyond* (Philadelphia: University of Pennsylvania Press, 2008), 26–45, 54–55. See also James J. Mcgivern, *Concomitance and Communion: A Study in Eucharistic Doctrine and Practice* (Fribourg, 1963).

12. McCord Adams, *Some Later Medieval Theories*, 86, 269–270; Innocent III, *De sacro altaris mysterio*, 10 (*Il sacrosanto mystero*, 272).

13. Innocent III, *De sacro altaris mysterio*, 7–8 (*Il sacrosanto mystero*, 266–68). Innocent compares the host to a mirror broken to pieces where in each the entire image is reflected.

14. Cited in Caroline Walker Bynum, *Christian Materiality: An Essay on Religion in Late Medieval Europe* (New York: Zone, 2011), 15. See also Ann W. Astell, *Eating Beauty: The Eucharist and the Spiritual Arts of the Middle Ages* (Ithaca: Cornell University Press, 2006), 27–61.

15. Innocent III, *Il sacrosanto mystero*, xxxiv.

16. Guitmund of Aversa, *De corporis et sanguinis Christi veritate*, in *La "verità" dell'eucharisia*, ed. and trans. L. Orabona (Naples: Edizioni Scientifiche Italiane, 1995), 142–144. "Species" is the "accidental" reality of being that is directly accessible to the senses, as distinct from the substance in which it is rooted. On Guitmund, see Stock, *The Implications of Literacy*, 309–315.

17. St. Albert the Great, IV Sent. D. 13 a. 38.

18. Innocent III, *De sacro altaris mysterio*, 34 (*Il sacrosanto mystero*, 316).

19. Ambrose of Milan, *De sacramentis* 6.1.3. This text is cited almost verbatim by Gratian in his *Decretum* (De cons. D. 2 c. 43).

20. Petrus Comestor, *De corpore et sanguine domini* 8, in *De sacramentis*, edited by R. M. Martin (Louvain, 1937), 37; *De sacro altaris mysterio*, 34 (*Il sacrosanto mystero*, 316): "*ad vitandum ridiculum.*" See also *vitae partum* 18.3 PL 73: 979–980.

21. Bonaventure, *Sent.*, in *Opera Omnia* (Quaracchi: S. Bonaventura, 1883–1902), 4, D. 12, p.1, art. 3, q. 1, conclusio, 4:283–284; Thomas Aquinas, *Sent.*, 4, D. 12, q. 1, art. 1–4.

22. See Innocent III, *De sacro altaris mysterio*, 34 (*Il sacrosanto mystero*, 316); Bonaventure, *Sent.*, 4, D. 10, p. 1, q. 1., art. 4; 4:217.

23. See Jeremy Cohen, *Christ Killers: The Jews and the Passion from the Bible to the Big Screen* (Oxford: Oxford University Press, 2007), 103–117.

24. William of Middleton (Guillelmus de Militona), *Quaestiones de sacramentis*, ed. G. Gal (Florence: Quaracchi, 1961), tract. 4. q. 59, pars 8; 2:734–735. For a shorter discussion see, Aquinas, *Summa Theologiae*, 3, q. 81, art. 1. The same arguments are made by Alexander of Hales and by Richard Fishacre in their commentaries on the *Sentences* and by William of Auxerre in his *Summa aurea*.

25. For example, Aquinas, *Summa Theologiae*, 3, q. 73, a. 3, ad secundum. See McCord Adams, *Some Later Medieval Theories*, 266.

26. Gerald of Wales, *The Jewel of the Church*, trans. by J. J. Hagen (Leiden, Brill, 1979), 45, pp. 93–94. The story appears in the Life of St. Norbert of Xanten who is sometimes shown with a spider and a chalice. See *Vita Norberti* 3.18, in PL 170:1268.

27. Petrus Comestor, *De corpore et sanguine domini* 25, in *De sacramentis*, 156.

28. Guitmund of Aversa, *La "verità" dell'eucharisia*, 138–140.

29. Innocent III, *De sacro altaris mysterio*, 11 (*Il sacrosanto mystero*, 272–274). See also McCord Adams, *Some Later Medieval Theories*, 192–195.

30. Rubin, *Gentile Tales: The Narrative Assault on Late Medieval Jews* (New Haven: Yale University Press, 1999), 33; Cohen, *Christ Killers*, 107.

31. Gratian, *Decretum*, de Cons. D. 2, non iste panis.

32. Petrus Comestor, *De corpore et sanguine domini*, 24, 56. Innocent III discussion of this is an almost verbatim repetition of Comestor's. Innocent III, *De sacro altaris mysterio*, 15 (*Il sacrosanto mystero*, 284–286). See also McCord Adams, *Some Later Medieval Theories*, 192–195.

33. Bonaventure, *Sent.*, 4., D. 12, p. 1, art. 3, q. 1, conclusio, ad 3, 4:284.

34. Susan Michele Carroll-Clark, "The Practical Summa *Ad instructionem iuniorum* of Simon of Hinton, O.P.: Text and Context" (PhD diss., University of Toronto, 1999), 135–136.

35. *Decretum*, de Cons. D. 2, non iste panis.

10. Untouchable

1. Aristotle, *Nicomachean Ethics*, 1118b. However, touch also serves Aristotle as a metaphor for the intellectual process. See Stanley Rosen, "Thought and Touch: A Note on Aristotle's *De Anima*," in *The Quarrel Between Philosophy and Poetry: Studies in Ancient Thought* (New York: Routledge, 1988), 119–126.

2. Maimonides, *Guide of the Perplexed*, 2.36; Maimonides, *The Guide of the Perplexed*, trans. Shlomo Pines (Chicago: University of Chicago Press, 1963).

3. Thomas H. Ogden, "On the Concept of an Autistic-Contiguous Position," *International Journal of Psychoanalysis* 70 (1989): 128.

4. Glenn Most has dedicated an entire book to the fact that while he believes that the text clearly indicates that Thomas did not in fact stick his finger into the wound in Christ's side, most artists chose to depict him as if he did. See Glenn W. Most, *Doubting Thomas* (Cambridge, Mass.: Harvard University Press, 2007).

5. Augustine, *In Iohannis evangelium tract.* 124, 121.5, in CCSL 36:667–668.

6. φέρε τὴν χεῖρά σου καὶ βάλε εἰς τὴν πλευράν μου.

7. Caroline Walker Bynum, *Jesus as Mother: Studies in the Spirituality of the High Middle Ages* (Berkeley: University of California Press, 1982). However, see Karma Lochrie, "Mystical Acts, Queer Tendencies," in *Constructing Medieval Sexuality*, ed. K. Lochrie et al. (Minneapolis: University of Minnesota Press, 1997), 180–200. Lochrie argues that the mystical devotion to the wound of Christ involves not only seeing and kissing (or drinking), but also erotic penetration. The sole textual example that she discusses in connection with this particular claim, the *Stimulus amoris* of James of Milan, does use erotic imagery and does speak of the wound as entry gate. However, there are no images of penetration. The entry gate imagery is clearly allegorical. The more plastic images refer to "joining" the wounds of the mystic and Christ.

8. See the classic study of Herbert Thurston, *The Physical Phenomena of Mysticism* (London: Burns Oates, 1952).

9. For a discussion of the way artists reshape the miracle through their representations, see Arnold I. Davidson, "Miracles of Bodily Transformation, Or How St. Francis Received the Stigmata," *Critical Inquiry* 35 (2009): 451–480. See also Carolyn Muessig, "The Stigmata Debate in Theology and Art in the Late Middle Ages," in *The Authority of the Word: Reflecting on Image and Text in Northern Europe, 1400–1700*, ed. C. Brusati, K. Enenkel, and W. S. Melion (Leiden: Brill, 2012), 481–504; Chiara Frugoni, *Francesco e l'invenzione delle stimmate: Una storia per parole e immagini fino a Bonaventura e Giotto* (Turin: Einaudi, 1993).

10. All early sources assert that Francis made an effort to conceal his stigmata and refused to talk about them even with his closest friends. Thomas of Celano's *First Life* mentions two who bear witness to Francis's wounds during his lifetime—his successor and close friend Brother Elias and Brother Rufino, another of the saint's close companions, who accidentally touched the side wound. See 1 CL 95. *The Second Life of Thomas*, written at the request of the Order's authorities between 1246 and 1247, mentions two more eyewitnesses—Brother Pacifico and a certain unnamed friar from Brescia. The chronicler, Thomas of Eccleston, notes that a certain Brother Bonizo was invited to testify to the truth of the stigmata at the general

chapter of Genoa in 1251. See Thomas of Eccleston, *De adventu fratrum minorum in Angliam*, ed. A. G. Little (Manchester: Manchester University Press), 74.

11. Kajetan Esser, *Opuscula S. Francisci* (Grottaferrata: Collegium S. Bonaventurae, 1978), 89–93. For a comprehensive discussion of the early sources concerning the stigmata, see Octavian Schmucki, *The Stigmata of St. Francis of Assisi: A Critical Investigation in the Light of Thirteenth-Century Sources*, trans. C. F. Connors (St. Bonaventure, N.Y.: St. Bonaventure University, 1991). Jacques Dalarun believes that this text is Leo's late reconstruction of the event. See Jacques Dalarun, "The Great Secret of Francis," in *The Stigmata of St. Francis of Assisi: New Studies, New Perspectives*, ed. Jacques Dalarun et al. (Ashland, Ohio: Franciscan Institute Publications, 2006), 23–25. For earlier uses of "stigmatic spirituality," see Carolyn Muessig, "Signs of Salvation: The Evolution of Stigmatic Spirituality Before Francis of Assisi," *Church History* 82, no. 1 (2013): 40–68.

12. 1 CL 113. See also Celano, *Tractatus de miraculis* 2.5. Bonaventure, in LM 13.8, speaks of great multitudes, but the only name he gives is that of Pope Alexander IV, who stated that he had seen the stigmata on Francis's corpse. Later (in LM 15.4), he mentions a certain Jerome, who, doubting the truth of the miracle, like Thomas, touched the marks of Christ's wounds (*vulnerum Christi*) in the hands, feet, and side, with his finger. Here again, there is reference to many unnamed witnesses. For a discussion of the problem of verification, see Roberto Rusconi, "La verità dei segni ovvero i segni della verità," in *Gian Luca Potestà, Autorität und Wahrheit: Kirchliche Verstellungen, Normen und Verfahren 13–15 Jahrhundert* (Oldenburg: Wissenschaftsverlag, 2012), 45–53.

13. *Francis of Assisi: Early Documents*, ed. Regis J. Armstrong, 3 vols. (New York: New City Press, 1998), 2:770–771.

14. 1 CL 94–95.

15. St. Bonaventure, the saint's biographer and a trained theologian, noted this is his description of the stigmata. LM 13.3.

16. Stanislao da Campagnola, *L'angelo del sesto sigillo e l'"Alter Christus": Genesi e sviluppop di due temi francescani nei secoli XIII–XIV* (Rome: Laurentinianum, 1971). See also Marjorie Reeves, *The Influence of Prophecy in the Later Middle Ages* (Oxford: University of Notre Dame Press, 1969); Delno C. West and S. Zimdras-Swartz, *Joachim of Fiore: A Study in Spiritual Perception and History* (Bloomington: Indiana University Press, 1983).

17. 1 CL 89.

18. Until recently, it was assumed that the unprecedented nature of the stigmata finds expression in the encyclical letter of Francis's successor as minister general, Brother Elias: "I bring you glad tidings, a new thing among miracles, a sign

never before seen, except in the Son of God. Shortly before his death, our brother and father was seen crucified, bearing in his flesh five wounds, the stigmata of Christ." Recently, the authenticity of the version known to us as the encyclical letter of Elias has been called into question. It has been suggested that the letter is a later rephrasing of a lost original, reflecting, rather than influencing, Celano's *First Life*. See *Francis of Assisi: Early Documents*, 2:485–488.

19. 2 CL 11. The suggestion that the wounds were not an external intervention, but a manifestation of internal love is interesting, though Celano does not develop it, and later suggests an external source—the Seraphic Christ.

20. 1 CL 112–14.

21. 1 CL 115.

22. 2 CL 219.

23. André Vauchez, "Les stigmates de Saint François et leurs détracteurs," *Mélanges d'archeologie et d'histoire Ecole Fraçaise de Rome* 80:619–623.

24. Scripta Leonis, *Rufini et Angeli Sociorum S. Francisci*, ed. and trans. Rosalind B. Brooke (Oxford: Clarendon Press, 1970), 85.

25. Aviad Kleinberg, *Prophets in Their Own Country: Living Saints and the Making of Sainthood in the Later Middle Ages* (Chicago: University of Chicago Press, 1992), 126–148.

26. Francis's own notion of imitation deserves a separate study. At this point, it might be enough to say that while Francis expected his followers to follow exactly in his footsteps, his idea of following Christ was much freer. Thus, Francis insists that not only his strict poverty but also his begging of alms is an imitation of Christ's. Yet the scriptural Christ seems to have renounced asceticism altogether and is never described in the Gospels as begging. And yet in the Rule of 1221, Francis insists that Christ "was poor and he had no home of his own and he lived on alms, he and the Blessed Virgin and his disciples." Rule of 1221, c. 9.

27. LM, prologus, 2.

28. LM 13.3. See also LM 9.2: "in quem optabat per excessivi amoris incendium totaliter transformari."

29. Bonaventure, *Itinerarium mentis in deum*, trans. Philotheus Boehner (St. Bonaventure, N.Y.: St. Bonaventure University, 1956), prol. 3., p. 33.

30. I. Doellinger, *Beiträge zur Sektengeschichte*, 2 vols. (Munich, 1890), 2:540. See also Bernardino of Siena: "transformatus est in crucifixum Iesum, ut miraculo inaudito seculis, benignitas salvatoris in carne illius imprimeret similitudinem suae sacratissimae passionis, constituens eum vexilliferum in nova rememoratione crucifixionis eius." Bernardino of Siena, Sermo 59, "de stigmatibus sacris gloriosi Francisci," in *Opera omnia* (Quarrachi, 1950–1965), 5:204.

31. Cited by Stanislao da Campagnola, *L'angelo del sesto sigilo*, 190.

32. *Analecta Franciscana*, vols. 4–5 (Quarrachi, 1906, 1912). See Achim Wesjohann, *Mendikantische Gründungserzählungen im 13. und 14. Jahrhundert: Mythen als Element institutioneller Eigengeschichtsschreibung der mittelalterlichen Franziskaner, Dominikaner und Augustiner-Eremiten* (Berlin: Lit, 2012), 125.

33. On the work's success in manuscripts and prints see the introduction to the second volume of the work in *Analecta Franciscana*, 5:xlv–ci.

34. De conformitate, in *Analecta Franciscana*, 4:8. See also 4:18.

35. Ibid., 4:10.

36. This argument is repeated, without reference to Bartholomew, by Augustine Thompson in his recent, very problematic "new biography" of the saint: Thompson, *Francis of Assisi: A New Biography* (Ithaca: Cornell University Press, 2012), 117–118. An earlier proponent of this view was Agostino Gemelli, a Franciscan physician and first rector of the Catholic University of the Sacred Heart in Milan: Gemelli, "Le stimmate di S. Francesco nel giudizio della scienza," *Vita e Pensiero* 10, no. 10 (1924): 580–603.

37. *Analecta Franciscana*, 4:13–15. The same arguments are repeated with much greater length in 5:369–414. The discussion of St. John is in 383–384.

38. Ibid., 4:15.

39. Ibid., 4:40.

11. Inaudible

1. A reference to *Song of Songs* 5:16: "His mouth is sweet."

2. See also *Bab. Tal.*, *Shabbath*, 88b where Rabbi Yehoshua argues that it was divine dew that revived the dead Israelites.

3. See Michael Fishbane, "The Holy One Seats and Roars: Mythopoesis and the Midrashic Imagination," in *The Exegetical Imagination: On Jewish Thought and Theology* (Cambridge, Mass.: Harvard University Press, 1998), 22–40.

4. *De Decalogo*, 9 in *The Works of Philo Judaeus*, trans. C. D. Yonge, 4 vols. (London: H. G. Bohn, 1854–1890), 3:143–144.

5. See also David Chidester's discussion of the relation between voice and sound in the thought of Philo: Chidester, *Word and Light: Seeing, Hearing, and Religious Discourse* (Urbana: University of Illinois Press, 1992), 30–43.

6. Yehuda Halevi, *Kitab al Khazari*, trans. H. Hirschfeld (London, Routledge, 1905), 1:87, pp. 60–61.

7. Ibid., 1:88–89, pp. 62–63.

8. See Haim Kreisel, "The 'Voice of God' in Medieval Philosophical Exegesis" [Hebrew], *Daat* 16 (1986): 29–38.

9. Maimonides, *Guide of the Perplexed* 1:65; Maimonides, *Guide of the Perplexed*, trans. Shlomo Pines (Chicago: University of Chicago Press, 1963). Translation slightly modified.

10. *Bab. Tal., Makot*, 24a.

11. Maimonides, *Guide of the Perplexed*, 2:33.

12. Ibid., 2:364–365.

13. Ibid., 2:365.

14. Ibid., 1:21.

15. Maimonides refers to Moses's request to see the face of God in Exodus 33:23.

16. The translator of the Bible to Aramaic who, whenever God is referred to in material terms, adds references to God's "glory" or "word."

17. Exodus 34:6: "And Jehovah passed by before his face."

18. "And Jehovah said to Moses: pass before the people."

19. Maimonides, *Guide of the Perplexed*, 1:21.

20. Ibid., 2:33.

21. Ibid. (emphasis added).

22. Ibid.

23. *Mekhilta of Rabbi Ishmael*, tract. "Shira" 3.

24. *Deutromomy Rabbah*, Devarim 15.

25. Alan of Lille, *De Fide Catholica*, 1.30, in PL 210:333.

12. Scentless

1. *Gilgamesh* tablet 11, lines 160–162.

2. See the excellent discussion of smell in the ancient Jewish tradition in Deborah A. Green, *The Aroma of Righteousness: Scent and Seduction in Rabbinic Life and Literature* (University Park: Pennsylvania State University Press, 2011), 64–83.

3. Naturally, taste is the exception. People have no reason to taste God—unless as sacrifice, as we saw in chapter 9.

4. See Diane Ackerman, *A Natural History of the Senses* (New York: Vintage, 1990), 5–64.

5. William Ian Miller, *The Anatomy of Disgust* (Cambridge Mass.: Harvard University Press, 1997), 67.

6. Constance Classen et al., *Aroma: The Cultural History of Smell* (London: Routledge, 1994), 45–48; Henry Cadbury, "The Odor of the Spirit at Pentecost," *Journal of Biblical Literature* 47, no. 3/4 (1928): 241–243; Susan Ashbrook

Harvey, *Scenting Salvation: Ancient Christianity and the Olfactory Imagination* (Berkeley: University of California Press, 2006), 11–30, 172–173; Marcel Detienne, *The Gardens of Adonis: Spices in Greek Mythology*, trans. J. Lloyd (Atlantic Highlands, N.J.: Humanities Press, 1977); Saara Lilja, *The Treatment of Odours in the Poetry of Antiquity* (Helsinki: Societas Scientiarum Fennica, 1972); Jean Delumeau, *Une histoire de paradis*, 3 vols. (Paris: Fayard, 2000), 3:146–149.

7. Josephus, *Antiquities* 8.4.1.

8. Severus of Minorca, *Letter on the Conversion of the Jews*, ed. and trans. Scott Bradbury (Oxford: Oxford University Press, 1996), 20–26, pp. 110–121. For other examples, see Harvey, *Scenting Salvation*, 125–134; Jean-Pierre Albert, *Odeurs de sainté: La mythologie Chrétienne des aromates* (Paris: EHESS, 1996).

9. On the stench of sin, see Harvey, *Scenting Salvation*, 206–210.

10. Origen refers to a specific odor of Christ in his discussion of the Sinful Woman anointing the feet of Christ: she acquired "the odor not so much of the ointment as of the very Word of God, and what she has put on her own head is the fragrance of Christ rather than that of the nard." Origen, *The Song of Songs: Commentary and Homilies*, trans. R. P. Lawson (New York: Newman Press, 1956), 160, cited by Harvey, *Scenting Salvation*, 174. However, given Origen's allegorical approach, it is unlikely that he understands this fragrance to be physical.

11. See Harvey, *Scenting Salvation*, 11–12, 227–229; Herbert Thurston, *The Physical Phenomena of Mysticism* (London: Burns and Oates, 1952), 222–232.

12. Venantius Fortunatus, *Opera poetica* 5.5, in MGH AA 4.1, p. 110.

13. *The Chronicle of Zuqnin Parts III and IV, A.D. 488–775*, trans. A. Harrak (Toronto: PIMS, 1999), 324.

14. Joshua Trachtenberg, *The Devil and the Jews: The Medieval Conception of the Jew and Its Relation to Modern Antisemitism* (New Haven: Yale University Press, 1943), 47–50; Israel Levi, "Le Juif de la légende," *Revue des études juives* 20 (1890): 249. "Foetor Judaicus" is discussed in my analysis of the conversion of Catherine of Parc-aux-Dames: Kleinberg, "A Thirteenth Century Struggle Over Custody: The Case of Catherine of Parc-aux-Dames," *Bulletin of Medieval Canon Law* 20 (1990): 53–70.

15. The Hebrew term has strong sexual connotations.

16. *Avot de Rabbi Natan* 16.b.

17. *Libellus de Principiis Ordinis Praedicatorum*, 110–119, in MOPH 16, ed. H. C. Scheeben (Rome: Institutum Historicum Fratrum Praedicatorum, 1935). Parts of my discussion in this chapter were published in Aviad Kleinberg, "The Possession of Blessed Jordan of Saxony," in *Medieval Christianity in Practice*, ed. M. Rubin (Princeton: Princeton University Press, 2009), 265–273.

18. *Libellus*, 110; MOPH 16:77.

19. *Libellus*, 115; MOPH 16:79.

20. *Libellus*, 113–114; MOPH 16:78.

21. *Libellus*, 116; MOPH 16:80.

22. *Libellus*, 117; MOPH 16:80.

23. *Libellus*, 115; MOPH 16:79.

24. *Libellus*, 117; MOPH 16:80.

25. *Libellus*, 118; MOPH 16:80–81.

26. *Libellus*, 119; MOPH 16:81.

27. It is ironic that the most conspicuous miracle of St. Dominic was the wonderful smell that erupted from his tomb when it was opened. Thus, Brother Ventura of Verona testifies that when the tomb was opened, "a marvelous and most sweet odor came out of it, unfamiliar to any of those present; it seemed to be more powerful than any aroma [familiar to them], nor did it seem to have the smell of anything human." *Acta canonizations S. Dominici* 10, in MOPH 16:131. One must note Jordan was not quick to believe miracles. He notes, for example, that though many reports of Dominic's posthumous miracles have reached him, he does not write them down since they are too often inconsistent with one another (*Libellus*, 99; MOPH 16:72). Such pedantry was not common among medieval writers.

28. See Dyan Elliott, "Seeing Double: John Gerson, the Discernment of Spirits and Joan of Arc," *American Historical Review* 197, no. 1 (2002): 26–54; Nancy Cacciola, *Discerning Spirits: Divine and Demonic Possession in the Middle Ages* (Ithaca: Cornell University Press, 2003). One must read Cacciola with the greatest caution, as her whole thesis of double possession is highly unconvincing. See also Wendy Love Anderson, *The Discernment of Spirits: Assessing Visions and Visionaries in the Late Middle Ages* (Tübingen: Mohr Siebeck, 2011).

POST SCRIPTUM

1. Leszek Kolakowski, *Religion: If There Is No God . . . : On God, the Devil, Sin and Other Worries of the So-called Philosophy of Religion* (South Bend, Ind.: St. Augustine's Press, 2001), 55. The book was originally published by Oxford University Press in 1982.

2. Ibid., 215.

BIBLIOGRAPHY

Abbreviations

ı CL   Thomas of Celano, *Vita prima S. Francisci*
2 CL   Thomas of Celano, *Vita secunda S. Francisci*
AF   Analecta Franciscana
Bab. Tal. Babylonian Talmud
CCSL   Corpus Christianorum Series Latina
CSEL   Corpus Scriptorum Ecclesiasticorum Latinorum
LM   Bonaventure, *Legenda major*
MGH   Monumenta Germaniae Historica
MOPH   Monumenta Ordinis fratrum Praedicatorum Historica
PG   Patrologia Graeca
PL   Patrologia Latina

Primary and Secondary Sources

Abelard, Peter. *Historia calamitatum*. Edited by J. Monfrin. Paris: Vrin, 1959.
——. *The Story of Abelard's Adversities*. Translated by J. T. Muckle. Toronto: Pontifical Institute of Mediaeval Studies, 1964.

Ackerman, Diane. *A Natural History of the Senses.* New York: Vintage, 1990.

Advaita Vedanta. *A Sourcebook of Advaita Vedanta.* Edited by Eliot Deutschand and J. A. B. Van Buitenen. Honolulu: University of Hawaii Press, 1971.

Alan of Lille. *De fide Catholica.* PL 210:305–430.

Albert, Jean-Pierre. *Odeurs de sainteté: La mythologie Chrétienne des aromates.* Paris: EHESS, 1996.

Albert the Great. *Opera Omnia.* Münster: Aschendorff, 1951– .

Aquinas, Thomas. *Summa Theologiae.* 4 vols. Edited by P. Caramello. Turin: Marietti, 1952–1956.

Astell, Ann W. *Eating Beauty: The Eucharist and the Spiritual Arts of the Middle Ages.* Ithaca: Cornell University Press, 2006.

Augustine. *Confessiones.* Edited by J. O'Donnell. 3 vols. Oxford: Oxford University Press, 1992, 2000.

——. *Confessions.* Translated by Henry Chadwick. Oxford: Oxford University Press, 1991.

——. *Contra epistulam Manichaei quam Vocant Fundamenti.* CSEL 25:191–248.

——. *De doctrina Christiana.* CCSL 32.

——. *De genesi ad litteram.* CSEL 28.

——. *De trinitate.* CCSL 50.

——. *In Johannis evangelium tractatus CXXIV.* CCSL 36.

Bartholomew of Pisa. *De conformitate vitae Beati Francisci ad vitam Domini Iesu Christi.* In *Analecta Franciscana,* vols. 4–5. Quarrachi, 1906, 1912.

Belting, Hans. *Likeness and Presence: A History of the Image Before the Era of Art.* Translated by E. Jephcott. Chicago: University of Chicago Press, 1994.

Bernard of Clairvaux. *Sermones in cantica.* Sources Chrétiennes 414, 431, 452, 472.

Bernardino of Siena. *Opera Omnia.* Vol. 5. Quarrachi, 1950–1965.

Bigham, Steven. *The Image of God the Father in Orthodox Iconography.* Torrance, Calif.: Oakwood, 1995.

Bonaventure. *Itinerarium mentis in deum.* Translated by P. Boehner. Saint Bonaventure, N.Y.: Franciscan Institute, 1956.

——. *Opera Omnia.* Quaracchi: S. Bonaventura, 1883–1902.

The Book of Kindred Sayings. 5 vols. Translated by C. A. F. Rhys Davids and F. L. Woodward. 1917; Oxford: Oxford University Press, 1993.

Boyarin, Daniel. "The Eye in the Torah: Ocular Desire in Midrashic Hermeneutic." *Critical Inquiry* 16, no. 3 (1990): 532–550.

Bynum, Caroline Walker. *Christian Materiality: An Essay on Religion in Late Medieval Europe.* New York: Zone, 2011.

———. *Jesus as Mother: Studies in the Spirituality of the High Middle Ages*. Berkeley: University of California Press, 1982.

———. *The Resurrection of the Body in Western Christianity, 200–1336*. New York: Columbia University Press, 1995.

———. *Wonderful Blood: Theology and Practice in Late Medieval Northern Germany and Beyond*. Philadelphia: University of Pennsylvania Press, 2008.

Cacciola, Nancy. *Discerning Spirits: Divine and Demonic Possession in the Middle Ages*. Ithaca: Cornell University Press, 2003.

Cadbury, Henry. "The Odor of the Spirit at Pentecost." *Journal of Biblical Literature* 47, no. 3/4 (1928): 237–256.

Carroll-Clark, Susan Michele. "The Practical Summa *Ad instructionem iuniorum* of Simon of Hinton, O.P.: Text and Context." PhD diss., University of Toronto, 1999.

Chidester, David. *Word and Light: Seeing, Hearing, and Religious Discourse*. Urbana: University of Illinois Press, 1992.

The Chronicle of Zuqnin Parts III and IV, A.D. 488–775. Translated by A. Harrak. Toronto: PIMS, 1999.

Chrysostom, Dio. "The Twelfth, or Olympic, Discourse." In *Discourses 12–30*, translated by J. W. Cohoon. Loeb Classical Library 339. Cambridge, Mass.: Harvard University Press, 1939.

Chrysostom, John. *On the Incomprehensible Nature of God*. Translated by P. W. Harkins. Fathers of the Church 72. Washington D.C.: Catholic University of America Press, 1984.

Classen, Constance, et al. *Aroma: The Cultural History of Smell*. London: Routledge, 1994.

Clement of Alexandria. *Christ the Educator*. Translated by S. P. Wood. Fathers of the Church 23. New York: Catholic University of America Press, 1954.

Cohen, Jeremy. *Christ Killers: The Jews and the Passion from the Bible to the Big Screen*. Oxford: Oxford University Press, 2007.

The Collection of the Middle-Length Sayings. 3 vols. Translated by I. B. Horner. London: Pali Text Society, 1954.

Comestor, Petrus. *De sacramentis*. Edited by R. M. Martin. Louvain, 1937.

Coolman, Boyd Taylor. *Knowing God by Experience: The Spiritual Senses in the Theology of William of Auxerre*. Washington, D.C.: Catholic University of America Press, 2004.

Da Campagnola, Stanislao. *L'angelo del sesto sigillo e l' "Alter Christus": Genesi e sviluppo di due temi francescani nei secoli XIII–XIV*. Rome: Laurentinianum, 1971.

Dagron, Gilbert. "Holy Images and Likeness." *Dumbarton Oaks Papers* 45 (1991): 23–33.

Dalarun, Jacques. "The Great Secret of Francis." In *The Stigmata of St. Francis of Assisi: New Studies, New Perspectives*, edited by Jacques Dalarun et al., 9–26. Ashland, Ohio: Franciscan Institute, 2006.

Dan, Joseph. *History of Jewish Mysticism and Esotericism* [Hebrew]. Jerusalem: Shazar, 2009– .

Davidson, Arnold I. "Miracles of Bodily Transformation, or How St. Francis Received the Stigmata." *Critical Inquiry* 35 (2009): 451–480.

Delumeau, Jean. *Une histoire de paradis*. 3 vols. Paris: Fayard, 2000.

Denzinger, *Enchiridion symbolorum*. Freiburg, 1911.

Detienne, Marcel. *The Gardens of Adonis: Spices in Greek Mythology*. Translated by J. Lloyd. Atlantic Highlands, N.J.: Humanities Press, 1977.

Doellinger, I. *Beiträge zur Sektengeschichte*. Munich: Beck, 1890.

Dominic, *Acta canonizations S. Dominici*. Edited by A. Waltz. MOPH 16 (1935): 88–194.

Eilberg-Schwartz, Howard. *God's Phallus: And Other Problems for Men and Monotheism*. Boston: Beacon, 1994.

Elliott, Dyan. "Seeing Double: John Gerson, the Discernment of Spirits and Joan of Arc." *American Historical Review* 197, no. 1 (2002): 26–54.

Esser, Kajetan. *Opuscula S. Francisci*. Grottaferrata: Collegium S. Bonaventurae, 1978.

Fishbane, Michael, "The Holy One Seats and Roars: Mythopoesis and the Midrashic Imagination." In *The Exegetical Imagination: On Jewish Thought and Theology*, 22–40. Cambridge, Mass.: Harvard University Press, 1998.

Foucart, George "Names (Primitive)." In *Encyclopedia of Religion and Ethics* 9:130–136.

Francis of Assisi: Early Documents. Edited by Regis J. Armstrong. 3 vols. New York: New City Press, 1998.

Frugoni, Chiara. *Francesco e l'invenzione delle stimmate: Una storia per parole e immagini fino a Bonaventura e Giotto*. Turin: Einaudi, 1993.

Gavrilyuk, Paul L. *The Suffering of the Impassible God: The Dialectics of Patristic Thought*. Oxford: Oxford University Press, 2004.

Gavrilyuk, Paul L., and Sarah Coakley, eds. *The Spiritual Senses: Perceiving God in Western Christianity*. Cambridge: Cambridge University Press, 2012.

Gemelli, Agostino. "Le stimmate di S. Francesco nel giudizio della scienza." *Vita e Pensiero* 10, no. 10 (1924): 580–603.

Gerald of Wales. *The Jewel of the Church*. Translated by J. J. Hagen. Leiden: Brill, 1979.

Gero, S. "The True Image of Christ: Eusebius's Letter to Constantia Reconsidered." *Journal of Theological Studies* 32 (1981): 460–470.

Goering, Joseph. "The Invention of Transubstantiation." *Traditio* 46 (1991): 147–170.

Goshen Gottstein, Alon. "The Body as Image of God in Rabbinic Literature." *Harvard Theological Review* 87, no. 2 (1994): 171–195.

Green, Deborah A. *The Aroma of Righteousness: Scent and Seduction in Rabbinic Life and Literature.* University Park: Pennsylvania State University Press, 2011.

Gregory of Nyssa. "The Lord's Prayer." PG 44:1119–1193.

Gregory the Great. *Registrum.* CCSL 140a.

Guitmund of Aversa. *De corporis et sanguinis Christi veritate.* In *La "verità" dell'eucharistia*, edited and translated by L. Orabona. Naples: Edizioni Scientifiche Italiane, 1995.

Halbertal, Moshe. *Maimonides* [Hebrew]. Jerusalem: Zalman Shazar Center, 2009.

——. "Were It Not Written, It Would Be Impossible to Utter" [Hebrew]. *Tarbiz* 68a (1999): 39–59.

Halevi, Yehuda. *Kitab al Khazari.* Translated by H. Hirschfeld. London: Routledge, 1905.

Harvey, Susan Ashbrook. *Scenting Salvation: Ancient Christianity and the Olfactory Imagination.* Berkeley: University of California Press, 2006.

Honorius of Autun. *Elucidarium.* PL 172.

Ignatius of Loyola. *The Spiritual Exercises, and Selected Works.* Edited and translated by G. E. Ganss. New York: Paulist, 1991.

Innocent III. *Il sacrosanto mystero dell'altare (De sacro altaris mysterio).* Edited and translated by S. Fioramonti. Vatican City: Libreria Editrice Vaticana, 2002.

Innocent IV. *Commentaria in quinque libros decretalium.* Frankfurt, 1570.

Jean de Montclos. *Lanfranc et Bérenger: La controverse eucharistique du XIe siècle.* Louvain: Spicilegium sacrum Lovaniense, 1971.

Jensen, Robin Margaret. *Face to Face: Portraits of the Divine in Early Christianity.* Minneapolis: Fortress, 2005.

John of Damascus. *Three Treatises on the Divine Images.* Translated by A. Louth. Crestwood, N.Y.: St. Vladimir's Seminary Press, 2003.

Jordan of Saxony. *Libellus de Principiis Ordinis Praedicatorum.* Edited by H. C. Scheeben. MOPH 16. Rome: Institutum Historicum Fratrum Praedicatorum, 1935.

Kant, Immanuel. *Conflict of the Faculties.* Translated by Mary J. Gregor. New York: Abaris Books, 1979.

Kessler, Herbert L. "Gregory the Great and Image Theory in Northern Europe During the Twelfth and Thirteenth Centuries." In *A Companion to Medieval*

Art: Romanesque and Gothic in Northern Europe, edited by Conrad Rudolph, 151–172. Malden, Mass. Blackwell, 2006.

——. *Spiritual Seeing: Picturing God's Invisibility in Medieval Art*. Philadelphia: University of Pennsylvania Press, 2000.

Kleinberg, Aviad. *Flesh Made Word: Saints Stories and the Western Imagination*. Translated by J. M. Todd. Cambridge Mass.: Harvard University Press, 2008.

——. "The Possession of Blessed Jordan of Saxony." In *Medieval Christianity in Practice*, edited by M. Rubin, 265–273. Princeton: Princeton University Press, 2009.

——. *Prophets in Their Own Country: Living Saints and the Making of Sainthood in the Later Middle Ages*. Chicago: University of Chicago Press, 1992.

——. "A Thirteenth Century Struggle Over Custody: The Case of Catherine of Parc-aux-Dames." *Bulletin of Medieval Canon Law* 20 (1990): 53–70.

Kolakowski, Leszek. *Religion: If There Is No God . . . : On God, the Devil, Sin and Other Worries of the So-Called Philosophy of Religion*. South Bend, Ind.: St. Augustine's Press, 2001.

Kreisel, Haim. "The 'Voice of God' in Medieval Philosophical Exegesis" [Hebrew]. *Daat* 16 (1986): 29–38.

Levi, Israel. "Le Juif de la légende." *Revue des études juives* 20 (1890): 249–252.

Liebes, Yehuda. "Natura Dei: The Jewish Myth and Its Transmutations." In *God's Story: Collected Essays on the Jewish Myth* [Hebrew], 35–117. Jerusalem: Carmel, 2008.

Lilja, Saara. *The Treatment of Odours in the Poetry of Antiquity*. Helsinki: Societas Scientiarum Fennica, 1972.

Lochrie, Karma. "Mystical Acts, Queer Tendencies." In *Constructing Medieval Sexuality*, edited by K. Lochrie et al., 180–200. Minneapolis: University of Minnesota Press, 1997.

Lootens, Matthew R. "Augustine." In *The Spiritual Senses: Perceiving God in Western Christianity*, edited by Paul L. Gavrilyuk and Sarah Coakley, 56–70. Cambridge: Cambridge University Press, 2012.

Lorberbaum, Yair. *Image of God: Halakha and Aggadah* [Hebrew]. Tel Aviv: Schocken, 2004.

Love Anderson, Wendy. *The Discernment of Spirits: Assessing Visions and Visionaries in the Late Middle Ages*. Tübingen: Mohr Siebeck, 2011.

Luther, Martin. *The Bondage of the Will*. Translated by J. I. Packer and O. R. Johnston. Grand Rapids, Mich.: Revel, 1992.

Maimonides. *The Guide of the Perplexed*. Translated by Shlomo Pines. Chicago: University of Chicago Press, 1963.

McCord Adams, Marilyn. *Some Later Medieval Theories of the Eucharist: Thomas Aquinas, Giles of Rome, Duns Scotus, and William Ockham.* Oxford: Oxford University Press, 2010.

Megivern, James J. *Concomitance and Communion: A Study in Eucharistic Doctrine and Practice.* New York: Herder, 1963.

Meister Eckhart. *Meister Eckhart: Teacher and Preacher.* Edited and translated by Bernard McGinn et al. New York: Paulist, 1986.

Menozzi, Daniele. *Les images l'Église et les arts visuels.* Paris, Cerf, 1991.

Merchavia, Chaim. *The Church Versus Talmudic and Midrashic Literature* [Hebrew]. Jerusalem: Bialik Institute, 1970.

Miller, William Ian. *The Anatomy of Disgust.* Cambridge Mass.: Harvard University Press, 1997.

Miller, William T. *Mysterious Encounters at Mamre and Jabbok.* Chico, Calif.: Scholars Press 1984.

Miquel, Pierre. "Images, culte des." In *Dictionnaire de spiritualité* 7:1503–1519.

———. "Théologie de l'icône." In *Dictionnaire de spiritualité* 7:1229–1239.

Mitchell, Nathan. *Cult and Controversy: The Worship of the Eucharist Outside Mass.* Collegeville, Minn.: Liturgical Press, 1990.

Morgan, David. *The Sacred Gaze: Religious Visual Culture in Theory and Practice.* Berkeley: University of California Press, 2005.

Most, Glenn W. *Doubting Thomas.* Cambridge, Mass.: Harvard University Press, 2007.

Muessig, Carolyn. "Signs of Salvation: The Evolution of Stigmatic Spirituality Before Francis of Assisi." *Church History* 82, no. 1 (2013): 40–68.

———. "The Stigmata Debate in Theology and Art in the Late Middle Ages." In *The Authority of the Word: Reflecting on Image and Text in Northern Europe, 1400–1700,* edited by C. Brusati, K. Enenkel, and W. S. Melion, 481–504. Leiden: Brill, 2012.

Norbert of Xanten. *Vita S. Norberti.* PL 170:1253–1350.

O'Connor, James T. *The Hidden Manna: A Theology of the Eucharist.* San Francisco: Ignatius Press, 1988.

Ogden, Thomas H. "On the Concept of an Autistic-Contiguous Position." *International Journal of Psychoanalysis* 70 (1989): 128.

Origen. *The Song of Songs: Commentary and Homilies.* Translated by R. P. Lawson. New York: Newman Press, 1956.

Ostrogorski, Gregorije. "Les décisions du 'Stoglav' concernant peinture d'images et les principes de l'iconographie Byzantine." In *L'art byzantine chez les Slaves,* 393–411. Paris, 1930.

Pelikan, Jaroslav. *The Growth of Medieval Theology, 600–1300*. Vol. 3 of *The Christian Tradition: A History of the Development of Doctrine*. Chicago: University of Chicago Press, 1978.

——. *Imago Dei: The Byzantine Apologia for Icons*. Princeton: Princeton University Press, 1990.

Philo Judaeus. *De Decalogo*. Translated by C. D. Yonge. In *The Works of Philo Judaeus*. London: H. G. Bohn, 1854–1890.

Plato. *Complete Works*. Edited by J. M. Cooper. Indianapolis, Hackett, 1997.

Plotinus, *Enneads*. Translated by Stephen MacKenna and B. S. Page. London: Hale, Cushman and Flint, 1921.

Pseudo-Dionysius. *The Complete Works*. Translated by C. Luibheid. Classics of Western Spirituality. New York: Paulist, 1987.

Rahner, Karl. "The Doctrine of the Spiritual Senses in the Middle Ages." In *Theological Investigations*, 16:104–134. New York: Crossroad, 1979.

Reeves, Marjorie. *The Influence of Prophecy in the Later Middle Ages*. Oxford: University of Notre Dame Press, 1969.

Rosen, Stanley. "Thought and Touch: A Note on Aristotle's *De Anima*." In *The Quarrel Between Philosophy and Poetry: Studies in Ancient Thought*, 119–126. New York: Routledge, 1988.

Rubin, Miri. *Corpus Christi: The Eucharist in Late Medieval Culture*. Cambridge: Cambridge University Press, 1991.

——. *Gentile Tales: The Narrative Assault on Late Medieval Jews*. New Haven: Yale University Press, 1999.

Rudy, Gordon. *Mystical Language of Sensation in the Later Middle Ages*. New York, Routledge, 2002.

Rusconi, Roberto. "La verità dei segni ovvero i segni della verità." In *Autorität und Wahrheit: Kirchliche Verstellungen, Normen und Verfahren 13–15 Jahrhundert*, edited by Gian Luca Potestà, 45–53. Oldenburg: Wissenschaftsverlag, 2012.

Sagi, Avi. "Leibowitz: Jewish Thought vis-à-vis Modernity" [Hebrew]. In *Yeshayahu Leibowitz: His World and Philosophy*, edited by A. Sagi. Jerusalem: Keter, 1995.

Salter Williams, David. "Reconsidering Marcion's Gospel." *Journal of Biblical Literature* 108, no. 3 (1989): 477–496.

Schmucki, Octavian. *The Stigmata of St. Francis of Assisi: A Critical Investigation in the Light of Thirteenth-Century Sources*. Translated by C. F. Connors. St. Bonaventure, N.Y.: St. Bonaventure University, 1991.

Schuman, Marjorie. "The Psychophysiological Model of Meditation and Altered States of Consciousness: A Critical Review." In *The Psychobiology of Consciousness*, edited by J. M. Davidson and R. J. Davidson, 333–378. New York: Plenum, 1980.

Scripta Leonis, Rufini et Angeli Sociorum S. Francisci. Edited and translated by Rosalind B. Brooke. Oxford: Clarendon Press, 1970.

Sells, Michael A. *Mystical Languages of Unsaying*. Chicago: University of Chicago Press, 1994.

Severus of Minorca. *Letter on the Conversion of the Jews*. Edited and translated by Scott Bradbury. Oxford: Oxford University Press, 1996.

Shapiro, Marc B. *The Limits of Orthodox Theology: Maimonides' Thirteen Principles Reappraised*. Oxford: Oxford University Press, 2004.

Silberman, Neil A., and Israel Finkelstein. *The Bible Unearthed: Archeology's New Vision of Ancient Israel and the Origin of Its Sacred Texts*. New York: Touchstone, 2002.

Sommer, Benjamin D. *The Bodies of God and the World of Ancient Israel*. Cambridge: Cambridge University Press, 2009.

Stock, Brian. *The Implications of Literacy: Written Language and Models of Interpretation in the Eleventh and Twelfth Centuries*. Princeton: Princeton University Press, 1983.

Symeon the New Theologian. *On the Mystical Life: The Ethical Discourses*. 3 vols. Translated by A. Golitzin. Crestwood, N.Y.: St. Vladimir's Seminary Press, 1996.

Tedoldi, Fabio Massimo. *La dottrina dei cinque sensi spirituali in San Bonaventura*. Rome: Pontificium Athenaeum Antonianum, 1999.

Tertullian. *Treatise on the Incarnation*. Edited and translated by E. Evans. London, 1956.

Theodore the Studite, *On the Holy Icons*. Translated by C. P. Roth. Crestwood, N.Y.: St. Vladimir's Seminary Press, 1981.

Thomas of Celano. *Tractatus de miraculis*. AF 10:269–331.

——. *Vita prima S. Francisci*. AF 10:1–117.

——. *Vita secunda S. Francisci*. AF 10:127–268.

Thomas of Eccleston. *De adventu fratrum minorum in Angliam*. Edited by A. G. Little. Manchester: Manchester University Press, 1951.

Thompson, Augustine. *Francis of Assisi: A New Biography*. Ithaca: Cornell University Press, 2012.

Thurston, Herbert, *The Physical Phenomena of Mysticism*. London: Burns Oates, 1952.

Trachtenberg, Joshua. *The Devil and the Jews: The Medieval Conception of the Jew and Its Relation to Modern Antisemitism*. New Haven: Yale University Press, 1943.

Vauchez, André. "Les stigmates de Saint François et leurs détracteurs." *Mélanges d'archeologie et d'histoire Ecole Fraçaise de Rome* 80:619–623.

Venantius Fortunatus. *Opera poetica*. MGH AA:4.

Victricius of Rouen. *De laude sanctorum*. PL 20:443–458.

Wesjohann, Achim, *Mendikantische Gründungserzählungen im 13. und 14. Jahrhundert: Mythen als Element institutioneller Eigengeschichtsschreibung der mittelalterlichen Franziskaner, Dominikaner und Augustiner-Eremiten*. Berlin: Lit, 2012.

West, Delno C., and S. Zimdras-Swartz. *Joachim of Fiore: A Study in Spiritual Perception and History*. Bloomington: Indiana University Press, 1983.

William of Middleton. *Quaestiones de sacramentis*. Edited by G. Gal. Quaracchi, 1961.

Wolfson, Harry Austryn. "Maimonides on the Unity and Incorporeality of God." *Jewish Quarterly Review* 56 (1965): 112–136.

INDEX

cannibalism, 92

Carmel, Mount, 30

Chaucer, Geoffrey, 95

Christ: as bridegroom, 103, 104; depictions of, 72, 74, 79; eating the flesh of, 89–90, 93; as phantasm, 59; as second Adam, 119. *See also* Jesus

Chronicle of Zuqnin, 140

Chrysostom, John, Saint, 17

City of God (Augustine), 118

Clement of Alexandria, Saint, 67

Comestor, Petrus, 89, 93, 94, 95, 96, 97

Communion, 77, 87, 92, 97, 99

Concordia discordantium canonum (Gratian's *Decretum*), 15, 95

Confessions (Augustine), 2, 4, 63

Conflict of the Faculties (Kant), 44

Creation, 119

Cross, Richard, 157n8

Cyril of Alexandria, Saint, 35, 39

Daniel, Prophet, 55

Darwin, Charles, 151

De carne Christi (On the Flesh of Christ) (Tertullian), 56–57, 58–59

Decalogue, 68, 124

Decretales Gregorii IX, 86

Decretum (Gratian), 15, 95

demiurge, 60

demonic possession, 141–145

Der Barfusser Monche Eulenspiegel und Alkoran (The Mendicants' Distorted Mirror and Koran) (Alber), 116

Descartes, René, 5

Deus absconditus (the hidden God), 22, 26, 27, 55, 151

Deuteronomy Rabbah, 133

Devil, smell of, 139, 140, 142, 143, 146

Dio, Chrysostom, 70, 71, 73, 77

Dionysius the Areopagite (Pseudo Dionysius), 20–22, 24, 26

Diotima, 5, 6, 7

Dominican Order, 113, 141

Donne, John, 2

double truth (Averroists), 38, 148

Eckhart, Meister, 10, 12, 24, 27

Ein Sof, 18, 22, 23, 26

Elias, Brother, 106, 113, 165n18

Eliezer son of Hyrkanos, Rabbi, 53–54, 133

Elijah, Prophet, 29–30, 31, 62, 123

Elucidarium (Honorius Augustodunensis), 64

Erasmus of Rotterdam, 27

Eros, 5

Eucharist, 76, 80, 81, 84, 86, 87, 88, 92, 94, 95–97, 99, 103

Eucharistic miracles, 85–86, 87, 88–89

"Existentialism Is a Humanism" (Sartre), 45

faith: as communal activity, 34; as not a logical argument, 63; as requiring fuzzy logic, 38; as what people actually do, 40

false memory, 7

Fear and Trembling (Kierkegaard), 44

Flatland (Abbott), 62

Foucault, Michel, 104

Francis of Assisi, Saint: according to Bartholomew of Pisa, 115–118; according to Bonaventure, 113–114; according to Thomas of Celano, 109–112; as *alter Christus*, 117, 118; as conceling stigmata, 164n10; notion of imitation, 166n26; as second Adam, 115; as second Christ, 115; stigmatization of, 104–114, 119

Franciscans/Franciscan Order, 112, 113, 115

frankincense, 137, 139

Freud, Sigmund, 151

Gavrilyuk, Paul, 35

Gerald of Wales, 93

Gilgamesh, 136

Gnosticism, 60, 148

God: according to rabbis of the Talmud, 53–55; belief in, 31–32; bodily aspects described in Bible, 53; as both transcendent and immanent, 151; Christian God as edible, 86; as commensurable,

Joseph, Patriarch, 55
Josephus Flavius, 138
Josiah, King, 121
Judaism: according to Yehuda Halevi, 126; as choosing incoherence, 60; founding moment of relationship between God and His chosen people according to, 125; as having problem with dual logic, 135; in Holy Land/Land of Israel, 44; idea of sonship, 56; as religion with weak philosophical sensibilities, 55; Thirteen Foundations of, 47

Kalam, philosophers of, 128, 129
Kant, Immanuel, 44–45, 62
Keter (Sephira), 22, 23, 26
Khazari, Book of, 126–128
Kierkeggard, Søren, 44
Kolakowski, Leszek, 147–148, 150, 151, 152

La Verna, vision of, 105, 107, 108, 112, 114
Lamentations Rabbah, 50, 51, 52, 53
Lanciano, miracle of, 85, 87, 88
Lanfranc of Bec, Bishop, 88–89
Lateran IV, Council, 86, 109
Legenda major (Bonaventure), 113, 114
Leibniz, Gottfried Wilhelm, 33
Leibowitz, Yeshaayahu, 27, 28
Leo, Brother, 105, 106
Leo III, Emperor, 73
Leviticus, 56
Life of Gregory the Great (Paul the Deacon), 87
light, as metaphor for man's intellectual ability, 79
Lord's Prayer, 67
Lord's Supper/Last Supper, 84, 90, 91, 94
lovemaking, as union of spirits, 103
Luther, Martin, 27, 28

Maimonides, ix, 35, 36–38, 47, 48, 51, 55, 75, 100, 129–132, 134, 135, 152
Marcion, 56, 57, 58, 59, 60
Matthew of Aquasparta, 115, 116

Mekhilta de Rabbi Ishmael, 134
Memento (film), 7
memory, 4–5, 6–7, 9
metaphors, 17, 26, 48, 51, 53, 55, 64, 66, 78, 79, 86, 103, 141
Midrash/Midrashim, 50, 52, 122, 132, 133, 134, 140
Miller, William, 137
The Mind's Journey into God (Bonaventure), 65, 114
miracles: appearance of stigmata, 106, 107, 108, 110, 111, 112; attributed to Francis, 116; during earlier stages of Exodus, 130; Eucharistic miracles, 85–86, 87, 88–89; Jesus as miracle-working, 45, 74; of La Verna, 112; of Lanciano, 85, 87, 88; at Lourdes, 39; at Mount Sinai, 120, 125, 126, 127, 134; new miracle, 110, 111, 119; as performed by relics, 80, 81; as proving something but not necessarily thing that needs proving, 31; renewed miracles, 109; singular wonder as, 105; transubstantiation. *See* transubstantiation:
Moses, 52, 62, 63, 69, 122, 125, 129
Most, Glenn, 163n4
myrrh, 137, 139
mystical union, 103, 104
mysticism, 103, 104

Nadab, 69
Nathan, Rabbi, 123
Nativity, 78
negative theology, 25
Neoplatonism, 19–20
nescience (non-knowledge in Shankara), 8, 9
Nestorius, 35, 39
Nicholas of Cusa, ix, 88
Nolan, Christopher, 7
non-self, 8

odor of sanctity, 140, 144, 145, 146
Ogden, Thomas, 100
Olivi, Pierre Jean, 114
omnipotence, 17, 25, 53, 54

spiritual eating, 92
Spiritual Exercises (Ignatius of Loyola), 77 78
spiritual knowledge, 64
spiritual sense(s): according to St. Bonaventure, 65–66; defined, 64; Richard Cross on, 157n8; of smell, 98
Stephen, Saint, 138
stigmata, 104–107, 110–112, 114, 115, 117, 118, 119
stigmatization: as divinization of man, 119; of Francis of Assisi, 104–114, 119
Stoicism, 56
stories, as main source of information, 12
The Suffering of the Impassible God (Gavrilyuk), 35
Summa contra gentiles (Thomas), 149
Symposium (Plato), 4, 5, 9

Tabor, Mount, 62
taste: in Aristotle, 137; God as having, 16; joy of, 65; knowing how it feels to taste God, 99; no reports as describing what Christ tastes like, 88; no reports as describing what God tastes like, 86, 98; soul as tasting truth, 64
Tathagata, 19
Tertullian, 56–58, 59
Theodora, Empress, 73
Theodore the Studite, 74
theoretical knowledge, 67
Thirteen Foundations of Judaism, 47
Thomas Aquinas, Saint, ix, 39, 152
Thomas of Celano, 105–106, 108–112
Thomas the Apostle, 77, 101–103, 119, 149
Timaeus (Plato), 75
time, as moving in one direction, 2
touch: according to Aristotle, 100, 137; according to Maimonides, 100; God as having, 16; metaphysical untouchability

of Almighty, 25; people as yearning to touch God, 103; as sign of weak faith, 102; soul as feeling truth, 64; Thomas as touching Jesus, 101–103; Word Incarnate as accessible to, 101
Tractatus logico philosophicus (Wittgenstein), 23
Transfiguration, 62
transubstantiation, 85, 86, 87, 95, 150
Trinity, 25, 74–75, 82
true essence, 10, 11, 25, 138
true knowledge, 8, 9
"Twelfth, or Olympic, Discourse" (Dio), 70

ultima ratio philosophorum, God as serving as, 13, 154n2
Urwelt, 148
Utnapishtim, 136

Vauchez, André, 112
Venantius Fortunatus, 140
Ventura of Verona, Brother, 169–170n27
Victricius of Rouen, 79
Virgin Mary, 35, 39, 105, 117
visio beatifica, 79
visual imagery, 75, 77
visualization, according to Augustine, 71–72

William of Middleton, 90–91, 92
Wittgenstein, Ludwig, 23
Word of God, 76

Yehoshua, Rabbi, 53–54
Yesh (being), 22
Yirmiah, Rabbi, 54

Zen, 23
Zeus, statue of, 70–71, 72, 74
Zipporah, wife of Moses, 52
Zohar, 16, 18, 22